the fifth BMW ART GUIDE by Independent Collectors

THE GLOBAL GUIDE TO PRIVATE COLLECTIONS OF CONTEMPORARY ART. REVISED EDITION WITH THIRTY-ONE ADDITIONAL COLLECTIONS.

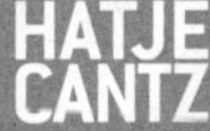

THE ART OF SHARING

270 Places of Encounter

With the first issue of the *BMW Art Guide by Independent Collectors* in 2012, we laid the foundation for a publication whose goal is to make contemporary, privately owned art around the world accessible. In addition to institutional-caliber, private museums, which were captivated by the project from the very outset, the initiative has also inspired many collectors to open their private residences for the first time to an art-enthusiast audience. Thus, with each new edition of the BMW Art Guide the number of collections presented has grown along with the variety of content. The publication takes us to vibrant metropolises as well as tranquil provinces, making for a highly varied art experience. Even if the collectors and their personalities, interests, and motivations are just as diverse as their art, they are united in the belief that their own collections are best served when shared with others: art communicates, stimulates exchange, and provides space for many special encounters. Featuring 270 private collections, the *BMW Art Guide by Independent Collectors* in its fifth edition has never been so multifaceted. We would therefore like to express our gratitude to all participating collections for their enthusiastic support of this project and their efforts to make such special places publicly accessible. In addition to our research, our partnership over the years has yielded many exciting conversations and portraits. An ongoing selection of these can be found at www.bmw-art-guide.com.

Jörg Reimann
Vice President Brand Experience Customer, BMW Group

Karoline Pfeiffer
Director,
Independent Collectors

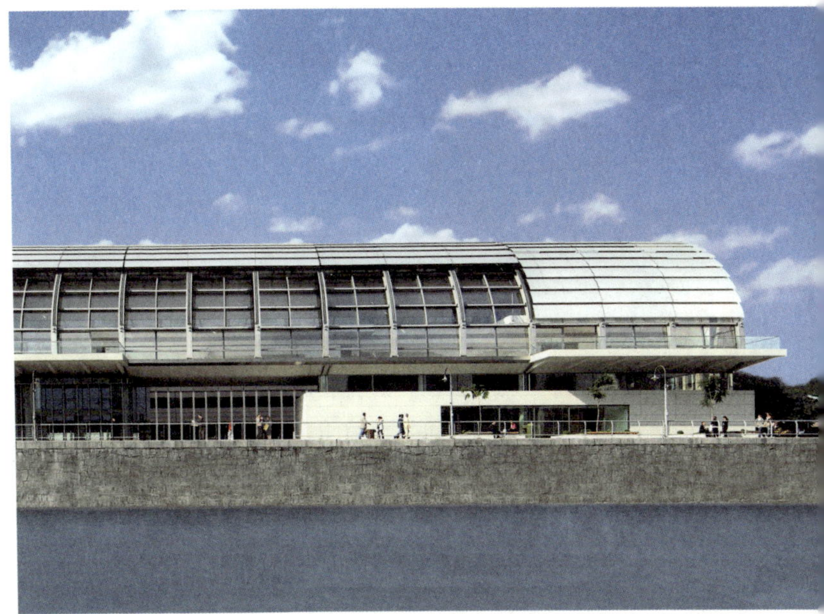

COLECCIÓN DE ARTE AMALIA LACROZE DE FORTABAT

Argentina's wealthiest woman presents six centuries of art-treasure collecting

Collector:
Amalia Lacroze de Fortabat

Address:
Olga Cossettini 141
Puerto Madero Este
C1107CCC Buenos Aires
Argentina
Tel +54 11 43106600
info@coleccionfortabat.org.ar
www.coleccionfortabat.org.ar

Opening Hours:
Tues–Sun: 12–8pm

The Colección de Arte Amalia Lacroze de Fortabat lies in the middle of Puerto Madero, the trendy quarter of the Argentine capital. Until the end of the 1990s, this neighborhood was still a no-go area of rundown buildings ringing the harbor. It's been heavily restored and added to over the past few years by world-class architects like Sir Norman Foster, Philippe Starck, and Santiago Calatrava. The architect of the Colección Fortabat, which opened in fall 2008, is the Uruguay-born New Yorker Rafael Viñoly. He built a modern, light-filled venue for the art collection of Argentina's wealthiest woman: 1 000 works ranging from Pieter Bruegel to Andy Warhol, who made a portrait of her in 1980. The socially critical artist Antonio Berni has a gallery all to himself.

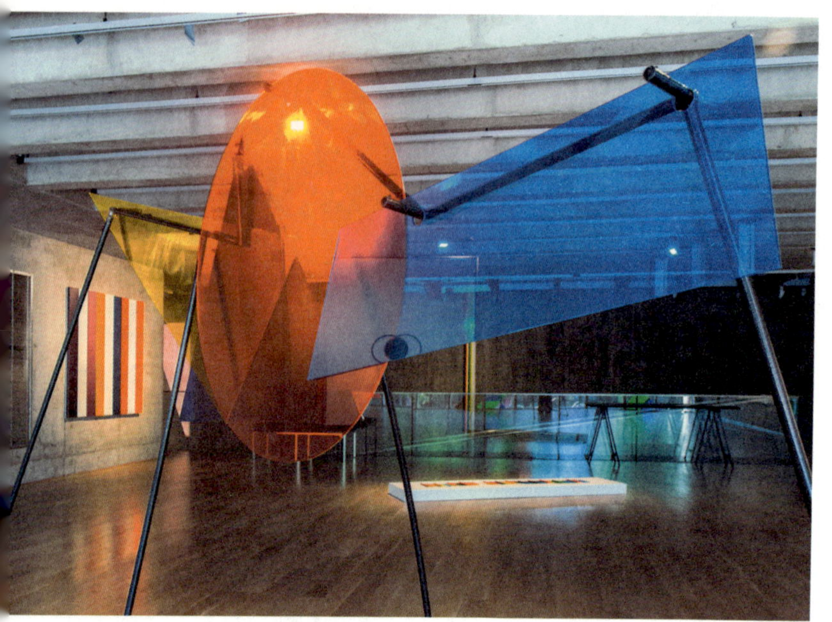

MACBA—MUSEO DE ARTE CONTEMPORÁNEO DE BUENOS AIRES

An art center with a focus on international geometric art

Collector:
Aldo Rubino

Address:
Avenida San Juan 328
C1147AAO Buenos Aires
Argentina
info@macba.com.ar
www.macba.com.ar

Opening Hours:
Mon, Wed–Fri: 11am–7pm
Sat–Sun: 11am–7:30pm

MAMBA, MALBA, MACBA. Anyone flaneuring through Buenos Aires on a museum tour could get them mixed up. While the first two have been around for a long time, the MACBA arrived on the scene in 2012. The Museo de Arte Contemporáneo de Buenos Aires was founded by native Aldo Rubino, who now lives in Miami and is a frequent guest on the collectors' panel at Art Basel Miami Beach. Rubino's private collection concentrates on geometric abstraction: Op Art, Hard Edge, and Neo-Geo, from Manuel Álvarez Bravo and Victor Vasarely, all the way to the American Sarah Morris. Special exhibitions feature all varieties of current art. Shows take place in the 2 400-square-meter translucent building brought to life by local architect duo Vila Sebastián. The location is great: the MACBA, which sits adjacent to the MAMBA, is in the lively flea-market quarter of San Telmo.

BUENOS AIRES

There is no shortage of museums, galleries, and other exciting art venues in Buenos Aires, the bustling metropolis on the Río de la Plata. Spread across so many different districts, with melodious names like Recoleta, Retiro, Palermo, and Belgrano, art invites you to explore the city and its rich cultural heritage. Since 2016, Buenos Aires is a partner city of the Art Basel Cities initiative. Over a number of years, this collaboration with the Swiss fair has been dedicated to strengthening the Argentine art scene. Aside from the private museums presented in this guide, you should definitely visit the Museo Nacional de Bellas Artes (MNBA), with its extensive collections of European and predominantly Argentine art through the twenty-first century. More closely affiliated with international art discourse is the private Fundación Proa, in the colorful harbor district of La Boca. Artists like Julian Rosefeldt, Alejandra Seeber, and Eduardo Basualdo have already been fêted in its gleaming-white building. In Palermo, the Museo de Arte Latinoamericano de Buenos Aires (MALBA) impresses with its highly varied exhibition program featuring artists from Octavio Paz to David Lamelas. Located just behind, in a renovated 1920s villa, Casa Cavia and its unconventional mix of restaurant, flower shop, and bookstore invites you to linger awhile. In the districts of Retiro and Recoleta, galleries Ruth Benzacar and Jorge Mara-La Ruche offer primarily top-notch Argentine avant-garde art. On the other hand, Galería Isla Flotante, located in La Boca, is one of a handful of Latin American galleries that first took part in Art Basel Miami Beach in 2017. Every year at the end of May, the ArteBA fair, initially specialized in Latin American art but increasingly international, opens its doors in the halls of La Rural, a trade fair center from the 1870s in the heart of Palermo. In fall, friends of photography will be rewarded at Buenos Aires Photo (BAPhoto), founded in 2005. Off-Spaces also exist—due to their often nomadic character, it is better to look for flyers once there.

FUNDACIÓN COSTANTINI/MALBA—MUSEO DE ARTE LATINOAMERICANO DE BUENOS AIRES

A grandiose overview of a century of Latin American art

Collector:
Eduardo F. Costantini

Address:
Avenida Figueroa Alcorta 3415
C1425CLA Buenos Aires
Argentina
Tel +54 11 48086500
info@malba.org.ar
www.malba.org.ar

Opening Hours:
Thurs–Mon: 12–8pm
Wed: 12–9pm

Unsuspecting "gringos" come across places in South America that they couldn't have imagined in their wildest dreams. The Museo de Arte Latinoamericano de Buenos Aires (MALBA) is one such place. The museum features work from the Caribbean to Tierra del Fuego and is located in the posh district of Palermo Chico. It looks like an outpost of New York's Museum of Modern Art (MOMA). Here, too, people know how to erect elegant structures; modernism is defined self-consciously here—naturally, from a Latin-American perspective. Nearly 300 key works from businessman Eduardo F. Costantini's collection are on permanent display, such as politically charged conceptual art by Léon Ferrari; the Chilean Surrealist Roberto Matta is also well represented, as is the Brazilian Lygia Clark, whose fragile metal objects have leapt to premium prices internationally.

MUSEO JAMES TURRELL—THE HESS ART COLLECTION, COLOMÉ

Turrell's largest Skyspace and additional light rooms in breathtaking surroundings

Collector:
Donald M. Hess

Address:
Ruta Provincial 53 km 20
Molinos 4419
Salta
Argentina
Tel +54 3868 494200
museo@bodegacolome.com
www.bodegacolome.com

Opening Hours:
Tues–Sun: 2–6pm
And by appointment.
Reservations encouraged.

Additional exhibition locations:
Napa, United States of America, p. 248

Far away from all the major urban art centers, in a majestic location beneath the expansive bright blue sky of the Argentine Andes, lies the world's first James Turrell Museum, opened in 2009. Here the light-and-land artist from Arizona completed his biggest *Skyspace* to date at his collector and friend Donald M. Hess's vineyard, Colomé: 2,300 meters up the side of a mountain sits an observatory with an open roof, enhanced by an orchestration of subtle light that achieves its greatest intensity at sunrise and sunset. Eight more light rooms, works acquired by Hess over the past forty years, are grouped around the spectacular centerpiece. Here you experience an unparalleled sense of meditative peace and inner reflectiveness. The Museo James Turrell, which Hess maintains along with his collection in North America, is a truly magical space in a fascinating location.

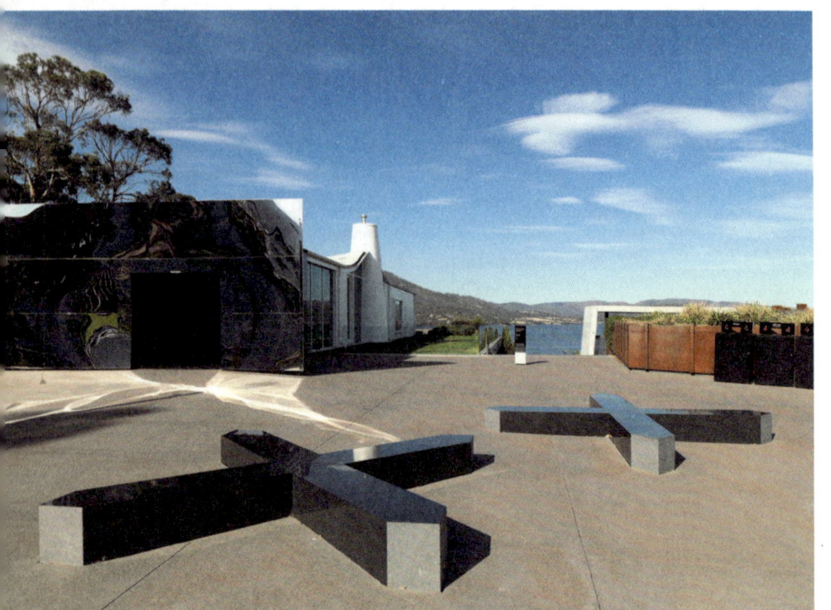

MUSEUM OF OLD AND NEW ART (MONA)

A collection that puts personal predilection over speculative intention

Collector:
David Walsh

Address:
655 Main Road
Berriedale TAS 7011
Hobart
Australia
Tel +61 3 62779900
info@mona.net.au
www.mona.net.au

Opening Hours:
May–September
Wed–Mon: 10am–5pm
October–April
Wed–Mon: 10am–6pm

Small gestures are not his thing: Australian millionaire David Walsh owns one of the largest museums in the southern hemisphere. This building without daylight is burrowed deep into the Tasmanian bedrock. Aside from contemporary art, the museum also houses Egyptian mummies and Greek coins. Walsh, who made his fortune developing complex winning-systems for gambling, combines antique treasures with Australian contemporary art, as well as works by internationally renowned artists like Jannis Kounellis, Hans Bellmer, Anselm Kiefer, the Viennese group Gelitin, or Wim Delvoye's excrement machine, *Cloaca*. Walsh prefers works that confront viewers immediately with subjects like sex and death. He views his Museum of Old and New Art, opened in 2011, as a kind of secular temple in which visitors are made keenly aware of humanity's existential conditions.

BUXTON CONTEMPORARY

A museum of contemporary Australian art set within an art college

Collector:
Michael Buxton

Address:
Corner Dodds Street and
Southbank Boulevard
Southbank VIC 3006
Melbourne
Australia
Tel +61 3 90359339
buxton-contemporary@unimelb.edu.au
www.buxtoncontemporary.com

Opening Hours:
Wed, Fri–Sun: 11am–5pm
Thurs: 11am–8pm

The Michael Buxton Collection (MBC) is regarded as one of the most important art collections in Australia. Initially focused on just six Australian artists, the collection now includes over 300 works by fifty-eight artists such as Tracey Moffatt, Howard Arkley, Patricia Piccinini, Mike Parr, and Bill Henson. In 2014, Buxton donated his collection to the University of Melbourne and provided the Victorian College of the Arts (VCA) with funding to create and operate long-term a new exhibition space on Southbank Boulevard. Somewhat hidden behind a historic red brick façade, this sprawling museum welcomed its first visitors in spring 2018. Boasting five exhibition spaces and a classroom covering over 2 200 square meters, Buxton Contemporary sees itself as a forum for discussing and debating art—even if you don't enter the building: an oversized screen at the entrance shows digital and video art, providing plenty of fodder for conversation.

JAHM—JUSTIN ART HOUSE MUSEUM

Digital and abstract art—with a glass of wine

Collectors:
Leah & Charles Justin

Address:
3 Lumley Court
Prahran VIC 3182
Melbourne
Australia
Tel +61 4 11158967
info@jahm.com.au
www.jahm.com.au

Only guided tours with prior online registration. Special tours by appointment.

Given its spacious and unorthodox design, the JAHM looks more like a public exhibition venue than a private residence. Elisa Justin, who is an architect like her father, designed the building featuring both exhibition and living areas for her parents Leah and Charles. Accordingly, the question of how an individual artwork relates to the space has perhaps greater influence on what works are acquired than with other collectors. The couple, whose collection comprises around 250 pieces, prefers abstract works, such as by Penelope Davis, Justin Andrews, or Gina Jones, and artists who deal with the concept of space. Digitally produced or modified works and video art are another focus. Hospitality is a top priority for the Justins: not only do they personally take visitors around the building, but they also invite them afterwards to engage in informal conversations and discuss the works over drinks and snacks—on the roof terrace in good weather.

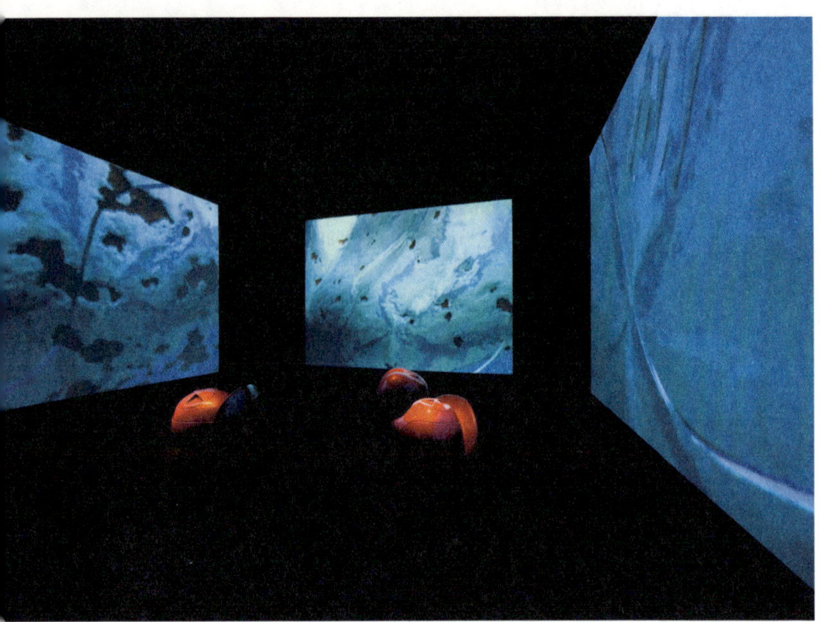

LYON HOUSEMUSEUM

The private home as museum: living with art and showing it off

Collectors:
Corbett & Yueji Lyon

Address:
219 Cotham Road
Kew VIC 3101
Melbourne
Australia
Tel +61 3 98172300
museum@lyonhousemuseum.com.au
www.lyonhousemuseum.com.au

By appointment only. To arrange an appointment, send an e-mail, or call on Mondays or Tuesdays between 9:30–11:30am.

If you want to visit Corbett and Yueji Lyon, you first have to make an appointment. For good reason: the architect built a house for his family that also functions as a museum. In the cavernous rooms the artworks are re-hung biannually. Lyon draws on a long tradition, such as Peggy Guggenheim's Venetian home, where her private collection was shown. The Australian pair has specialized in the artists of their own country, collecting paintings from the likes of Tim Maguire, sculptures by Peter Hennessey, or large C-print photographs by Anne Zahalka. Two decades ago the Lyons decided to collect the work of a new generation, such as that by Peter Atkins, Callum Morton, and Patricia Piccinini, who have since become established internationally. The couple has remained true to their pioneering spirit.

SYDNEY

Sydney has long battled it out with Melbourne for top billing on the Australian cultural calendar. But, while the latter boasts an equally if not more active gallery and museum scene, Sydney's harborside arts festival, the Biennale of Sydney, places it a cut above, particularly on the international art world stage, having attracted top-notch curators for its past editions—Documenta 13 artistic director Carolyn Christov-Bakargiev, Fondazione Prada director Germano Celant, and Stephanie Rosenthal, appointed director of the Martin-Gropius-Bau in Berlin in 2018. The twenty-first edition of the Biennale of Sydney in 2018, marked the forty-fifth anniversary of the exhibition; it was stewarded by Japanese curator Mami Kataoka, chief curator of the Mori Art Museum (MAM) in Tokyo. For those headed Down Under during biennale off-months, there's still plenty left to see. The Art Gallery of New South Wales (Art Gallery NSW) leads off Sydney's museum scene. The institution's John Kaldor Family Collection is of particular note here for its breadth of American and European postwar and contemporary masters. The Museum of Contemporary Art Australia (MCA)'s waterfront building, since its renovation in 2012, exudes a fresh modern vibe. More experimental is Artspace, a contemporary art venue in the city's Woolloomooloo district, which was founded by artists in 1983 and moved to its current venue, a historic building known as The Gunnery, in 1992. The much younger Carriageworks opened in 2007 in the disused Eveleigh Rail Yards, and hosts a multi-disciplinary program of contemporary art, theater, and performance—as well as the city's biggest art fair, Sydney Contemporary, which is held in September. Australia's relative isolation from the art market power-centers of Europe, America, and Asia translates into fewer commercial galleries than some cities of similar global standing, but a trip here wouldn't be complete without a stop at Roslyn Oxley9 Gallery, which has helped launch the careers of Tracey Moffatt and Fiona Hall, among others.

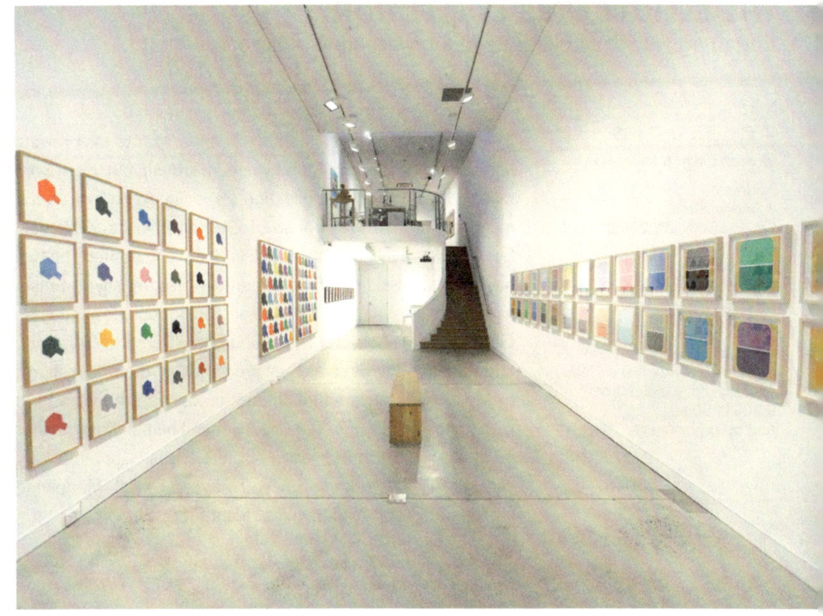

TEN CUBED

Spotlight on artists from Australia and New Zealand

Collectors:
Dianne Gringlas & Ada Moshinsky

Address:
1489 Malvern Road
Glen Iris VIC 3146
Melbourne
Australia
Tel +61 3 98220833
info@tencubed.com.au
www.tencubed.com.au

Opening Hours:
Tues–Sat: 10am–4pm

Most art collections don't open their doors with a pre-determined closing date, but Ten Cubed is one that did. Established in 2010, the original idea was to collect ten works by ten artists over ten years, hence the name. Once enough works by a single artist—from painting to photography, to sculpture and video art—had been purchased, they would be given a solo show in the airy, custom-built gallery space in Glen Iris. The original focus was on Australian and New Zealand artists, from sculptors Alexander Knox and Anne-Marie May to photographers such as David Rosetzky and Pat Brassington. Aesthetic appeal and collectability were the main criteria. Surprised by the success of their experiment—within five years ten artists had already been selected—collector Dianne Gringlas and her curatorial advisor Ada Moshinsky, who is also her sister-in-law, announced Ten Cubed 2, which will now include international artists for the project.

THE ELLIOTT EYES COLLECTION

Engaging with the collectors in a private atmosphere

Collectors:
Gordon Elliott & Michael Eyes

Address:
7 Bridge Street
Erskineville NSW 2043
Sydney
Australia
Tel + 61 411 500511
gordon@theelliotteyescollection.com
www.theelliotteyescollection.com

Only guided tours with prior registration, every first and third Tuesday of the month from 9:30–11:30am.
And by appointment.

It is not often that art collectors open the door to their private home and also personally show visitors around, but this is what makes the Elliott Eyes Collection a special experience. In the elegant Victorian townhouse of Gordon Elliott and Michael Eyes, art fills every available wall, surface, and corner. The two have amassed almost three hundred works, mostly by artists from Australia and New Zealand, including Rick Armor, James Gleeson, Clara Adolphs, Peter Churcher, Clement Meadmore, and Michael Zavros, and they are proud of their collection's highly individual, personal character. Many of the works are surprisingly humorous. The (mostly male) human figure, either as sculpture or on canvas, is a clear focus. Contemporary ceramics, with works by Gwyn Hanssen Pigott, Madeleine Child, and Stephen Benwell, are another.

WHITE RABBIT COLLECTION OF CHINESE CONTEMPORARY ART

One of the largest collections of contemporary Chinese art

Collector:
Judith Neilson

Address:
30 Balfour Street
Chippendale NSW 2008
Sydney
Australia
Tel +61 2 83992867
info@whiterabbitcollection.org
www.whiterabbitcollection.org

Opening Hours:
Wed–Sun: 10am–5pm

Judith Neilson has chosen to limit herself: she only collects Chinese art, and only works created after the year 2000. When she first traveled to Beijing in 2001 she realized that her understanding of Chinese art was based on an outdated cliché. When she returned, she restructured her existing collection and bought an old warehouse in Chippendale, a former industrial district of Sydney, now a cosmopolitan area. She then began to systematically acquire contemporary work by artists like Xu Zhen, Xu Bing, Shang Yang, or Yu Hong. The fame of the artist did not matter, rather Neilson was after "creativity and quality." Instead of acquiring art at auctions, she buys directly in China and Taiwan from gallerists and artists' studios. Today her collection includes almost 2 600 works by more than 500 artists. It is considered one of the world's most important collections with this focus.

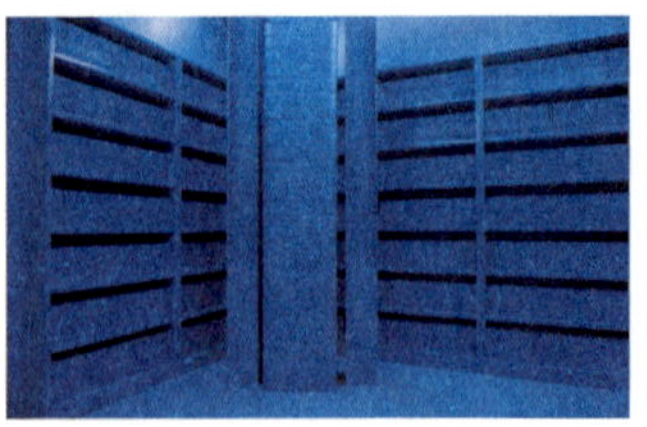

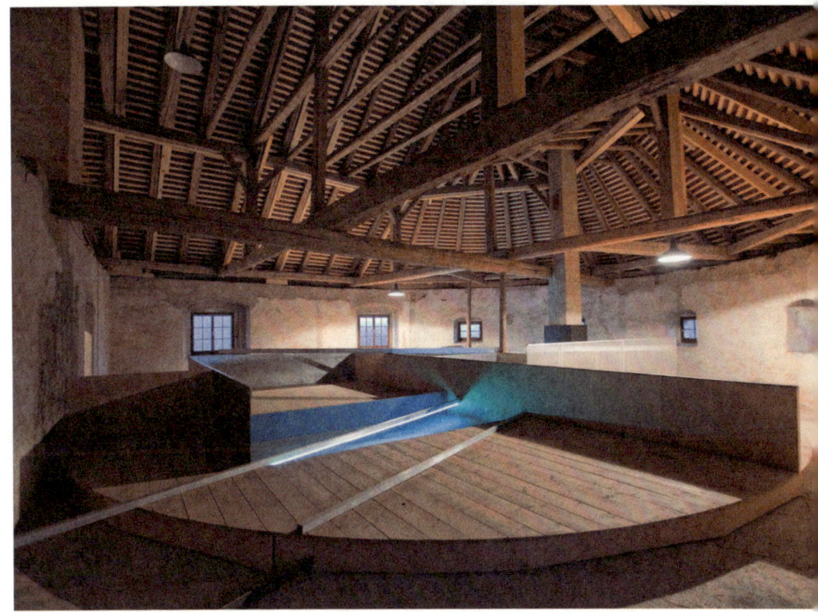

KUNSTRAUM BUCHBERG

Permanent contemporary installations and projects in the park

Collectors:
Gertraud & Dieter Bogner

Address:
Buchberg am Kamp 1
3571 Gars am Kamp
Austria
Tel +43 676 7806699
bogner.buchberg@aon.at

By appointment only.

Gertraud and Dieter Bogner are museum experts. The couple runs an internationally active agency for museum planning, cultural and strategic museum concepts, and exhibition management in Vienna. Some of their prestige projects in recent years include the New Museum in New York City or the Bauhaus Museum in Dessau. Of course, with this type of background, the Bogners also have a strong interest in living with art. This is done at their twelfth-century castle Schloss Buchberg located in Lower Austria, where, since 1979, they have invited artists to come and work with its spaces. Thus far twenty-seven permanent, site-specific, full-scale installations have been realized: in the gardens and courtyards stars like Dan Graham or Heimo Zobernig have executed striking works relating to the architecture. In the spaces inside, installations have been created by artists like Monika Brandmeier, Roland Goeschl, John Hilliard, Thomas Kaminsky, Dorit Margreiter, and François Morellet.

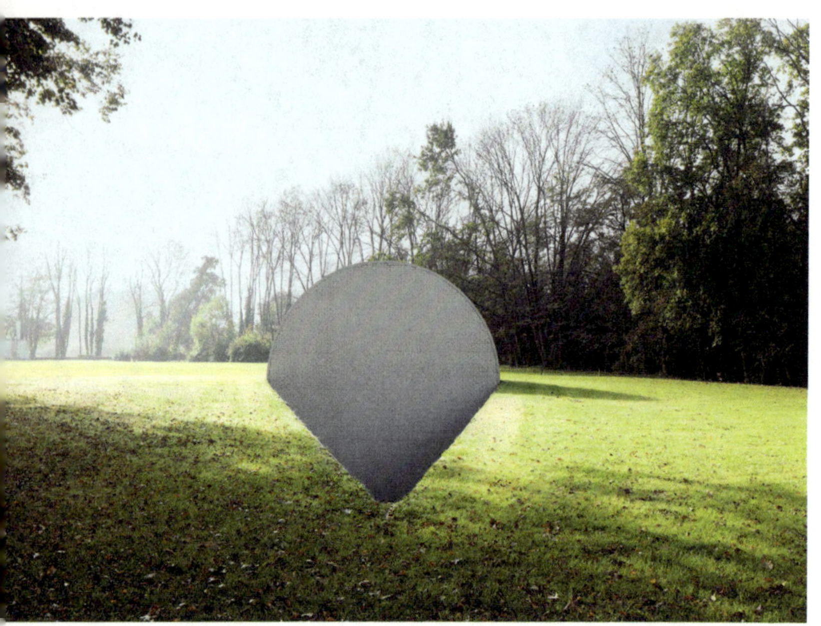

SCHLOSSPARK EYBESFELD

Carefully executed art projects in a palace-garden setting

Collectors:
Christine & Bertrand
Conrad-Eybesfeld

Address:
Jöss 1
8403 Lebring
Austria
Tel +43 3182 240812
Tel +43 3182 240818
cce@eybesfeld.at
bce@eybesfeld.at
www.eybesfeld.at

Only guided tours by appointment.

A palace, a garden, and an enthusiastic couple. Christine and Bertrand Conrad-Eybesfeld do not buy their art off the rack. It originates on site, sometimes in a few weeks, sometimes over a period of years. The owners of a cultural management agency do not consider themselves collectors or patrons, but rather artists' partners for these outdoor projects. Indeed, the couple has enough space: the palace is located in the sparsely populated state of Styria, in southeastern Austria. It all started with the artist Heimo Zobernig, who in 1989 made his mark on the palace's former tennis court with a fifteen-centimeter-thick concrete plate. Sol LeWitt executed a large-scale work shortly before his death, in 2007. For the Conrad-Eybesfelds, at least as important as the end result is getting people involved in the whole process, including the local community.

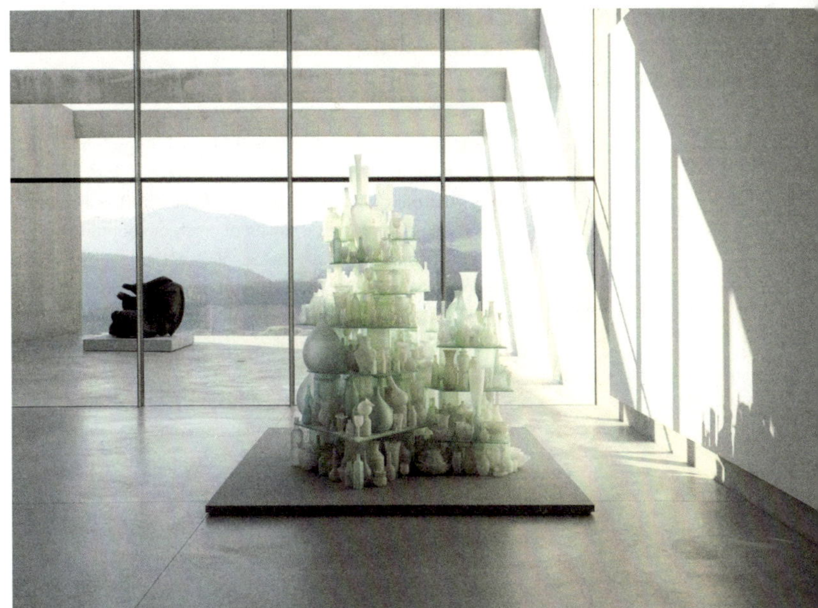

MUSEUM LIAUNIG

Austrian art after 1945 and prominent works by international artists

Collector:
Herbert W. Liaunig

Address:
Neuhaus 41
9155 Neuhaus
Austria
Tel +43 4356 21115
office@museumliaunig.at
www.museumliaunig.at

Opening Hours:
May–October
Wed–Sun: 10am–6pm

With its slim, slightly rounded form, the Museum Liaunig resembles a gigantic USB-stick plugged into verdant hills. Carinthian businessman Herbert W. Liaunig opened this radically modern-looking museum far away from the urban hustle and bustle in the summer of 2008, and had it greatly expanded in 2014. The building was masterminded by the Viennese architects Querkraft, who lean toward understatement: 90 percent of the rooms are located underground. Liaunig collected "what resulted from personal encounters and predilections." The more than 3000 works include key pieces of Austrian postwar art by figures like Arnulf Rainer or Maria Lassnig, but also undiscovered or overlooked works, as well as young positions. Since the museum was founded, Liaunig has collected with more focus and closed some previous gaps, such as his acquisition of several Viennese Actionists. His goal is to bring Austrian art since 1945 alive for the visitor.

MUSEUM ANGERLEHNER

The unique collection of an entrepreneur fascinated by art and artists

Collector:
Heinz J. Angerlehner

Address:
Ascheter Strasse 54
4600 Thalheim bei Wels
Austria
Tel +43 7242 2244220
office@museum-angerlehner.at
www.museum-angerlehner.at

Opening Hours:
Fri–Sun: 10am–6pm
And by appointment.

The Upper Austrian entrepreneur Heinz J. Angerlehner describes himself as "a collector with heart and soul." Over a thirty-year period he acquired more than 2500 works of art. They have either attracted him emotionally or spontaneously—without regard for any art-historical classification, but with a high regard for quality. This is how his collection grew over the years to include many famous names from his homeland, such as Arnulf Rainer, Gunter Damisch, Hubert Schmalix, or Andreas Leikauf. In September 2013 the Museum Angerlehner opened in Thalheim, near Wels. It is housed in a former assembly hall covered with iridescent black metal panels, which in addition to showing the collection also hosts temporary exhibitions in its roughly 2000-square-meter space. An added highlight is the fifty-meter-long display storeroom with retractable walls.

SAMMLUNG SANZIANY & PALAIS RASUMOFSKY

Figurative art in a noble, palatial atmosphere

Collectors:
Adrian Riklin & Antonis Stachel

Address:
Rasumofskygasse 23–25
1030 Vienna
Austria
b.miks@alcar-wheels.com

Only guided tours with prior registration.

Upon entering Palais Rasumofsky, it's easy to be dazzled by its magnificent marble columns, opulent crown moldings, and lavish chandeliers. If you didn't know better, you would never guess that the classical garden palace, once the residence of Russian art collector and ambassador of the Russian Empire Prince Andrej K. Rasumovsky, is home to a significant collection of contemporary art. Entrepreneur Adrian Riklin, who acquired the building in 2004, originally envisioned it as a luxury hotel but things turned out differently. Now Riklin and his partner Antonis Stachel present their magnificent collection on exclusive guided tours. Represented are works by Austrian sculptors such as Alfred Hrdlicka and Erwin Wurm or international artists like Nan Goldin and Julian Opie. The exhibition features primarily figurative art—not hung in museum style, but in a way typical of private living spaces: closely together and surrounded by designer furniture.

VIENNA

No other city in the German-speaking world boasts such a dense network of museums and galleries like Vienna, the Austrian metropolis of 1.8 million inhabitants. The best place to begin a tour is MuseumsQuartier Wien (MQ), where you'll find three institutions of international standing: the Museum Moderner Kunst Stiftung Ludwig Wien (MuMoK), founded in 1962, featuring the largest collection of twentieth- and twenty-first century art in central Europe, the Kunsthalle Wien, focusing on contemporary discourse, and the Leopold Museum, with the largest Egon Schiele collection in the world. Other highlights on the Vienna tour include the Belvedere, with Austrian art from 1900 onwards, and its annex for contemporary art, the 21er Haus. Art Nouveau enthusiasts should not miss the Vienna Secession. Every fall, Vienna-Contemporary, an international contemporary art fair, draws visitors to the Marx Halle, a brick building and once popular market hall designed in the nineteenth-century by renowned architect Rudolf Frey. This is also the perfect chance to discover the local gallery scene of experienced protagonists who have set the tone with committed international and avant-garde programs. In the city's first municipal district, Rosemarie Schwarzwälder has shown abstract and concept art since 1984 at Galerie nächst St. Stephan, on Grünangergasse. Located just a stone's throw away are the exhibition spaces of Ursula Krinzinger, the grande dame of Vienna's galleries. Since 1971, Krinzinger has been synonymous with performance and body art, as well as the Viennese Actionism of Hermann Nitsch and Rudolf Schwarzkogler. Further to the southwest, Georg Kargl Fine Arts, on Schleifmühlgasse, has made a name for itself since the late 1990s with artists like Gerwald Rockenschaub, Clegg & Guttmann, or Mark Dion. Next door you'll find the galleries of Christine König and Kerstin Engholm, also well worth a visit. As the day draws to a close, the Viennese art scene enjoys meeting up for schnitzel, goulash, and Czech beer at the legendary Viennese Beisl Café Anzengruber.

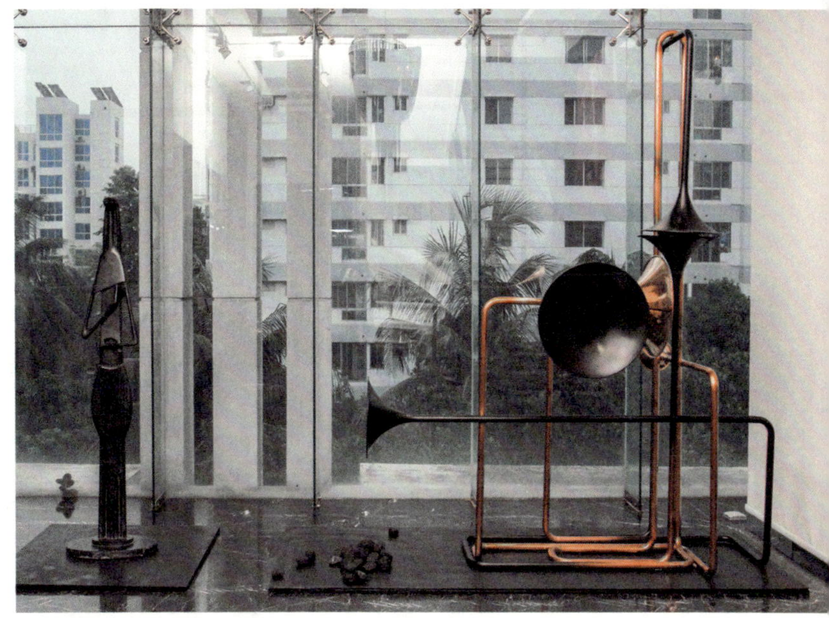

SAMDANI ART FOUNDATION (SAF)

A discovery of modern and contemporary art from Bangladesh

Collectors:
Nadia & Rajeeb Samdani

Address:
Level 5, Suite 501 & 502
Shanta Western Tower
186 Gulshan—Tejgaon Link Road
Tejgaon I/A, Dhaka-1208
Bangladesh
Tel +880 2 8878784-7
info@samdani.com.bd
www.samdani.com.bd

By appointment only.

Globalization has put previously ignored countries on the art map—Bangladesh, for example. Bangladeshi industrialist Rajeeb Samdani and his wife, Nadia, are well aware of this, so their aim is to acquaint an international audience with art from their country. In April 2011, they opened a foundation to promote local art via exhibitions and events like the Dhaka Art Summit. Their collection, spread over three floors of their private home, includes local artists such as Shumon Ahmed, Joydeb Roaja, Tayeba Begum Lipi, and Mahbubur Rahman, alongside international artists such as Laure Prouvost, Lee Ufan, Prabhakar Pachpute, Tony Oursler, Michael Armitage, Huma Bhabha, or Maria Taniguchi. With the Samdani Art Centre and Sculpture Park, the couple is opening another exhibition venue in the northeast of Bangladesh, in Sylhet, at the end of 2018. In the park, you can see works by Paweł Althamer, Subas Tamang, and others.

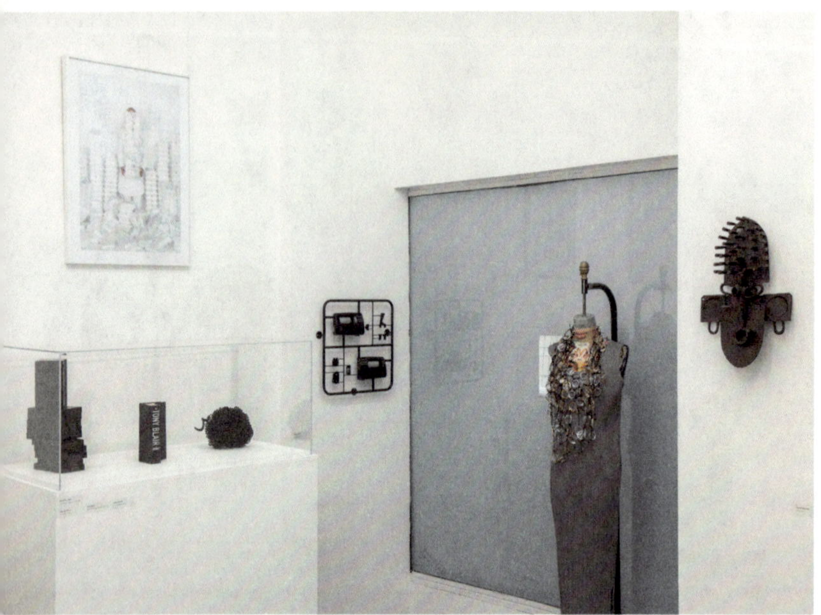

GALILA'S P.O.C.

A collection of varied thematic interests

Collector:
Galila Barzilaï-Hollander

Address:
295 Avenue Van Volxem
1190 Brussels
Belgium
galilaspoc@gmail.com

By e-mail appointment only.

Galila Barzilaï-Hollander bought her first artwork at the Armory Show in New York in 2005. Since then her collection of art by mainly young artists has grown to several thousand works. The intuitive collector does not limit herself to a specific medium but is mostly drawn to photography, video, drawings, works on paper, and object-based art. Thematically, her collection revolves around categories such as eyes, books, chairs, or concepts like recycling and other interests. To make her art publicly accessible, she purchased an historic 1950s-era industrial building in Brussels's Forest district. Its unobtrusive front façade blends easily into a street of revivalist residential buildings, however, the rear of the renovated structure, completed in 2018, reveals an expansive exhibition space with skylights and a mezzanine. The collection is in good neighborly company: just a few hundred meters away is Wiels, a contemporary art center that opened in 2007.

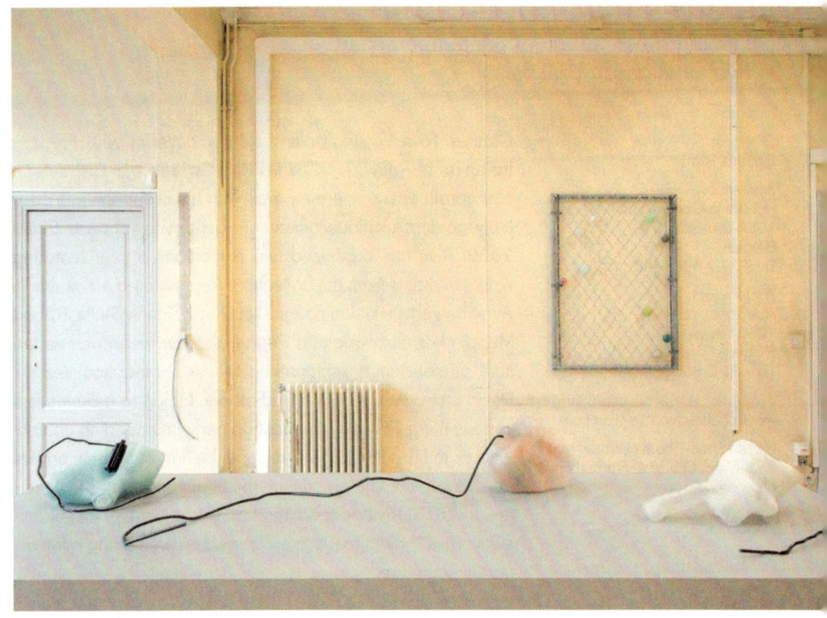

FRÉDÉRIC DE GOLDSCHMIDT COLLECTION

Reduced aesthetics and humble materials in the center of Brussels

Collector:
Frédéric de Goldschmidt

Address:
Brussels, Belgium
frederic@frederic.net

Visitation permitted only occasionally. Please inquire by e-mail.

He was always buying art but it wasn't until 2009 that the tireless Frenchman Frédéric de Goldschmidt began thinking of himself as a collector. His collection is now shown in several locations around the city. De Goldschmidt operates temporary showrooms in the Quartier des Quais and a permanent location is currently in planning: at the end of 2019, the collection will be moving into a three-story exhibition space at Quai du Commerce—located in a building where he provides not only co-working space but also room for artist residencies. His collection revolves conceptually around the group Zero and their associates, with works by Günther Uecker, Heinz Mack, or Piero Manzoni. In the meantime, de Goldschmidt has begun collecting mostly younger artists, such as Stef Heidhues, or Joël Andrianomearisoa. The common thread here is a reduced aesthetic and great sensitivity for rather simple materials. De Goldschmidt rearranges the collection each year in time for Art Brussels.

CHARLES RIVA COLLECTION

Charming presentation of contemporary art in two locations in Brussels

Collector:
Charles Riva

Addresses:
Rue de la Concorde 21
1050 Brussels
Belgium
Tel +32 2 5030498

Riva Project:
Rue Tenbosch 124
1050 Brussels
Belgium
Tel +32 2 8504238

info@charlesrivacollection.com
www.charlesrivacollection.com

Please check the website for the most current information on opening hours.

Charles Riva—collector and former gallerist with French-Italian roots—views his Charles Riva Collection in Brussels as a nonprofit space. Here he lives with his collection in a centrally located, luxurious, nineteenth-century townhouse. Since 2009, Riva has organized two exhibitions a year featuring works of artists from the collection. Represented are primarily American artists including Paul McCarthy, Frank Stella, Robert Mapplethorpe, or Richard Prince, but European names are also present such as Jonathan Meese, Francesco Vezzoli, David Ostrowski, AES + F, and others. Going to galleries is a serious thing, Riva says, almost on par with attending church. Visitors to his collection will experience first-hand how private spaces can completely change the effect that art has on viewers. In 2015, Riva opened another space just two kilometers away: Riva Project focuses exclusively on presenting contemporary sculpture.

FAMILY SERVAIS COLLECTION

Art that poses questions, in a converted factory loft in the north of Brussels

Collector:
Alain Servais

Address:
Brussels, Belgium
collection.servais@gmail.com

By e-mail appointment only.

Alain Servais is omnipresent in the art world. He is occasionally part of the expert panel for the collection of new media at Art Basel. At other times he can be seen during Berlin Art Week rushing from gallery to gallery on a rented Vespa. He is also an avid Twitter user. The extremely well-connected collector, who lives in Brussels, is hungry for art. In his opinion, good art should question certainties: "It should teach me something that I don't know about myself or my environment." Servais converted an old factory into a 900-square-meter loft in the multicultural district of Schaerbeek. Here he not only lets artists live and work, but he also shows parts of his collection—established names such as Gilbert & George and Barbara Kruger as well as younger positions, like video works by Mexican artist Arturo Hernández Alcázar. Once a year he rearranges 80 percent of his collection's holdings.

BRUSSELS

If you are looking for quality and want to discover something new, come to Brussels. The art scene there is flourishing—not least thanks to two fairs that regularly attract an international audience. In April 2016, Art Brussels moved into its new quarters inside the historic halls of Tour & Taxis. At the same time, the New York fair Independent installed its European off-shoot at the Dexia Art Center, a centrally located, former furniture department store from the 1930s. During art fair season, Brussels really comes alive: open houses hosted by scores of private collectors, gallery nights, and parties set the program. For young artists and international collectors, this European capital—with both its charm and rough edges—has become a Mecca: studios, galleries, and institutions congregate here en masse. The Palais des Beaux-Arts (for short: Bozar) lures visitors with exhibitions ranging from Jeff Wall to Daniel Buren, to new stars like Kehinde Wiley. Art-goers interested in seeing additional current positions such as Rita McBride are in good hands at the Wiels—Centre d'Art Contemporain, in the Forest district. Nine artists' studios for international new-comers are available for residencies at this art center, which opened in 2007 in an old brewery. If you want to explore the Brussels gallery scene, it's best to take a tour of the Ixelles district, or the Lower Town, also known as Downtown. Situated here are the spaces of the long-established Galerie Greta Meert and the gallery Dépendance, run by German-native Michael Callies. Walking in the direction of Ixelles you'll also pass the flagship gallery Jan Mot as well as the New York blue-chip gallery Barbara Gladstone. Upon arriving in the elegant Ixelles district, you'll find Almine Rech, Xavier Hufkens, and Levy Delval. Anyone wishing to stock up on art books in otherwise comics-enthusiast Belgium should head straight to the magnificent Galeries Royales Saint-Hubert Passage, near the Grand Place. Here the book-shop Tropismes provides an opportunity for end-less hours of browsing.

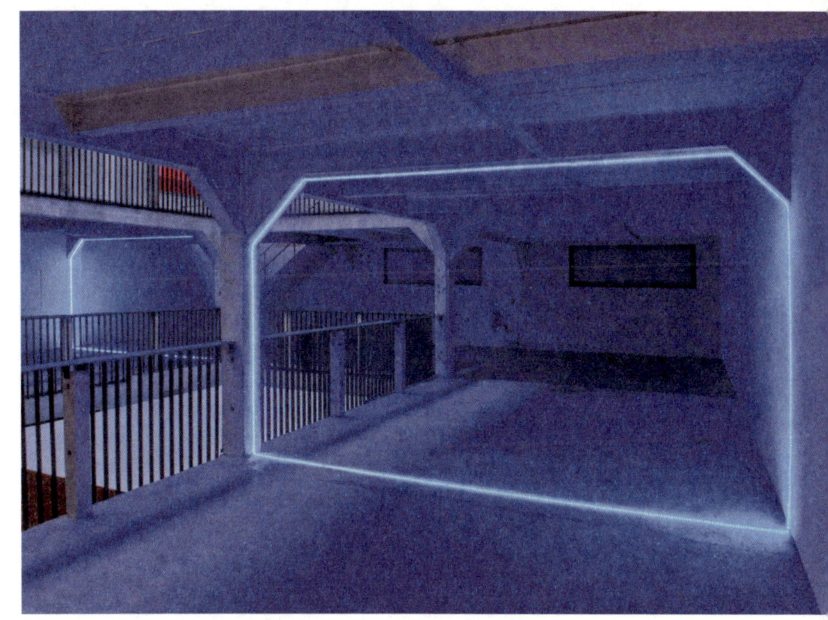

VANHAERENTS ART COLLECTION

Art and film since the 1970s: Warhol, Naumann, and subsequent trends

Collector:
Walter Vanhaerents

Address:
Rue Anneessens 29
1000 Brussels
Belgium
Tel +32 2 5115077
www.vanhaerentsartcollection.com

Online registration required.

Walter Vanhaerents's family has been in the construction business for eighty years, so naturally he went into the business too. But as a young man he studied film. He was so impressed with Andy Warhol's five-hour-long film *Sleep* that he wanted to see other works by the Pop icon. No surprise then, that Warhol, along with Bruce Naumann, is one of the anchors of the Vanhaerents Art Collection. But the reactions of subsequent generations of artists to these seminal figures interests Vanhaerents as well, whose collection also features works ranging from Cindy Sherman, Matthew Barney, and Ugo Rondinone, to the provocative, Neo-Pop Art, business-minded artist Takashi Murakami. The collection is housed in a charmingly remodeled 1926 industrial building on the outskirts of the hip fashion and gallery district of Dansaert. Starting in 2007, new exhibitions have been shown biannually on three floors.

MUSEUM DHONDT-DHAENENS

In the middle of Flanders, international art stars shown in quick succession

Collectors:
Jules & Irma Dhondt-Dhaenens

Address:
Museumlaan 14
9831 Deurle
Belgium
Tel +32 9 2825123
info@museumdd.be
www.museumdd.be

Opening Hours:
Wed–Sun: 10am–5pm

The Flanders industrialist couple Jules and Irma Dhondt-Dhaenens began collecting art in the 1920s. Belgium was just as divided then as it is today, which is why the couple focused almost exclusively on Flemish artists from 1880 to 1950, including James Ensor and Frits Van den Berghe. Later the collector couple decided to have a museum built to house their collection. Not in Brussels or Ghent, but in the country-side at Deurle, a beautifully located village on the river Leie and close to the artist colony Sint-Martens-Latem. The bright white, flat-roofed modernistic structure was opened in 1968. Today the museum continues to sharpen its contemporary profile with around eight annual exhibitions devoted to such international artists as Thomas Hirschhorn, Karla Black, Wade Guyton, Julie Mehretu, Jessica Rankin, Ryan Gander, Thomas Zipp, Richard Aldrich, and Charline von Heyl.

HERBERT FOUNDATION

A highly cerebral private collection in an industrial complex in Ghent

Collectors:
Anton & Annick Herbert

Address:
Coupure Links 627 A
9000 Ghent
Belgium
Tel +32 9 2690300
contact@herbertfoundation.org
www.herbertfoundation.org

Opening hours vary depending on exhibition. Please check the website for the most current information.

To utopia and back. The collection of the Ghent-based couple Annick and Anton Herbert focuses on art produced between 1968 and 1989. In a former steam-engine factory near the center of the Flemish city they present in temporary exhibitions works by concept and avant-garde artists such as Bruce Nauman, Marcel Broodthaers, Carl Andre, Robert Barry, and Lawrence Weiner as well as Martin Kippenberger, Franz West, and Thomas Schütte. What connects them all is their critical reflection upon social and artistic issues. What makes the collection so unique is its profound archive of artist books, letters, postcards, posters, invitations, and other documents, which show the friendly ties and decades of intellectual debate between the Herberts and "their" artists.

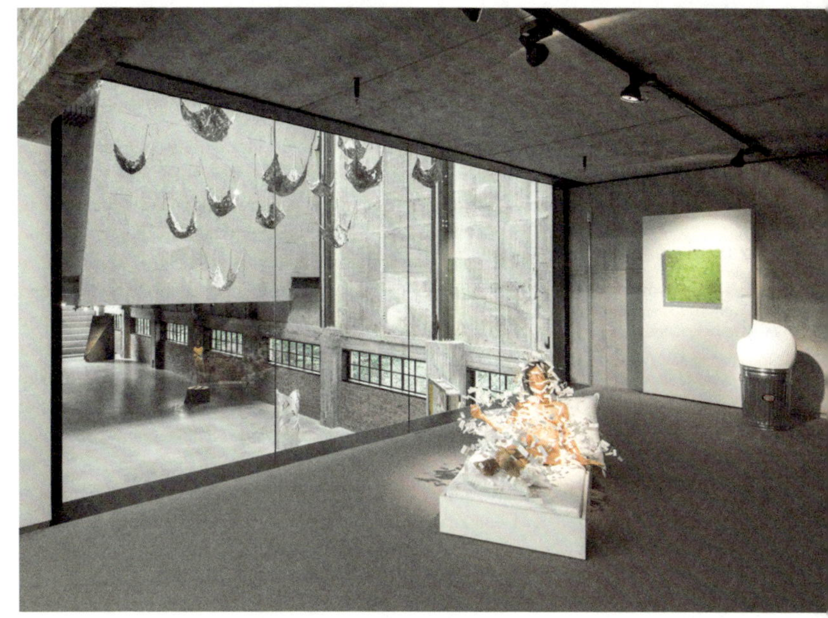

ART CENTER HUGO VOETEN

International art inside an old factory close to Antwerp

Collector:
Hugo Voeten

Addresses:
Vennen 22
2200 Herentals
Belgium
Tel +32 475 555125
info@artcenterhugovoeten.org
www.artcenter.hugovoeten.org

Sculpture Park:
Hazenhout 17–19
2440 Geel
Belgium

Please check the website for the most current information on opening hours.

More than 1 700 works of art, assembled by a single collector. This can only be described as collecting mania, even if Hugo Voeten steadily honed his collection over three decades. The collector, who died in 2017, was not committed to a particular geographical or medium-specific category, but had certain priorities: Bulgarian and Belgian art in general, and sculpture in particular. With 5 000-square-meters of exhibition space in a former 1950s-era grain mill, the Art Center Hugo Voeten near Herentals is suited for extended forays through twentieth- and twenty-first-century art history. There is also a dedicated park in Geel showcasing monumental sculptures. In addition to the much-talked-about artist Arno Breker, there are also crowd favorites like Aristide Maillol and Auguste Rodin, as well as contemporaries from Wim Delvoye to Thomas Houseago.

VERBEKE FOUNDATION

An impressive terrain for hiking and discovering unorthodox art

Collectors:
Geert Verbeke &
Carla Verbeke-Lens

Address:
Westakker
9190 Kemzeke, Stekene
Belgium
Tel +32 3 7892207
info@verbekefoundation.com
www.verbekefoundation.com

Opening Hours:
Thurs–Sun: 11am–6pm
And by appointment.

Dynamic, not static. This is the motto of the Belgian collector pair Geert Verbeke and Carla Verbeke-Lens. "Our exhibition space does not aim to be an oasis. Our presentation is unfinished, in motion, unpolished, contradictory, untidy, complex, inharmonious, living, and unmonumental," says Verbeke. The former logistics businessman opened a twelve-hectare art park in 2007 on his company's property. Storage buildings and greenhouses offer 20 000 square meters of covered space for two enormous special exhibitions per year. The Verbekes started with collages and assemblages, but now they prefer "Bio-Art"—art that includes living animals, plants, and even scents. Visitors unable to see the whole display in a single day can spend a night in a truly new environment: Joep van Lieshout's eccentric polyester sculpture *CasAnus,* a gigantic reconstruction of a human rectum.

COLLECTION VANMOERKERKE

Highlights of European and American contemporary art

Collector:
Mark Vanmoerkerke

Address:
Oud Vliegveld 10
8400 Ostend
Belgium
Tel +32 473 997745
info@artcollection.be
www.artcollection.be

By appointment only.

A good collection should have a focus, says entrepreneur Mark Vanmoerkerke who hails from the Belgian seaside resort of Ostend. His collection currently includes around 500 works of mainly European and American Post-Conceptual Art—works by artists like Ed Ruscha, Maurizio Cattelan, or Christopher Wool, for example. Vanmoerkerke regularly invites established curators, gallerists, and artists to put together exhibitions from the collection. This way things remain exciting not only for him but also for visitors. Previous guest curators have included the likes of museum directors Nicolaus Schafhausen and Dirk Snauwaert, gallerist Leo König, or artist David Claerbout. The Belgian cult curator Jan Hoet was one of the first to be allowed to mix it up in the former airplane hangar and modern extension that houses the collection.

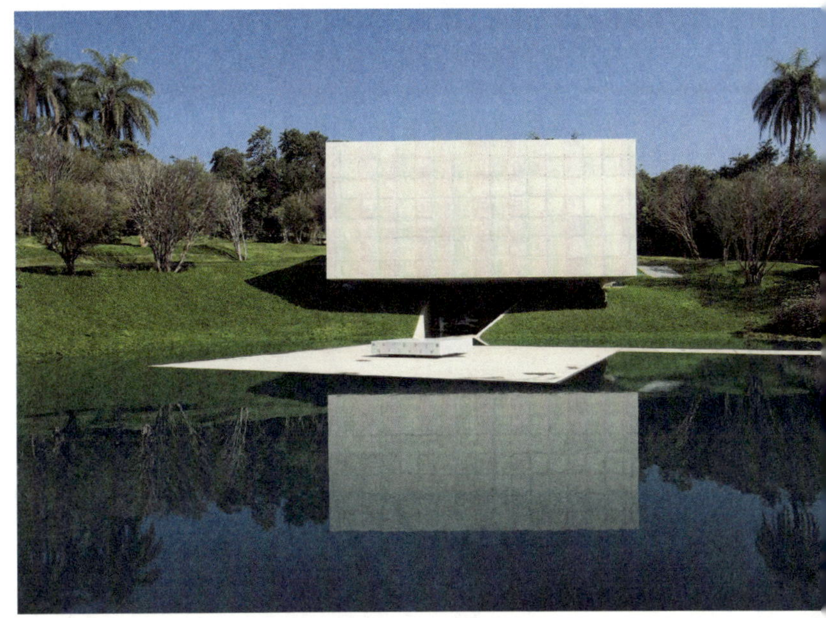

INSTITUTO INHOTIM—CENTRO DE ARTE CONTEMPORÂNEA E JARDIM BOTÂNICO

The harmony of art and nature at one of the world's most sensual locations

Collector:
Bernardo Paz

Address:
Rua B 20
Brumadinho, MG
35460-000
Brazil
Tel +55 31 37519700
info@inhotim.org.br
www.inhotim.org.br

Opening Hours:
Tues–Fri: 9:30am–4:30pm
Sat–Sun: 9:30am–5:30pm

Admittedly, it's hard to get here—but it's worth it. Inhotim, located approximately sixty kilometers outside of Belo Horizonte, completely redefines the production, exhibition, and experience of major, outdoor-art projects. The collector, commodities magnate and philanthropist Bernardo Paz, invites well-known artists to his 1 000-hectare tropical expanse to unleash their most extravagant ideas. A team of curators supports the artists however it can. Cildo Meireles, Matthew Barney, Ólafur Elíasson, Yayoi Kusama, Chris Burden, Giuseppe Penone, Dominique Gonzalez-Foerster, and Elisa Bracher have all left their marks. Getting to Doug Aitken's *Sonic Pavilion,* which funnels the sounds of inner earth to the surface, or to Hélio Oiticica's color-orgy *Magic Square #5,* might take a while. Best is to take one of the many golf carts available, but if you decide to walk, there are plenty of benches along the way to let your dreams fly.

INSTITUTO FIGUEIREDO FERRAZ (IFF)

Abstract painting and concept art in Brazil's interior

Collector:
João Carlos de Figueiredo Ferraz

Address:
Rua Maestro Ignácio Stábile, 200
Alto da Boa Vista
Ribeirão Preto, SP
14025-640
Brazil
Tel +55 16 36232261
contato@iff.art.br
www.iff.art.br

Opening Hours:
Tue–Sat: 2–6pm

Ribeirão Preto, located inland northwest of São Paulo, has been one of Brazil's largest agricultural centers since the nineteenth century. Its economic success brought money for large villas and culture into the city, which in addition to numerous parks also boasts a historical opera house. What it lacked, however, was the visual arts—a gap that has been filled by João Carlos de Figueiredo Ferraz. An exhibition of his collection of predominantly contemporary Brazilian art at the Museu de Arte Moderna de São Paulo (MAM) in 2001 prompted de Figueiredo Ferraz to establish a permanent home for it. For the collector it had to be in Ribeirão Preto and the only option was to build a new exhibition venue there. Located in a residential neighborhood, the Instituto has been a cool oasis of tranquility since 2011—at least when one of the many school classes are not visiting to study works by world-class artists such as Edgard de Souza, Tatiana Blass, and Ivens Machado.

THE FERNANDA FEITOSA & HEITOR MARTINS COLLECTION

A journey into the postwar Brazilian art scene

Collectors:
Fernanda Feitosa &
Heitor Martins

Address:
São Paulo, Brazil
julia@picklespr.com

By e-mail appointment only.

As founder and director of SP-Arte, Fernanda Feitosa takes supporting Brazilian artists to heart. Her intensive professional engagement with the Latin American art scene has also strongly influenced Feitosa's private collecting. Upon entering her private property in the southern part of the city, visitors will immediately notice a figure by the Brazilian artist Tunga, which has found its home in the sculpture garden. Selected works of art are installed inside an elegant 1960s-era building, which serves as the residence of the lawyer and her husband Heitor Martins, director of the Museu de Arte de São Paulo (MASP). However, most of the collection is housed in two modern extensions, especially designed for this purpose by the architectural office Metro Arquitetos. Providing the cornerstones of the collection presented here are works from the postwar period, by artists such as Adriana Varejão, Mira Schendel, Regina Silveira, and Rivane Neuenschwander.

SÃO PAULO

For fans of modern architecture, São Paulo is a paradise: Oscar Niemeyer's elegant buildings have defined the bustling metropolis more than anything else since the 1940s. The Edifício Copan in the city center is spectacular, not only for its S-shape. The reinforced concrete construction is also the largest residential building in the world. Inside is Pivô, an exhibition platform for contemporary art and curatorial experiments. A fifteen-minute drive away through heavy traffic is the Museu de Arte de São Paulo (MASP), a glass building floating above the ground, ensconced by surrounding red steel beams. Renowned exhibition organizer Adriano Pedrosa has breathed new life into the distinguished collection since 2014. Opened in 1968, the museum was designed by legendary architect Lina Bo Bardi, who also transformed the Serviço Social do Comércio (SESC Pompéia) cultural center, a former barrel factory in the north of the city, into a masterpiece of brutalism in 1977. From the MASP, it's only a few minutes walk along the bustling Avenida Paulista until you'll reach the Instituto Moreira Salles (IMS), which offers a substantial collection of classic Brazilian photography, including Thomaz Farkas and Marcel Gautherot. A stone's throw away you'll find the Galeria Vermelho, a top address for Brazilian art—for example by Ana Maria Tavares and Claudia Andujar. Also within walking distance: the Casa Triângulo, whose program includes contemporary Brazilian artists such as Lucas Simões or Yuri Firmeza. Head south to escape the confines and heat of a city of 12-million inhabitants in Ibirapuera Park—a gigantic green oasis with countless bird species, which also forms the cultural center of the city. Here Lina Bo Bardi outfitted the Museu de Arte Moderna de São Paulo (MAM) with a curved glass facade. Incidentally, Oscar Niemeyer designed its distinctive roof as well as the park's Biennial Pavilion—a glass and concrete marvel. In addition to the Bienal de São Paulo, the SP-Arte art fair has been held here since 2005, ensuring that São Paulo's artistic life is currently experiencing an upswing not seen since the 1950s.

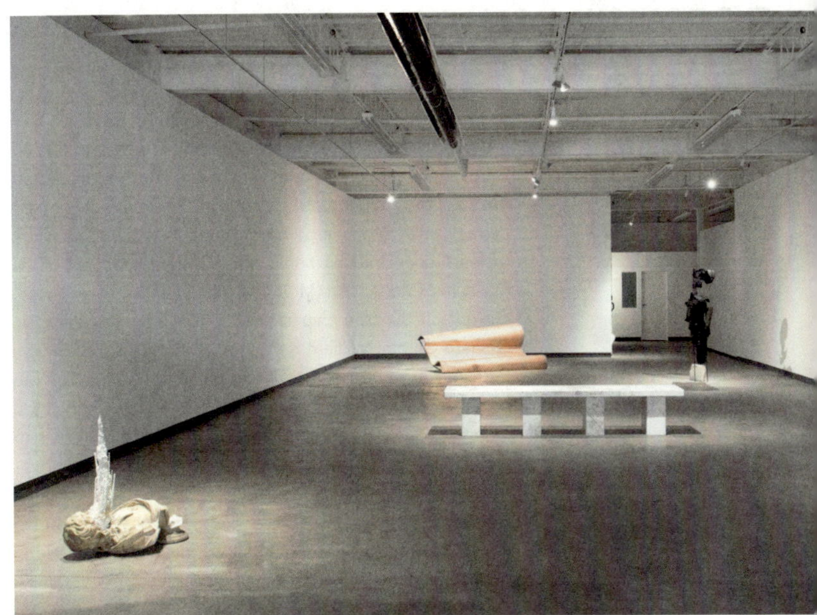

SCRAP METAL

Art focused on the relationship between word and image in an industrial hall

Collectors:
Samara Walbohm &
Joe Shlesinger

Address:
11 Dublin Street, Unit E
Toronto ON M6H 1J4
Canada
Tel +1 416 5882442
info@scrapmetalgallery.com
www.scrapmetalgallery.com

Please check the website for the most current information on opening hours.

The name of the collection is bemusing: inside the former industrial warehouse, where investor Joe Shlesinger and his wife Samara Walbohm have presented selections from their collection since 2011, anything other than scrap metal is on view, as the name of the space cheekily suggests. Rather, the focus is on Canadian and international artists whose work is similarly humorous and ambiguous. This includes art by General Idea, Bill Viola, Jeff Wall, Camille Henrot, or other global players. The names Dave Dyment, Micah Lexier, or Laurel Woodcock, however, are not so well known. All their works examine the complex interrelationship of language, text, and image. The link between art and text also resonates at Scrapbooks—a bookshop designed by Paul P.—where the artist currently exhibiting work at the collection determines the reading selection.

THE BRADSHAW COLLECTION

A collector couple that profits from the bundled synergy of their highly developed feel for art

Collectors:
Cecily & Robert Bradshaw

Address:
Toronto, Canada
robertbradshaw@me.com

Visitation permitted only occasionally. Please inquire by e-mail.

It was a shared love of art that brought Cecily and Robert Bradshaw together about ten years ago. Both collected art prior to their marriage but Robert Bradshaw attributes their current collection in large part to the influence of his wife's tastes. Cecily Bradshaw sits on the Director's Council of the Museum of Modern Art (MOMA) in New York, and their collection reflects this blue-chip sensibility. Works by Anselm Kiefer, Chiharu Shiota, William Kentridge, Tony Cragg, and Ross Bleckner are but a few of those installed in their Toronto home. To furnish their residence, the Bradshaws appointed renowned Dallas-based interior designer Jan Showers to create spaces that generously highlight the couple's art collection. The design also took special care to incorporate the Bradshaws' impressive trove of livres des artistes, featuring books illustrated by Pablo Picasso, Jasper Johns, Henri Matisse, and Marcel Duchamp, among others.

THE WEDGE COLLECTION

Contemporary African art in a penthouse in Toronto

Collector:
Kenneth Montague

Address:
25 Ritchie Avenue
Toronto ON M6R 2J6
Canada
Tel +1 416 7079400
info@wedgecuratorialprojects.org
www.wedgecuratorialprojects.org

By appointment only.

Contemporary art from Africa and the African diaspora has recently taken an increasingly prominent position in the art historical canon—and rightly so. Among Toronto's foremost collectors helping to push that evolution forward is dentist-cum-curator Kenneth Montague. The Wedge Collection—the name he has given his assemblage of works—focuses on artists like Jennifer Packer, Mickalene Thomas, Barkley L. Hendricks, Lynette Yiadom-Boakye, and Zanele Muholi, whose practices explore black identity. Begun in the late 1990s, the collection is now located in Montague's David Anand Peterson-designed home. Montague himself started collecting at just ten years old and has gone on to assemble an impressive selection of mid-century design in addition to art. Now, the collector frequently stages programming and exhibitions at his home that are free and open to the public, and curates shows in Toronto and elsewhere of artists he collects and collaborates with.

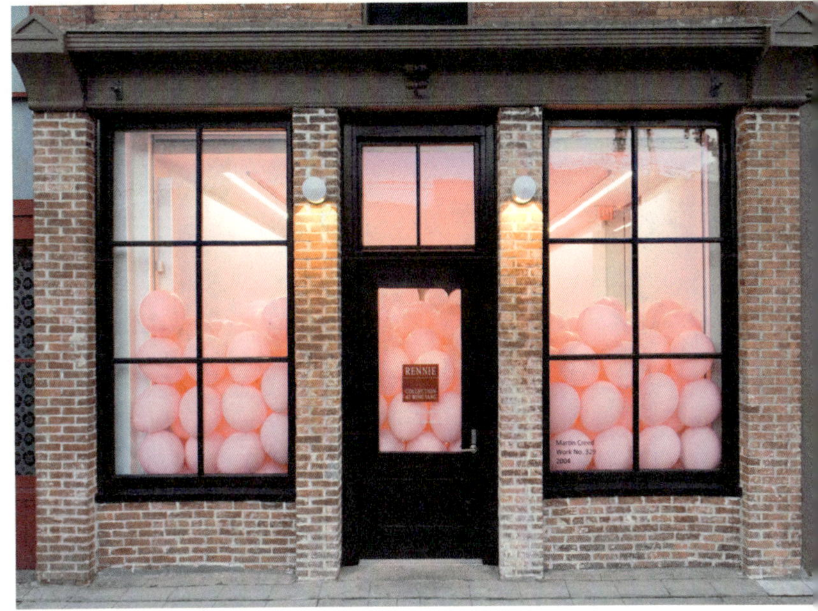

RENNIE MUSEUM

Continuity since 1972: from trailblazing giants to new talents

Collector:
Bob Rennie

Address:
51 East Pender Street
Vancouver BC V6A 1S9
Canada
www.renniemuseum.org

Only guided tours with prior online registration.

A guided tour through Chinatown's Wing Sang Building, where collector Bob Rennie presents his acquired works, takes exactly fifty minutes—not a lot of time for one of the largest collections in Canada. But Rennie focuses on key figures, like John Baldessari, Mike Kelley, Mona Hatoum, Rodney Graham, or Belgian artist David Claerbout, who takes excerpts of Hollywood classics lasting seconds and stretches them out to last an entire day. The works owned by the real-estate marketer are rearranged annually in two to three solo or group exhibitions. Rennie, who had the oldest building in the district lavishly renovated, has been collecting for over thirty years, acquiring many pieces now considered to be trailblazing. In addition he keeps himself abreast of contemporary art trends by collecting the works of talents like Turner Prize winners Martin Creed and Simon Starling.

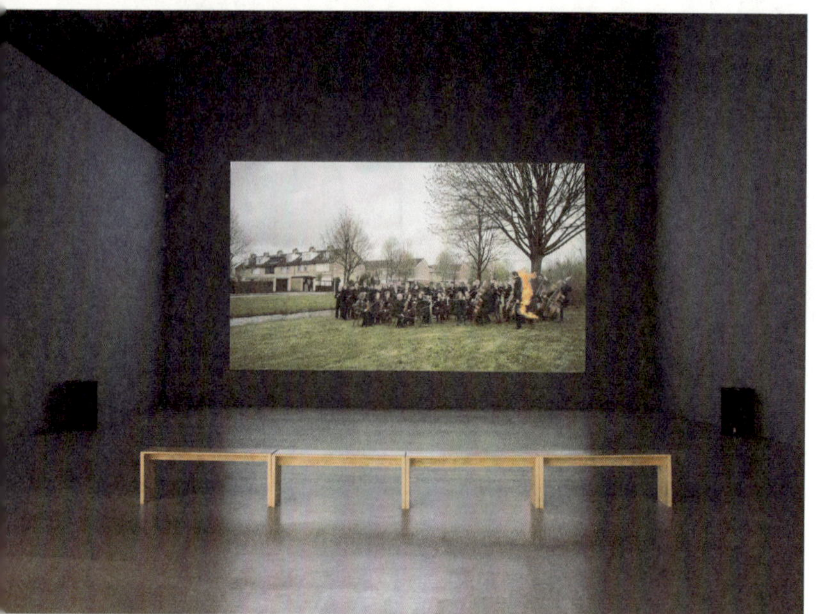

M WOODS

Contemporary art in a former factory in the 798 Art Zone

Collector:
Lin Han

Address:
D-06, 798 Art Zone
No. 2, Jiuxianqiao Road
Chaoyang District
Beijing 100015
China
Tel +86 10 83123450
info@mwoods.org
www.mwoods.org

Opening Hours:
Tues–Sun: 11am–6pm
And by appointment.

Youthful industrial designer Lin Han, who runs a PR agency and also works in the family-owned investment firm, has collected more than one hundred works by well-known artists thus far. In 2014, together with his wife, Wanwan Lei, and co-founder Michael Xufu Huang, he opened the M Woods Museum in a former munitions factory in the 798 Art Zone district. Even though Lin did not begin collecting art until 2013, he says it has a big impact on his life. His eclectic collection ranges from works by Tracey Emin, Zeng Fanzhi, Paul McCarthy, Kader Attia, Yoshitomo Nara, and Ólafur Elíasson, to Buddhist sculptures of the Northern Qi Dynasty, which Lin likes to display alongside one another in the expansive exhibition spaces. The museum's name alludes to Lin's family: The "M" is the first letter of the name of his mother, who awakened his love for art. "Woods" is the English translation of his family name, "Lin."

HONG KONG

Hong Kong is the undisputed hub of the Asian art market. In the skyscrapers of the Central District, Hong Kong Island's buzzing financial hub, numerous galleries have set up shop alongside international auction houses. Influential Chinese representatives like Pearl Lam Galleries and 10 Chancery Lane Gallery are found here, in addition to Western protagonists like Gagosian, White Cube, and Galerie Perrotin. In 2011, Art Basel took over the local fair Art HK, completing another step on the way to Hong Kong's transformation into an art market giant. In 2014, the repertoire was expanded to include the fair Art Central Hong Kong. The next big event on the agenda is the planned 2019 opening of M+, a major museum for visual culture. This will host, among other treasures, the core of the collection of Uli Sigg, one of the most important collectors of Chinese contemporary art. The Herzog & de Meuron designed museum will be part of the West Kowloon Cultural District, a vibrant quarter located directly on the harbor's waterfront. This area already enjoys several major museums, including the Hong Kong Museum of Art, which holds an excellent collection of Chinese paintings and calligraphy. The Hong Kong Arts Centre (HKAC) in Wan Chai plays a pivotal role in the local arts scene, bringing together exhibition spaces, theaters, a cinema, and artists' studios under one roof. Just as multidisciplinary is Tai Kwun—Centre for Heritage & Art, which opened in 2018 in a former police station, also designed by Herzog & de Meuron. Other institutions worth visiting include Para Site, a non-profit art space on the north-eastern section of Hong Kong Island, and the Asia Society Hong Kong Center, located further west in Admiralty. The trend towards contemporary art is rapidly expanding, seen in the rise of artistic hubs in Hong Kong's industrial areas. Chai Wan, for example, is now home to galleries like Platform China Contemporary Art Institute; and in Wong Chuk Hang, Blindspot Gallery shows mainly contemporary photography in its 650-square-meter exhibition space.

LIVING COLLECTION

Contemporary art from Hong Kong in the loft of a former industrial building

Collector:
William Lim

Address:
Hong Kong, China
info@cl3.com
www.livingcollection.hk

By e-mail appointment only.

Since the founding of Art Basel Hong Kong, the former British colony has become a hotspot on the international art scene. But if you're particularly interested in its local art, you should visit the imposing exhibition space of collector William Lim. In 2004, during his travels, the architect began to acquire works by Chinese artists. Two years later he decided to focus more exclusively on artists from Hong Kong. Since then, he has been collecting, among others, the works of Lee Kit, Nadim Abbas, or Tsang Kin-Wah—young artists who deal with society and their lives in Hong Kong. But here you'll also find international positions such as Lee Bul, Hernan Bas, or Callum Innes in Lim's nearly 400-square-meter loft. That his studio is a place of lively exchange is evidenced not least in the artists' dinners that Lim hosts on a regular basis.

Z COLLECTION

A collection of Chinese and Western contemporary art in a private home on Victoria Peak

Collector:
William Zhao

Address:
Hong Kong, China
Tel +852 97015650
ei@zcompanyhk.com

Visitation permitted only occasionally. Please inquire by e-mail.

Hong Kong-based financier turned art critic, collector, and curator William Zhao discovered his passion for art at an early age, purchasing his first piece, a drawing by Pablo Picasso, twenty years ago. His art collection is on display at his home, a large house on the Peak overlooking Hong Kong, where both Chinese and Western artists are featured including established positions like Carol Rama and Joseph Beuys as well as younger artists such as Duan Jianyu and Chris Huen Sin-kan. The passionate polo player mainly collects artists he knows personally, and whose creative language he finds inspiring. Zhao advises collectors on contemporary Chinese art and curates exhibitions with major Chinese artists such as Zhang Enli and Liu Weijian for galleries and foundations including Louis Vuitton. He is also involved with Duddell's, a Hong Kong art and cultural venue.

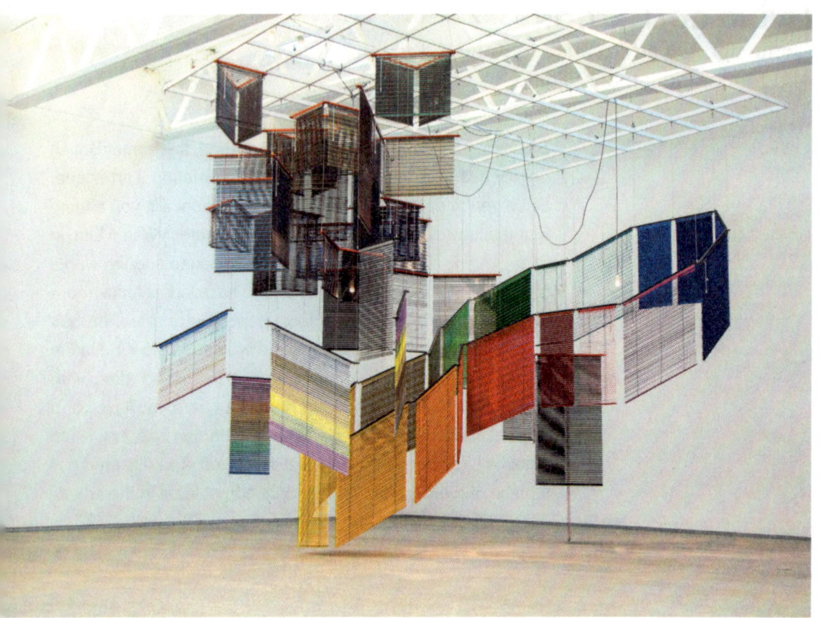

SIFANG ART MUSEUM

Emerging and blue-chip artists in a building by Steven Holl

Collector:
Lu Xun

Address:
No. 9, Zhenqi Road
Pukou District
Nanjing 210031
China
Tel +86 25 58609999
contact@sifangartmuseum.org
www.sifangartmuseum.org

Opening Hours:
Thurs–Sun: 10am–5pm

"The way art brings joy to the heart and challenges your existing perceptions is fascinating," explains Chinese collector Lu Xun in describing the motivation behind his collecting activity, a great passion of his since 2009. The first works that Lu acquired were a sculpture by Yayoi Kusama and a watercolor by Marlene Dumas. Since then, he has collected about 200 artworks by Chinese and international artists, such as Yang Fudong, Xu Zhen, William Kentridge, and Luc Tuymans. But Lu is increasingly interested in emerging artists, particularly from China. His collection is housed in a spectacular building, designed by Steven Holl, in the middle of the Laoshan National Park, on the outskirts of Nanjing. Opened in November 2013, the museum is part of the Sifang Parkland, a versatile area that includes a conference center, a hotel, a recreation center, and artist residences—the ideal space to find peace and harmony with nature and art.

SHANGHAI

In Shanghai, where things have always been business-focused, the art scene has exploded over the past decade in the southern part of the city. Much of the most recent thrust of that growth has centered on the West Bund district, a riverside redevelopment, which is now home to two of the city's top-notch contemporary art institutions. This being China, they are private museums and art spaces—Liu Yiqian and Wang Wei's Long Museum and Qiao Zhibing's Qiao Space and Tank Shanghai, where several former oil tanks were converted into a vast art center. Also part of Shanghai's private art scene is Adrian Cheng's K11 Art Foundation (KAF), which shows its projects in the K11 Art Mall, located on People's Square. The nearby Museum of Contemporary Art Shanghai (MOCA Shanghai) features a wide-ranging exhibition program, spanning both contemporary art and design. While Asia's most significant fair remains Art Basel Hong Kong, Shanghai has seen a number of exciting new additions to the calendar of art-market events. The West Bund Art & Design and Art021 Shanghai Contemporary Art Fair in November have managed, since their founding in 2013 and 2014, to attract to mainland China major international galleries like David Zwirner, Sadie Coles HQ, and Gagosian Gallery. More and more galleries are always opening up in the city. Some of the notable highlights include Antenna Space, situated along the Wusong River, Leo Xu Projects, located in the former Shanghai French Concession district, as well as Don Gallery in West Bund, all of which have attracted international attention with experimental programs. The centerpiece of the art market, however, remains the ShanghArt Gallery, which, in addition to its space in West Bund, also boasts locations in Beijing and Singapore. The fact that the gallery, which has fostered the careers of major figures like Zeng Fanzhi and Yang Fudong, has already celebrated more than twenty years of existence goes to show the level of determination driving Shanghai's art scene. Other art world capitals would be well advised to be on the lookout.

LONG MUSEUM

An overview of Chinese art history and contemporary art

Collectors:
Liu Yiqian & Wang Wei

Address:
3398 Longteng Avenue
Xuhui District
Shanghai
China
Tel +86 21 64227636
info@thelongmuseum.org
www.thelongmuseum.org

Opening Hours:
Tues–Thurs, Sun: 10am–5:30pm
Fri–Sat: 10am–6pm

The first collectors from Mainland China to make it onto the 2012 Artnews list of the 200 top collectors were the investor Liu Yiqian and his wife, Wang Wei. In December of that same year, the billionaires opened their collection to the public at the Long Museum in Shanghai. Liu's career began in the 1980s, with the opening of the Chinese market. First he turned his mother's small shop into a thriving business. Then a friend introduced him to the newly created financial sector, where he grew his fortune. For over twenty years the couple has bought art from China mainly at auctions, ranging from traditional art to work by contemporary artists such as Zhou Chunya, Wang Guangyi, Zhang Xiaogang, and Yue Minjun. Meanwhile, the museum in Shanghai now occupies two locations: older works remain in Pudong while current positions are presented at West Bund, since 2014. And a third venue opened in spring 2016 in Chongqing.

QIAO SPACE

Presenting young Chinese and international artists in two locations

Collector:
Qiao Zhibing

Addresses:
2555 Longteng Avenue
Xuhui District
Shanghai
China

Tank Shanghai:
2350 Lonteng Avenue
Xuhui District
Shanghai
China

qiaozhibing@gmail.com
www.qiaocollection.com

Please check the website for the most current information on opening hours.

At West Bund, one of Shanghai's main art hubs, you'll find Qiao Space, featuring a stellar collection of Chinese and international art. Here, Qiao Zhibing, an engaging personality who has been collecting contemporary art since 2006, show cases a variety of art genres in rotating exhibitions. His collection focuses primarily on the recent generation of Chinese artists, including Liu Wei, Zhang Enli, Yang Fudong, MadeIn Company, or Qiu Xiaofei. An additional emphasis is on international artists like Ólafur Elíasson, Sterling Ruby, Thomas Houseago, Michaël Borremans, Theaster Gates, and Danh Vo. Opening at the end of 2018, approximately one kilometer upriver, is Qiao's second location: Tank Shanghai, where five former oil tanks in a disused industrial area have been converted into an art and cultural center and an adjoining park. Here, over sixty thousand square meters of art, urban life, and nature enter into dialog with one another.

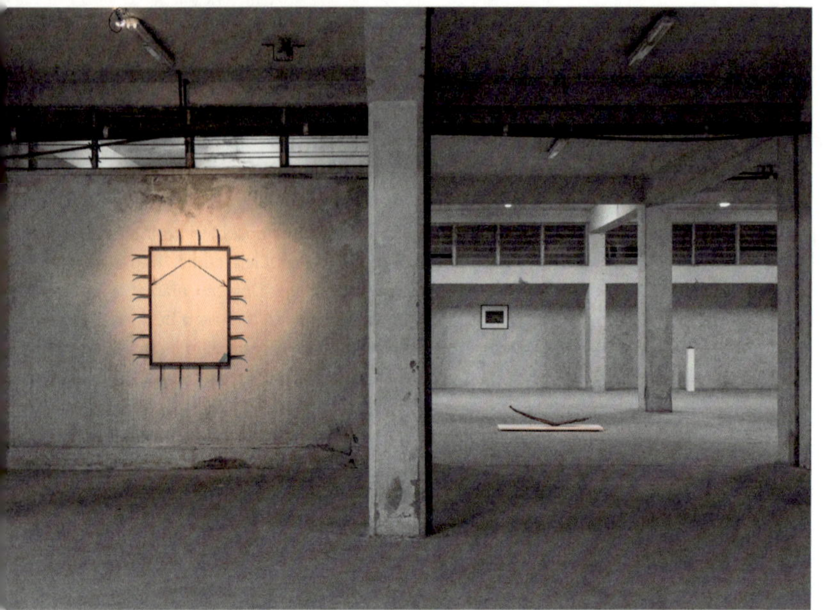

THE OFFICE COLLECTION

Positions from various cultures in dialogue

Collector:
Anastasios A. Gkekas

Address:
Solonos 46
1011 Nicosia
Cyprus
Tel +357 9 9848495
collection@theofficegallery.com

By appointment only.

Founded in 2009 by Anastasios A. Gkekas, the collection presides over a wide variety of formats, artists, and thematic content. Gkekas, who runs a gallery close to his apartment within the medieval walls of Nicosia's city center, loves juxtaposing otherwise contrasting positions. The private collection, which he presents at his home, as well as in external exhibitions, includes works by international artists, mainly from Europe and the Middle East. Often these are figurative photographs or sculptures with motifs like the human body, which serves as a point of departure for dealing with political themes. The works of Cypriot artists Nicolas Panayi and Glafkos Koumides, for example, address and examine the current situation in their divided homeland, while those of Nazgol Ansarinia center on modern Iran. British artist Robert Montgomery, by contrast, focuses on Western civilization in works involving poetic writing.

THE SUBLIME HYACINTH COLLECTION

Czech art meets Czech design

Collectors:
Boudewijn Jansen &
Yvette van Dishoeck

Address:
Mostecká 276/17
Malá Strana
118 00 Prague 1
Czech Republic
info@nogb.nl

By e-mail appointment only.

When Boudewijn Jansen and Yvette van Dishoeck, who are both Dutch, met in 1992 in Prague, it was love—for one another, the city, and Czech art. The couple began to put together an extensive collection by visiting artists in their studios, since galleries were few and far between right after the fall of the Wall. They first acquired large-scale paintings by Jan Merta or František Matoušek. Then came photographs by Ivan Pinkava as well as sculptures by Olbram Zoubek or Petr Císařovský, who also designed the extraordinary front door to the apartment building where the collectors live. The bronze relief depicts Czech philosopher Johann Amos Comenius and Dutch theologian Erasmus of Rotterdam. Barbora Škorpilová's clear and elegant interior design concept for the living spaces also creates the perfect setting for design objects by Milan Pekař and Jiři Pelcl. Incidentally, the collection is named after the mythological figure Hyakynthos, a lover of the god Apollo.

THE VERONIKA SMETÁČKOVÁ COLLECTION

Czech art, repatriated from abroad

Collector:
Veronika Smetáčková

Address:
Mostecká 276/17
Malá Strana
118 00 Prague 1
Czech Republic
Tel +49 162 1083766
mail@smetackova.de

By appointment only.

Veronika Smetáčková was born in Prague into a family of artists, but grew up in Berlin. More than ten years ago, she began intensively exploring her cultural identity—and discovered an unwavering passion for Czech art in the process. Since 2005, Smetáčková has been acquiring works at international art fairs and returning the pieces back to the Czech Republic—the home country of the artists. The collector, who spends her time between Berlin and Prague, fulfilled her dream when she purchased an apartment in a historic building in Prague's Old Town in 2013. This is where she presents works by primarily contemporary artists such as sculptor Eva Kot'átková, installation artist Krištof Kintera, or sculptor David Černý. However, the collection also includes works by international representatives who have been inspired in one way or another by the Czech Republic, such as Berlin-based Lennart Grau or Romanian artist Ioana Nemeş.

DJURHUUS COLLECTION

International contemporary art tending toward irony and the grotesque

Collector:
Leif Djurhuus

Address:
Copenhagen, Denmark
ldj@plesner.com
www.djurhuuscollection.com

Visitation permitted only occasionally. Please inquire by e-mail.

If you have reservations, don't do it! This is the maxim of the Copenhagen lawyer and art collector Leif Djurhuus, who has been devoid of doubt roughly 2000 times, the number of works in his collection. Since he does not own a private museum, they are stored in a warehouse. A selection of 200 works was exhibited from August 2011 to January 2012 at the Aros Aarhus Art Museum. Showcased were pieces by the 1960s Danish avant-garde, such as Poul Gernes or Sven Dalsgaard. The collection also includes international sky-rocketeers like Robert Kusmirowski or Kendell Geers, along with plenty of young artists from all over the world. What interests Djurhuus is cutting-edge, border-crossing, provocative young art. If you make an appointment with him, Djurhuus will show you his collection wherever it is being exhibited.

PETER IBSEN COLLECTION

Minimalist works that hone your sense for detail

Collector:
Peter Ibsen

Address:
Copenhagen, Denmark
peter@copenhagen-contemporary.dk

By e-mail appointment only.

Peter Ibsen randomly collected art he liked for ten years. That is until the founder of the Copenhagen Contemporary art blog came across a black, checkerboard-like work by Gregor Hildebrandt—one that defied his powers of interpretation, making it impossible to put out of his mind. Ibsen decided to break from his past: he sold off his collected works and set himself a strict focus going forward. Since then, he has concentrated on monochrome and minimalist works by a viable number of artists he shows in his private home. Ibsen—who also co-curates the Code Art Fair in Copenhagen—often promotes young artists starting out in their careers. In addition to Hildebrandt, his collection includes works by Sergej Jensen, André Butzer, Sam Moyer, and Ethan Cook, among others. "I enjoy the fact that when there is less to see, you have to look a little harder," is how Ibsen explains his fondness for the "non-colors" black, white, and gray.

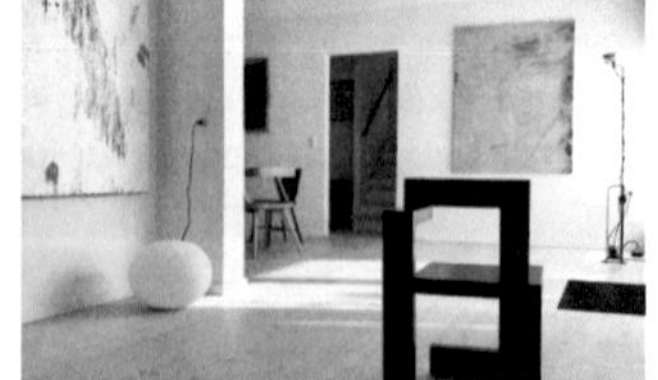

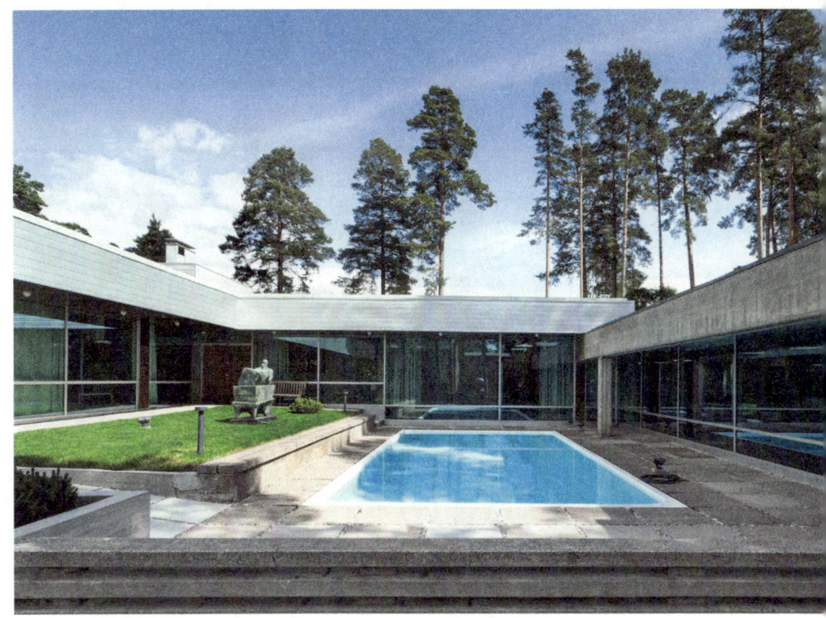

DIDRICHSEN ART MUSEUM

International and Finnish art in a once very modern Finnish home

Collectors:
Gunnar & Marie-Louise Didrichsen

Address:
Kuusilahdenkuja 1
00340 Helsinki
Finland
Tel +358 10 2193970
office@didrichsenmuseum.fi
www.didrichsenmuseum.fi

Please check the website for the most current information on opening hours.

A house in the elegant International Style, flooded with light, overlooking the ocean and a garden dotted with sculptures by Henry Moore. This dreamy house is not located in Pacific Palisades, California, but rather on a bay near Helsinki. The modernist villa, built in 1958, belonged to the collector pair Gunnar and Marie-Louise Didrichsen. Its architect, Viljo Revell, once an assistant to Alvar Aalto, later added a structure that in 1965 was opened as the Didrichsen Art Museum. Gunnar Didrichsen, a Dane who moved to Finland in 1928 and started a lucrative business, began collecting with his wife, Marie-Louise, and he loved progress as much as he liked art. The comprehensive collection of the now-late couple includes classical modernist works alongside pre-Columbian art and Chinese antiquities.

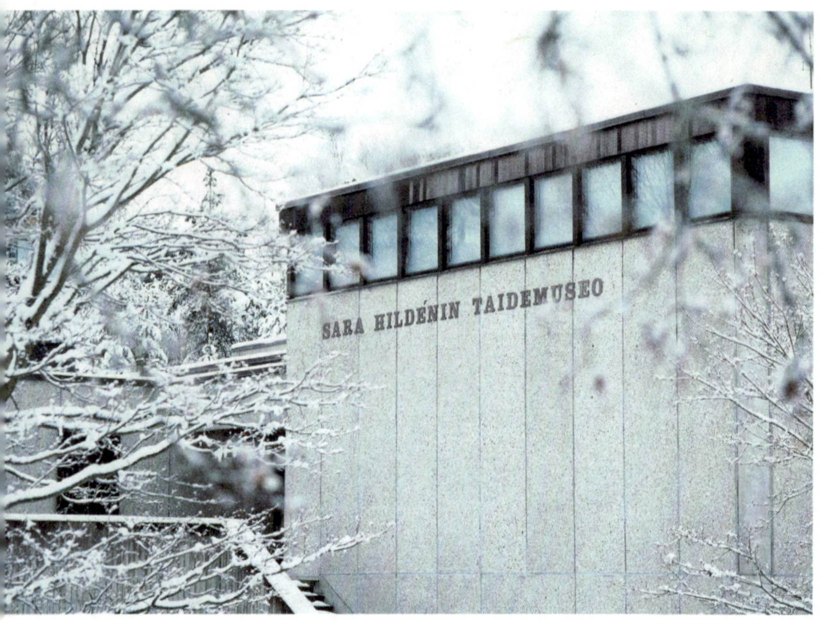

SARA HILDÉN ART MUSEUM

One of the most important Finnish art hubs, located on a beautiful lake

Collector:
Sara Hildén Foundation

Address:
Laiturikatu 13, Särkänniemi
33230 Tampere
Finland
Tel +358 3 56543500
sara.hilden@tampere.fi
www.tampere.fi/english/sarahilden

Opening Hours:
Tues–Sun: 10am–6pm

Typical Finland: the Sara Hildén Art Museum, in Tampere, is nestled harmoniously in an expansive sculpture park abutting a lakeshore. Sara Hildén (1905–1993) was a successful entrepreneur in the fashion industry who collected Finnish and international artists of her time. In 1962 she established a foundation. The museum was commissioned by the city of Tampere in 1979, and was designed by the local architect Pekka Ilveskoski as a two-story, low-rise building with large windows. Over 1 500 square meters serve to showcase the collection's works, some 5 000 objects. The focus remains on Finnish art: from the "Finnish Frida Kahlo," Helene Schjerfbeck, to very young artists. Wide-ranging special exhibitions feature internationally renowned artists like Alex Katz, Subodh Gupta, or Wilhelm Sasnal.

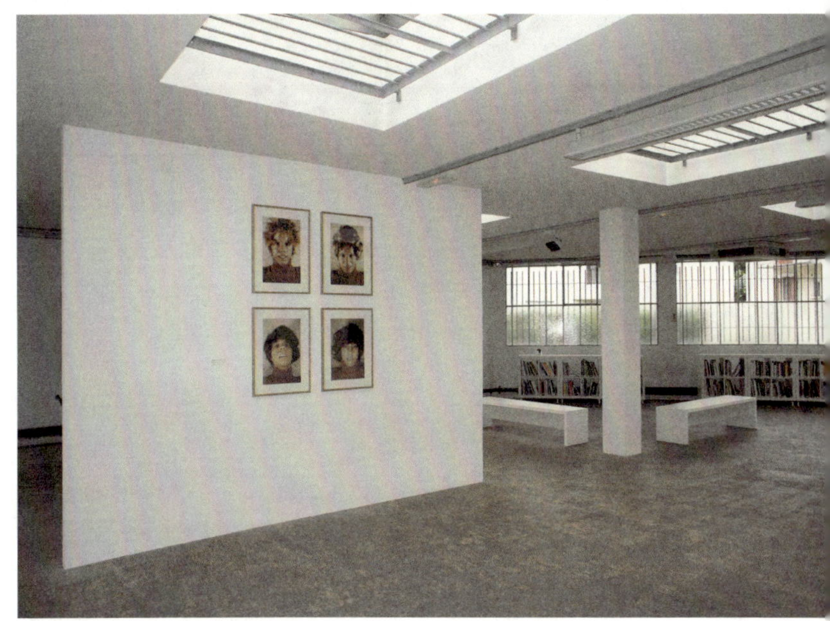

FONDATION POUR L'ART CONTEMPORAIN—CLAUDINE & JEAN-MARC SALOMON

From a solitary castle to the vibrant town center: contemporary art seeks a public audience

Collectors:
Claudine & Jean-Marc Salomon

Address:
34 Avenue de Loverchy
74000 Annecy
France
Tel +33 4 50028752
www.fondation-salomon.com

Please check the website for the most current information on opening hours.

In 2001, Claudine and Jean-Marc Salomon opened their contemporary art collection to the public in a beautiful, albeit secluded location in the Savoyard Alps. Housed in a castle, the Fondation Salomon opened at the time with a bang: forty works by the eccentric artist duo Gilbert & George caused quite a stir in the tranquil mountain valleys—and bestowed upon the collection the added attention from which it profits today. After twenty-five exhibitions, a move was made to the lively little town of Annecy, in 2014. The collection has set itself the goal of presenting not only more experimental forms of art in a municipal environment, but also of reaching a larger audience. An art prize also serves here as part of the new strategy, which allows francophone artists to spend half a year in New York.

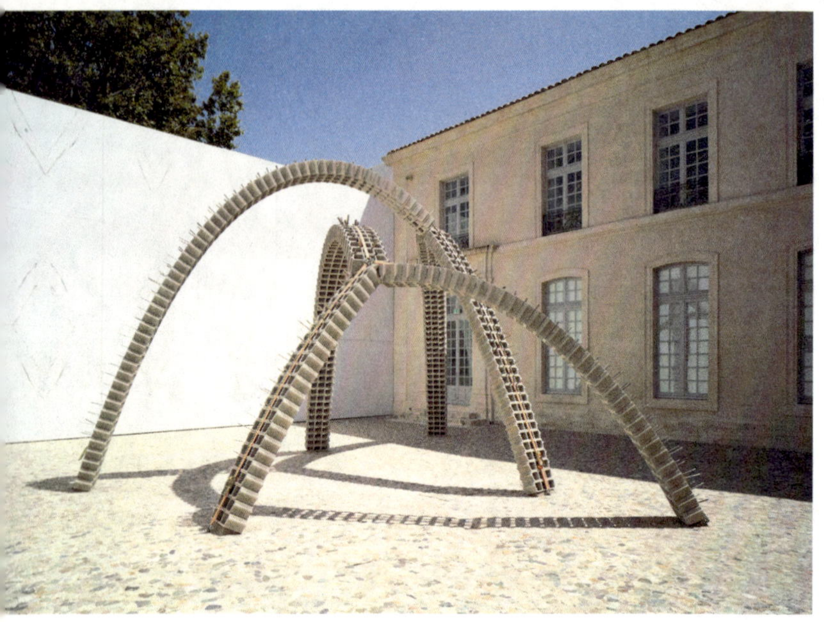

COLLECTION LAMBERT

Museum-quality international contemporary art since 1960

Collector:
Yvon Lambert

Address:
5 Rue Violette
84000 Avignon
France
administration@collectionlambert.com
www.collectionlambert.com

Opening Hours:
Tues–Sun: 11am–6pm

Collection Lambert's register of artists reads like a Who's Who of recent art history: from Francis Alÿs to Lawrence Weiner. And then a slew of top names in between to make any museum director jealous: Louise Bourgeois, Cy Twombly, and Jenny Holzer, to name just three. Yvon Lambert was once one of the most trendsetting gallerists in all of France. In 2014, he gave up his gallery, founded in 1966, in order to devote more time to his own collection and to publishing. With Collection Lambert, opened in 2000 in Avignon, he has fulfilled a dream of bringing his collection to his hometown in southern France. It was first housed in the somewhat dimly lit Hôtel de Caumont, an eighteenth-century palace. In July 2015, the exhibition space doubled in size when the neighboring Hôtel de Montfaucon was converted into a white-cube space.

L'INSTITUT CULTUREL BERNARD MAGREZ

French lifestyle and art in the heart of Bordeaux

Collector:
Bernard Magrez

Address:
16 Rue de Tivoli
33000 Bordeaux
France
Tel +33 5 56817277
contact@institut-bernard-magrez.com
www.institut-bernard-magrez.com

Opening Hours:
Fri–Sun: 1–6pm

Bernard Magrez may be known for his wine, which is how he made his fortune. At his Institut Culturel, in Bordeaux, he offers a broad audience access to his artistic interests. The elegant eighteenth-century townhouse Château Labottière presents parts of his collection of modern and contemporary art in temporary, thematic exhibitions. Magrez deliberately avoids the expertise of professional art consultants, instead letting his personal response to art guide his acquisitions. His eclectic taste is mirrored in a wide range of artists, from Lucio Fontana and Peter Doig to Wim Delvoye, Sam Taylor-Wood, Takashi Murakami, and Joana Vasconcelos. The patron also maintains three additional castles in the region, each dedicated to literary or musical events and to intellectual exchange.

PEYRASSOL—PARC DE SCULPTURES

A sculpture park on a centuries-old vineyard in Provence

Collectors:
Valérie Bach & Philippe Austruy

Address:
Commanderie de Peyrassol RN 7
83340 Flassans-sur-Issole
France
Tel +33 4 94697102
contact@peyrassol.com
www.peyrassol.com

Opening Hours:
Mid-April–mid-October
Mon–Fri: 9am–7pm
Sat–Sun: 10am–7pm
Mid-October–mid-April
Mon–Fri: 9am–6pm,
Sat: 10am–6pm

Located on the historic vineyard estate Peyrassol northwest of Saint-Tropez, in the Var Département of the Provence region, is one of France's most charming private sculpture parks. In 2001, the Brussels entrepreneur Philippe Austruy and his wife, gallery owner Valérie Bach, acquired the vineyard, which dates back to the year 1256. For the Belgian-French couple, wine, food, and hospitality are equally as important as contemporary art. Nestled on the wooded grounds are—in addition to a separate exhibition hall—over sixty sculptures by artists like Jean Dubuffet, César, Gavin Turk, Bernar Venet, Jean Tinguely, and Jaume Plensa, among others—and the collection is being constantly expanded. In recent years, works by French artists like Jeanne Susplugas or Fabrice Langlade have also been added. The perfect blend of art, Provençal flavors, and warm Mediterranean sun comprise the charm of this special place.

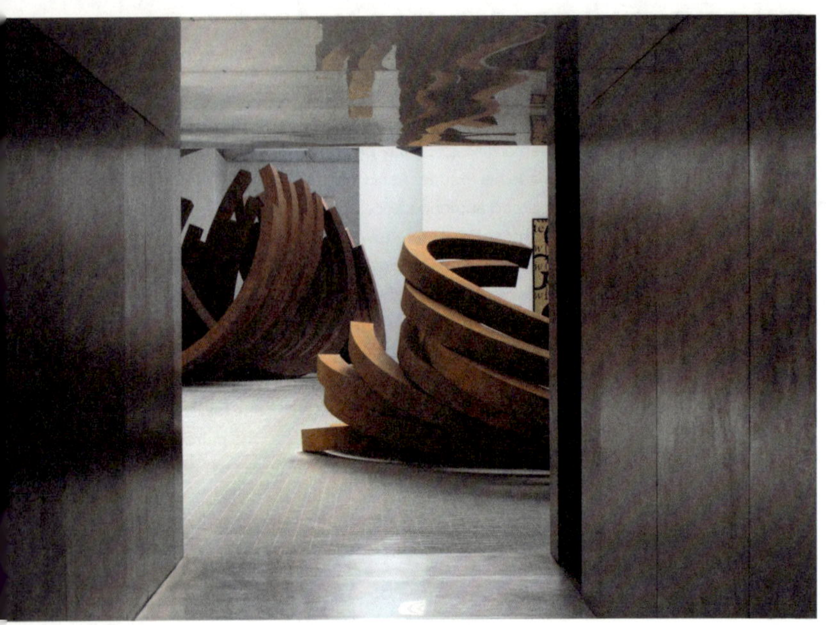

VENET FOUNDATION

An artist's take on collecting in the South of France

Collector:
Bernar Venet

Address:
Le Muy, France
info@venetfoundation.org
www.venetfoundation.org

Only guided tours with prior online registration, every Thursday and Friday.

While a majority of the collections featured in this guide have been assembled by successful players in the world of business, artists have also long been smitten by the collecting bug. In the summer of 2014, French conceptualist Bernar Venet opened the doors to his Le Muy property, which has become widely known as the Venet Foundation, a project over twenty-five years in the making. The site was developed in conversation with Minimalist master Donald Judd and expanded in 2017. Boasting a chapel designed by Frank Stella, and numerous large pieces by Venet himself, it features around 100 works by fellow postwar and contemporary art giants: Sol LeWitt, Carl Andre, Jean Tinguely, On Kawara, Anthony Caro, and Dan Flavin among them. The collection is a personal one, with Venet often exchanging his own works for those on view by artists who shaped the practice of Conceptual Art as we know it—all friends of Venet whom he met after moving to New York in 1966.

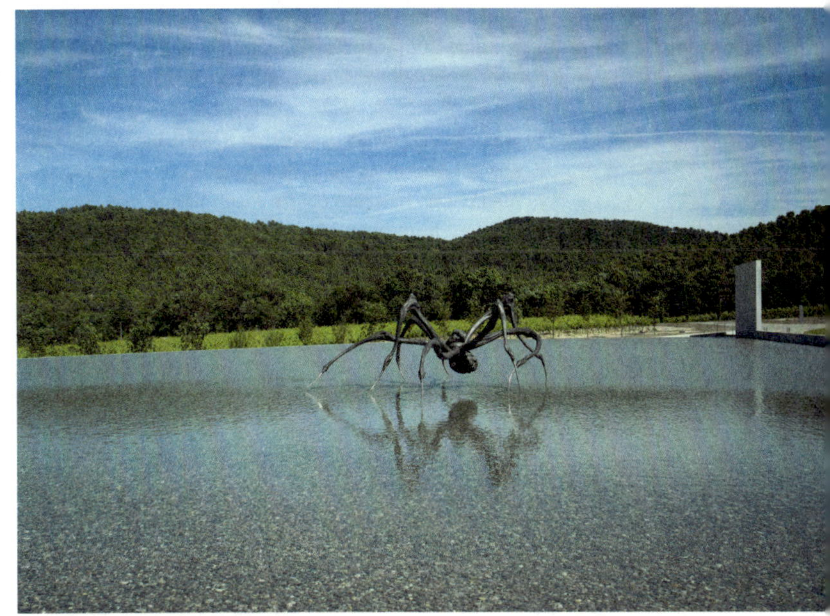

CHÂTEAU LA COSTE

Exceptional art projects on a slightly different kind of Provençal vineyard

Collector:
McKillen Family

Address:
2750 Route de la Cride
13610 Le Puy-Sainte-Réparade
France
Tel +33 4 42619292
reservations@chateau-la-coste.com
www.chateau-la-coste.com

Opening Hours:
Mon–Sun: 10am–7pm

Art, architecture, nature, and wine enter into a compelling dialogue here. When the Irish businessman Paddy McKillen acquired the idyllic winery Château La Coste, some seventeen years ago, the idea arose to forge a creative space that would bring together artists and architects in the scenic surroundings of Luberon. Since 2011, the 125-hectare site has been open to art lovers, who should budget at least two hours for a walking tour of the property's vineyards, olive groves, and woods. Japanese architect Tadao Ando designed the visitor center at the entrance, guarded by a large Louise Bourgeois bronze spider standing in water. Other highlights include site-specific works by Tracey Emin, Liam Gillick, Richard Serra, and Franz West. In addition, temporary shows in a separate exhibition hall, a luxury hotel, and several restaurants offer further reasons to stay awhile.

LE SILO

Minimalism, Conceptual Art, and geometric abstraction arranged perfectly in a former grain silo

Collectors:
Jean-Philippe & Françoise Billarant

Address:
Route de Bréançon
95640 Marines
France
lesilo@billarant.com

By appointment only.

They don't consider themselves pure collectors; they're more artists' companions and contemporaries. For over thirty years the Parisian business couple Jean-Philippe and Françoise Billarant have been intensely engaged with Minimalism, Conceptual Art, and geometric abstraction. Their friendships with artists have played a central role: Carl Andre, Robert Barry, François Morellet, and Michel Verjux are all pals. In 2010, in Marines, northwest of Paris, the couple had a 1948 grain silo transformed into exhibition spaces by the young architect Xavier Prédine-Hug, a former employee of Philippe Starck, who remodeled the simple structure into a reductive cathedral. And the artists? They thanked the collectors for their decades-long loyalty with perfect site-specific installations.

LA FABRIQUE—COLLECTION GENSOLLEN

A psychiatrist couple collects Conceptual Art as intellectual challenge

Collectors:
Marc & Josée Gensollen

Address:
11–13 Rue du Commandant Rolland
13008 Marseille
France
gensollen.la.fabrique@hotmail.fr

By e-mail appointment only.

"We do not just want to show art; we insist upon having a dialogue with others about it," say Marc and Josée Gensollen, who have amassed an impressive collection of Minimal and Conceptual Art since the early 1970s. The psychoanalytically trained couple from Marseille presents their collection of more than 500 key works in a stylishly converted former mill. In La Fabrique, light-filled living and exhibition rooms merge together over several floors. A remarkable library and an archive convey the impression of a great affinity for artists such as Lawrence Weiner, Gianni Motti, Pierre Huyghe, Dan Graham, and Jonathan Monk. Art as an intellectual challenge: the eloquent pair relishes how their collection inspires them to think about the present in more complex ways.

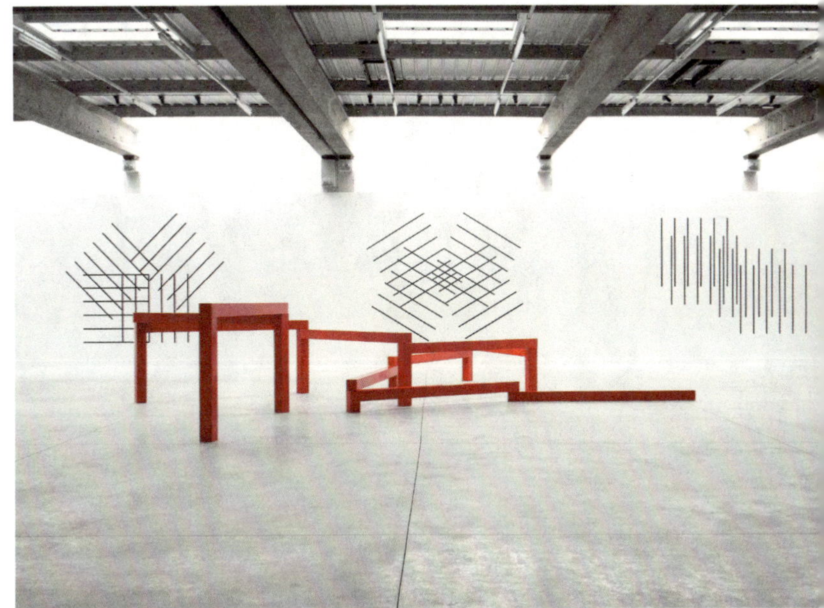

FONDS M-ARCO—LE BOX

Cutting-edge art on the grounds of a former slaughterhouse in Marseille

Collectors:
Marc & Marie-Hélène Féraud

Address:
Anse de Saumaty
Chemin du Littoral
13016 Marseille
France
Tel +33 4 91969002
contact@marco.org
www.m-arco.org

Opening Hours:
Mon–Fri: 10am–4pm

One of Marseille's former abattoirs is located on a remote harbor just outside the city limits. This is where Marc Féraud, a successful ship-outfitter, established both his company and—behind a shiny silver aluminum façade—his 1 000-square-meter exhibition space, Le Box. Here he presents works from his contemporary art collection, from François Morellet, Jean-Pierre Bertrand, Stanley Brouwn, Niele Toroni, Gérard Traquandi, Adrian Schiess, to Kelly Walker, Wade Guyton, and Anne Imhof, in one or two temporary exhibits a year. Together with his wife, Marie-Hélène, Féraud has been dedicated to young art since the late 1990s. In 2009, they founded the Fonds M-ArCo (Marseille-Art Contemporain). Le Box opened in 2011 with an exhibition of Gérard Traquandi and Alan Charlton. In addition to their own program, the Férauds work closely with the public museum collections of Marseille.

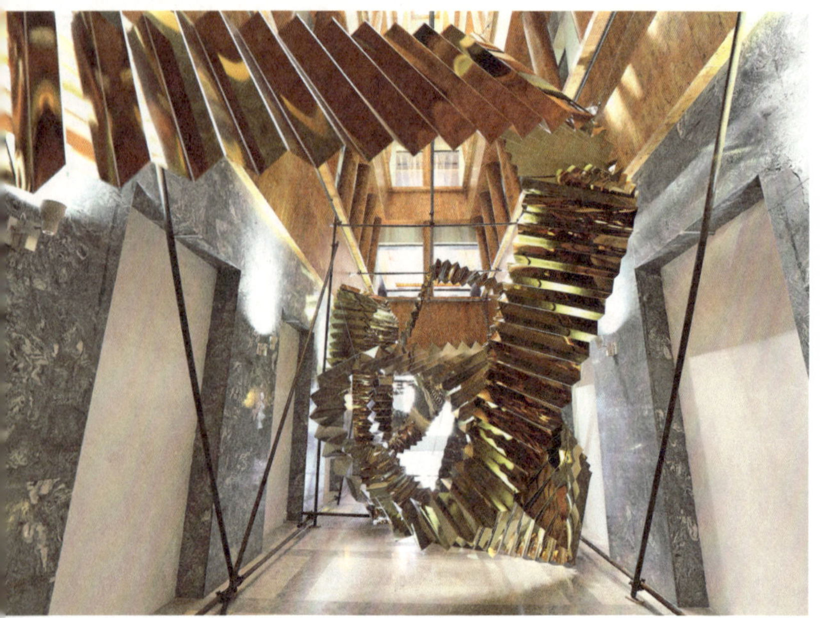

DSLCOLLECTION

The best of Chinese contemporary art, available 24/7, 365

Collectors:
Dominique & Sylvain Levy

Address:
Paris, France
art.dslcollection@gmail.com
www.dslcollection.org

Opening Hours:
Mon–Sun: 24 hours

The DSLCollection is only thirteen years old but the assemblage of ninety-some Chinese contemporary artists is by no means lacking in depth. Featuring works by leading figures like Ai Weiwei and Zeng Fanzhi, alongside those of promising younger artists who carry the Chinese avant-garde tradition forward like Song Yuanyuan and Zhao Zhao, the collection demonstrates its intent to remain current with an extensive online platform-cum-virtual museum, an iPad app, and 3-D films. Spearheaded by Paris-based couple Dominique and Sylvain Levy, the DSLCollection differs from others in that it strictly limits the number of artworks it holds at any one time to 250, and a number of works are sold each year to make room for new pieces. As opposed to collections where the works reflect a timeline of particular tastes, the Levys constantly strive to collect art that is relevant to their specific profile.

PARIS

Paris is not only popular the word over for its timeless charm, but also for its vibrant art scene. Everyone can find happiness here: whether at the numerous museums, in galleries, or at various art centers. One of the hotspots of the art scene is the Palais de Tokyo: a 22 000-square-meter laboratory for young international contemporary art—perfect for night owls, since it's open until midnight. Major exhibitions of modern and contemporary art are also on show at the Centre National d'Art et de Culture Georges-Pompidou, the Galerie Nationale du Jeu de Paume, and the Musée d'Art Moderne de la Ville de Paris, all located in the city center, as well as the Fondation Cartier, which lies a bit further south. The Grand Palais, on the other hand, serves as the venue for two high-profile fall fairs: the FIAC art fair and Paris Photo. If you want to visit commercial galleries, head to the Marais district. Here, for example, you'll find the distinguished spaces of the grandes dames of the Paris gallery scene, Chantal Crousel and Nathalie Obadia. In recent years, a hip new gallery district has popped up in the dynamic neighborhood of Belleville. And uncompromisingly contemporary galleries like Balice Hertling or Bugada & Cargnel are always worth a visit. Even among art collectors word has spread that you won't just make discoveries inside this neighborhood's trendy galleries and cool off-spaces but also in the popular restaurants and unconventional shops that lend this district its special flair. Opened in 2014 in the Bois de Boulogne in a deconstructivist Frank O. Gehry-designed building, the Fondation Louis Vuitton of mega-collector Bernard Arnault is still a much-discussed pilgrimage site for art enthusiasts. Elsewhere, the city also stimulates critical discourse about the present—for example at La Colonie, a multidisciplinary space founded near the Gare du Nord by artist Kader Attia in 2016, featuring three floors for exhibitions, concerts, and discussions.

FONDATION MAEGHT

Key figures of the twentieth-century avant-garde and an extravagant sculpture park

Collectors:
Aimé & Marguerite Maeght

Address:
623 Chemin des Gardettes
06570 Saint-Paul-de-Vence
France
Tel +33 4 93328163
accueil@fondation-maeght.com
www.fondation-maeght.com

Opening Hours:
October–June
Mon–Sun: 10am–6pm
July–September
Mon–Sun: 10am–7pm

It all started in the 1920s. Aimé Maeght, a lithographer, moved from the outskirts of Lille to Cannes and opened a small printing company with his wife, Marguerite, where they also sold radios and furniture. The then-unknown painter Pierre Bonnard asked them to take a few of his paintings on commission. They sold out in an instant, leading to one of the biggest success stories of twentieth-century art dealing. In 1946 the couple opened their legendary gallery in Paris and organized shows with Henri Matisse, Marc Chagall, and Wassily Kandinsky, and with Americans like Alexander Calder. The Fondation Maeght, founded in 1964, centers on works by all these artists and acts as a gift to posterity. With aesthetic inspiration from the likes of Marc Chagall, Joan Miró, and Georges Braque, Spanish architect Josep Lluís Sert constructed a museum of Mediterranean light that attracts roughly 200 000 visitors a year.

FONDATION FRANCÈS

Contemporary photography in the service of discussion

Collectors:
Estelle & Hervé Francès

Address:
27 Rue Saint-Pierre
60300 Senlis
France
www.fondationfrances.com

Opening Hours:
Tues–Sat: 11am–1pm, 2–7pm

For Estelle and Hervé Francès, the collector's mission is not just to pile up works of art, but rather to be creative in bringing diverse art positions together in order to foster dialogue. In 2009 the head of a cultural communication office and her husband, an ad agency boss, opened their collection in Senlis, a small city outside of Paris. The 300-square-meter space in an eighteenth-century building offers enough room for thematic exhibitions every half year. There are also guest studios, where artists can spend a summer. The Francès' collection aims to provoke discussion, to foster new interactions, and to unsettle the emotions. Exhibiting photographs of vulnerable or sexually charged human bodies—works by Andres Serrano, Vanessa Beecroft, Dash Snow, or Larry Clark—often does the trick.

SAMMLUNG FIEDE

Young contemporary art in very different locations

Collector:
Friedrich Gräfling

Address:
Aschaffenburg, Germany
fiede@culturalavenue.org
www.sammlung-fiede.de

Only guided tours with prior registration.

When Friedrich Gräfling was fifteen years old, he was faced with the decision to buy a PlayStation or the work of a graffiti artist. He opted for the latter, thereby laying the foundation for this impressive collection of contemporary art. The architect shows his art today in his hometown of Aschaffenburg, where he converted a former slaughterhouse into an unconventional 600-square-meter venue, featuring one new exhibition annually. Additionally, Gräfling initiated an independent exhibition space, called Salon Kennedy, in a prestigious historic apartment in Frankfurt. "I am interested in the idea of sharing works with people who otherwise might not have the opportunity to see artists from abroad or even this kind of art," says the collector, who proved early on to possess a good sense for quality, acquiring works by Taryn Simon, Yves Scherer, Katharina Grosse, and Andy Boot.

KUNSTMUSEUM WALTER

Former East meets West in a remodeled industrial monument

Collector:
Ignaz Walter

Address:
Beim Glaspalast 1
86153 Augsburg
Germany
Tel +49 821 8151163
office@kunstmuseumwalter.com
www.kunstmuseumwalter.com

Opening Hours:
Fri–Sat: 11am–8pm
Sundays and public holidays:
11am–6pm
And by appointment.

His motto: *Don't let others define your understanding of art.* Since the early 1970s, the Augsburg developer Ignaz Walter has been collecting modern and contemporary art from 1945 to today. He focuses mainly on painting and sculpture, but also the niche-medium of glass art—the latter is prominently represented in the collection via the works of the Italian Egidio Costantini. The juxtaposing of art from East and West Germany is of particular interest to Walter. Painters from the former East Germany—Bernhard Heisig, Wolfgang Mattheuer, or Werner Tübke—are represented as prominently as Georg Baselitz, Sigmar Polke, or A.R. Penck, who were all born in East Germany but carved out their careers in the West. Walter exhibits his roughly 1 600 works in a 6 000-square-meter glass palace, a remodeled industrial landmark from 1909-10 in Augsburg's garment district.

MUSEUM FRIEDER BURDA

A comprehensive collection of high-profile classical modernism and international contemporary art

Collector:
Frieder Burda

Address:
Lichtentaler Allee 8 B
76530 Baden-Baden
Germany
Tel +49 7221 398980
office@museum-frieder-burda.de
www.museum-frieder-burda.de

Opening Hours:
Tues–Sun: 10am–6pm

In 2004, architect Richard Meier realized the Museum Frieder Burda, a light-filled architectural marvel, where interior and exterior space, art and park landscape enter into dialogue. Here, works of the twentieth and twenty-first century are presented on four levels in temporary exhibitions. A fascination with color and the emotional expressive qualities of art have been the focus of entrepreneur Frieder Burda for more than forty years. This passion is reflected in works of German and American Abstract Expressionism as well as in the modern archaicism of Pablo Picasso's late work. Another focus is on the second half of the twentieth century and artists such as Gerhard Richter, Sigmar Polke, and Georg Baselitz. The collection, which today comprises around 1 000 paintings, sculptures, and works on paper, is constantly growing. Works by Katharina Grosse, Andreas Gursky, and Rodney Graham have been recently added.

SAMMLUNG KLÖCKER

Portraits of women in all possible facets in a private atmosphere

Collectors:
Maria Lucia & Ingo Klöcker

Address:
Bad Homburg v. d. Höhe,
Germany
ml.kloecker@gmx.de

By e-mail appointment only.

For thirty years, Maria Lucia and Ingo Klöcker have been collecting postwar and contemporary works of art with a focus on portraits of women. Ingo Klöcker humorously chalks this decision up to his wife, "by the time I realized it, it was too late." Apart from this, the couple has no other imposed restrictions. When collecting they both pay strict attention to quality, but are not swayed by art historical or market trends. What's most important is that the work of art tells a story about love, youth, old age, life, or death. Consequently, the range and variety is expansive: paintings, sculptures, paper and photographic works by German and international artists such as Lucian Freud, Katsura Funakoshi, Franz Gertsch, Eugène Leroy, Wolfgang Mattheuer, Kiki Smith, Nancy Spero, or Werner Tübke. Parts of the collection have already been exhibited in various museums, but they take on a particular lifelike presence inside the collector's home.

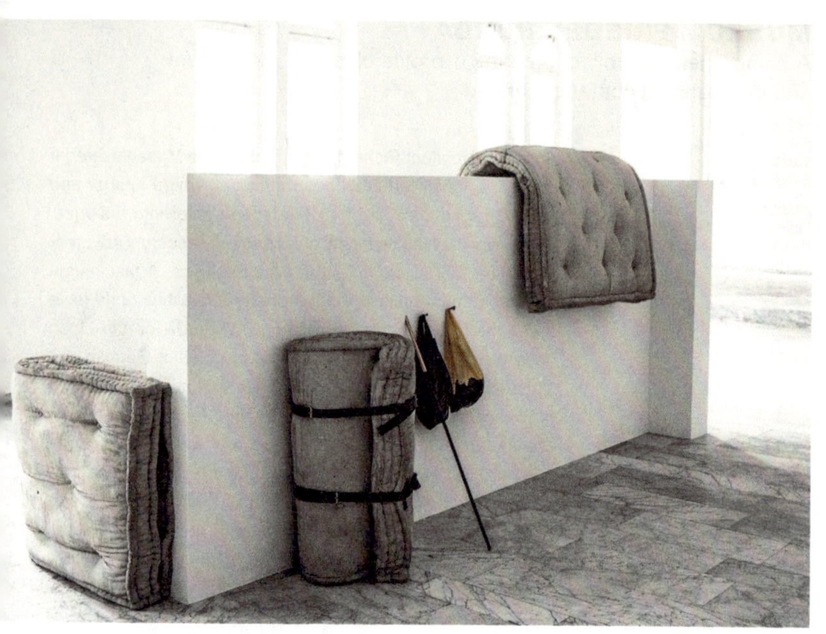

KAT_A—KUNST AM TURM_ANDRA

Top-notch conceptual and photographic art at the foot of the Seven Mountains

Collector:
Andra Lauffs-Wegner

Address:
Haus Hedwig
Konrad-Adenauer-Strasse 23
53604 Bad Honnef-Rhöndorf
Germany
info@kat-a.de
www.kat-a.de

By e-mail appointment only.

"Irony, intelligent wit, and a high regard for aesthetics are very important to me," says Andra Lauffs-Wegner. The shareholder in storied juice manufacturer Haus Rabenhorst was first introduced to collecting art while still in the cradle, so to speak, with her parents being enthusiastic supporters of Pop Art, Arte Povera, and Minimal Art. Since November 2014, Lauffs-Wegner has presented her own collection with a focus on conceptual and photographic art in a carefully renovated Wilhelminian villa in Bad Honnef. Here, a subtle patina prevails rather than a sterile white cube atmosphere: the rented premises of Haus Hedwig, a former rehabilitation center for mothers, deliberately exudes the charm of imperfection. Isa Genzken, Wolfgang Tillmans, Anne Imhof, Simon Denny, Katja Novitskova, and Yngve Holen are established highlights in a continuously growing collection. The extensive park grounds are also used for presenting works.

BMW ART GUIDE BLOG

In 2012, we published the first edition of this handy companion to private, publicly accessible art collections worldwide. With the art world in constant flux, we knew from the beginning that this would become an ongoing project, with subsequent editions to follow. In the course of research and preparation, we continually stumble upon exciting stories, innovative projects, and other publications we'd like to share with our readers. Since including all of these findings in the Art Guide would exceed the scope of our travel-friendly pocket format, we decided to launch the BMW Art Guide Blog, an interactive platform featuring all the additional material we cannot fit into our book, accessible by anyone, anywhere. As an additional place for thoughtfully curated content, the blog provides enough space to talk about individual collection visits, publishes personal interviews with collectors from around the world, and offers background information and insights into the topics that keep the art world buzzing. You can also find out more about the making of the Art Guide and receive further up-to-date book recommendations, hand-picked from our editors. With illustrated posts published on a regular basis, we aim for quality of content rather than quantity of posts in order to generate material that dives deeply into the world of collecting. If you always wanted to know why a former French mining town is starting to show up on the art radar, why a bottle of sake once helped collector Donald M. Hess acquire a beloved art work, and what Hans Ulrich Obrist thinks about the *BMW Art Guide by Independent Collectors*, follow the link to explore: www.bmw-art-guide.com.

The Blog was nominated for the German Design Award 2015 and received a special mention in the category Excellent Communications Design—Audiovisual and Digital Media.

STIFTUNG MUSEUM SCHLOSS MOYLAND

An extensive collection of Joseph Beuys's life and work meets contemporaries

Collectors:
Hans & Franz Joseph van der Grinten

Address:
Am Schloss 4
47551 Bedburg-Hau
Germany
Tel +49 2824 951060
info@moyland.de
www.moyland.de

Opening Hours:
April–September
Tues–Fri: 11am–6pm
Sat–Sun: 10am–6pm
October–March
Tues–Sun: 11am–5pm

The art-enthusiast brothers Hans and Franz Joseph van der Grinten had a lifelong friendship with Joseph Beuys. This resulted in a vast collection of nearly 6 000 works and roughly 100 000 letters, photos, and notes by the action artist, as well as numerous works by other artists. The Schloss Moyland collection has been open to the public as a museum of modern and contemporary art since 1997. With the Josef Beuys Archive, the museum has also established itself as an international research center for the artist's work. Renovated in 2011, the building shines in a new splendor. Even though Hans van der Grinten has since died and his brother Franz Joseph is retired, an extensive program is still offered. Last but not least, special exhibitions with younger artists or students of Beuys such as Katharina Sieverding ensure that visitors are continually drawn to this idyllic moated castle on the Lower Rhine.

GALERIE BASTIAN

Hybrid use: a mix of private collection showrooms and commercial gallery

Collectors:
Céline & Heiner Bastian

Address:
Berlin, Germany
Tel +49 30 20673840
info@galeriebastian.com

Please check the website for the most current information on opening hours.

Since 1989, the Bastian family of collectors and gallerists has presented its own collection in combination with commercial exhibitions. For over ten years, the gallery building at Kupfergraben, designed by architect David Chipperfield, provided the setting for this idiosyncratic concept. After donating the building to the Staatliche Museen zu Berlin, Céline, Heiner, and son Aeneas Bastian will be exhibiting in new locations: starting in 2018 in a London branch and, in 2020, at a new location in Berlin. Represented in their first-rate private collection are numerous well-known artists such as Joseph Beuys, Anselm Kiefer, Andy Warhol, Dan Flavin, Pablo Picasso, Damien Hirst, and Wim Wenders, but also emerging talents. A personal connection exists to many of the artists—for example, to Beuys, who Heiner Bastian once worked for early in his career as his personal secretary; before he then made a name as an art dealer, writer, and curator.

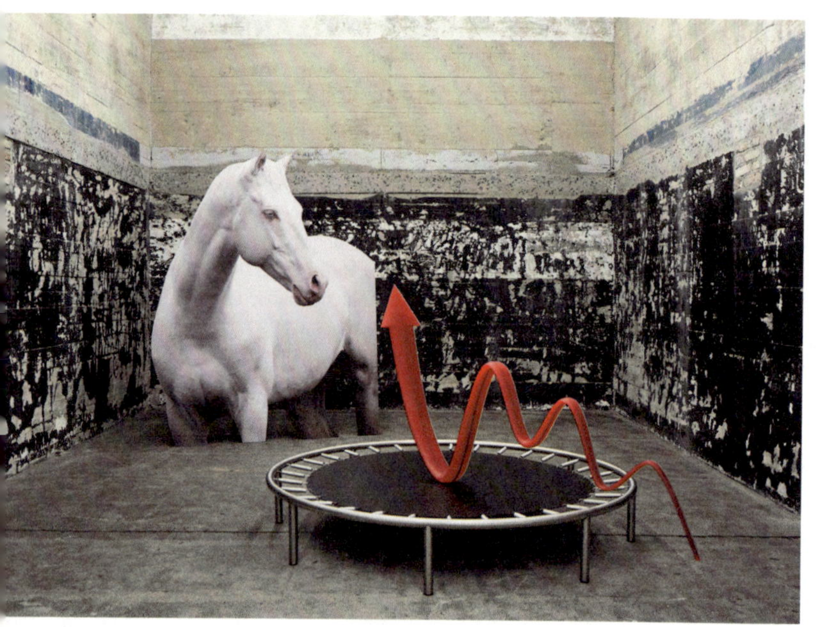

SAMMLUNG BOROS

Roughly 700 works of contemporary art in an extensively refurbished bunker

Collectors:
Christian & Karen Boros

Address:
Reinhardtstrasse 20
10117 Berlin
Germany
Tel +49 30 27594065
info@sammlung-boros.de
www.sammlung-boros.de

Opening Hours:
Thurs: 3–8pm
Fri–Sun: 10am–8pm
Only guided tours with prior online registration.

This is a spectacular place for a private collection of zeitgeist-minded art. It took Karen and Christian Boros four years to transform a former air-raid bunker, an historic monument in Berlin's Mitte district, into their private museum. Ad-man Boros, who has offices in Wuppertal and Berlin, has been collecting contemporary art since the 1990s. Since 2008, the collection has shown groups of works by international artists in exhibitions that change every four years. In 2017, the third presentation opened with works by Yngve Holen, Sergej Jensen, Guan Xiao, Kris Martin, and Uwe Henneken, among others. The remodeling of the bunker—which was used in East Germany as a warehouse for exotic fruits, and then as a techno club after the Wall came down—took both time and money. Architect Jens Casper had to remove a number of walls to transform 120 small rooms into eighty larger ones—approximately 3 000 square meters are now available for presenting work.

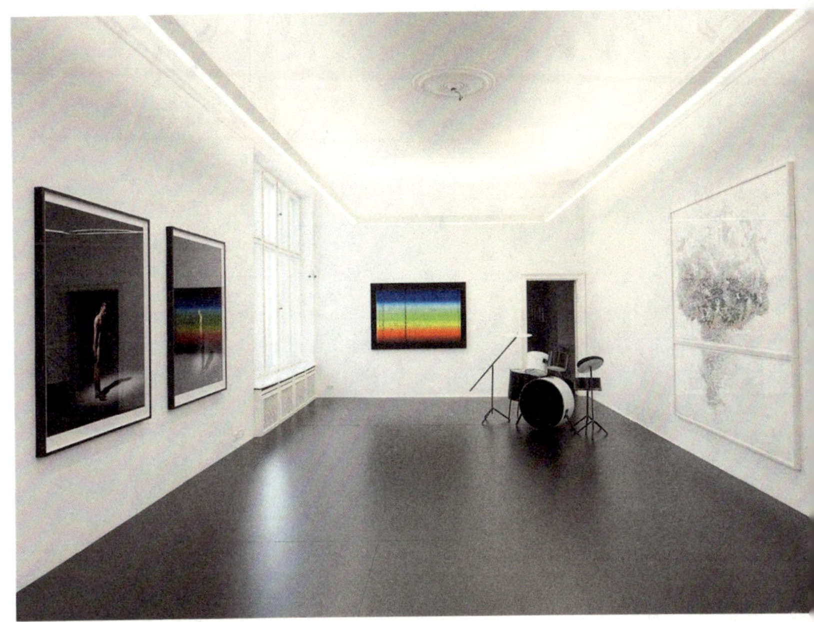

SALON DAHLMANN

A Finnish collector and the revival of the salon tradition in Berlin

Collectors:
Timo Miettinen & Iiris Ulin

Address:
Marburger Strasse 3
10789 Berlin
Germany
Tel +49 30 21909830
info@salon-dahlmann.de
www.salon-dahlmann.de

Opening Hours:
Sat: 12–6pm
And by appointment.

You simply can't ignore Berlin—Finnish collector Timo Miettinen is convinced of this. In 2010 he acquired, together with his three sisters, an impressive historical building in Berlin-Charlottenburg. The technology company owner initiated a salon with rotating exhibitions on the building's first floor. Since 2004 he has collected—together with his wife, the architect Iiris Ulin—international contemporary art with a focus on Germany and Finland. On Marburger Strasse 3 he also presents works from his collection, ranging from Albert Oehlen and Björn Dahlem to Marianna Uutinen. At the center of his interest, however, is his Salon Dahlmann—named after the home's previous owner—which hosts openings that are always well attended. Miettinen also regularly invites young curators to have a fresh look at other scenes and collectors.

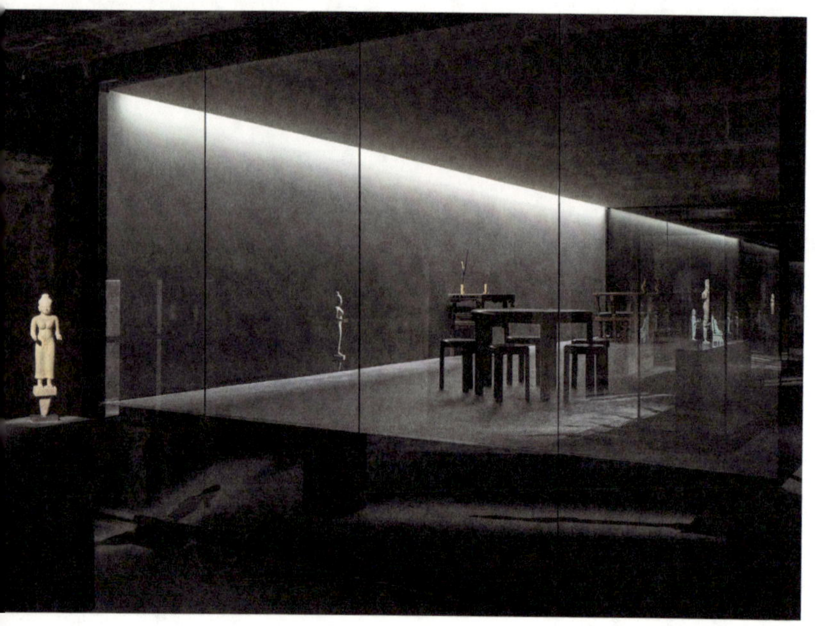

THE FEUERLE COLLECTION

Antique Asian art and furniture meets contemporary art in a Berlin World War II bunker

Collector:
Désiré Feuerle

Address:
Hallesches Ufer 70
10963 Berlin
Germany
info@thefeuerlecollection.org
www.thefeuerlecollection.org

Only guided tours with prior online registration.

Désiré Feuerle has assembled one of the most extensive collections of Asian art in Europe. It unites Khmer sculptures from the seventh to thirteenth century, Imperial Chinese lacquer and stone furniture, wood and stone Chinese Scholar-gentry furniture from the Han to the Qing dynasty, and contemporary works by artists such as Anish Kapoor, Zeng Fanzhi, and James Lee Byars, among others. A former gallerist, Feuerle was the first to exhibit contemporary art alongside antique Asian artifacts in the 1990s. This highly unusual collection has an equally unorthodox home: a former World War II telecommunications bunker in Berlin-Kreuzberg, which has been open to the public since May 2016. Feuerle commissioned British architect John Pawson, known for his subtle redesigns of historic buildings, with the conversion of the two-story, 6 000-square-meter space. The museum generates new perspectives on global artistic positions.

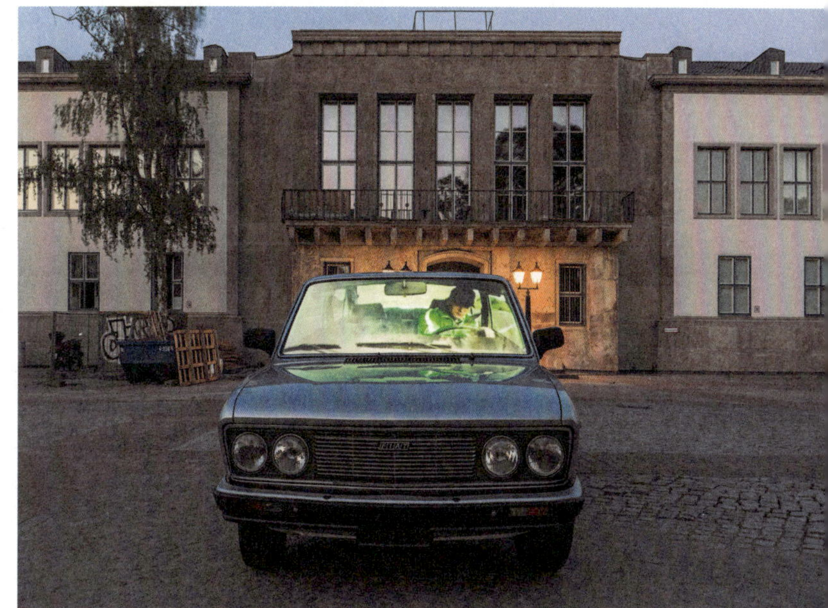

FLUENTUM COLLECTION

Contemporary video art in historic surroundings

Collector:
Markus Hannebauer

Address:
Clayallee 174
14195 Berlin
Germany
info@fluentum.org
www.fluentum.org

Only guided tours with prior online registration.

Markus Hannebauer founded the Fluentum Collection in 2010 focusing on works of time-based media art. He discovered his passion for artistic films and videos at the Loop Fair in Barcelona, where he also acquired his first work of art: *Secret Machine,* a video work by Reynold Reynolds. Initially the collection was housed in Hannebauer's apartment, and selected videos could be viewed on his website. Since then, however, the Berlin-based software entrepreneur, whose collection includes works by Omer Fast, Hito Steyerl, and Christian Jankowski, acquired a building where films and videos can be presented under ideal conditions. For this, architects Sauerbruch Hutton transformed part of the former US military headquarters in Berlin's Dahlem district, the location from where General Clay orchestrated the Berlin Airlift in 1948–9, into a residence and exhibition venue for hosting discussion panels and artist talks in addition to presenting the collection.

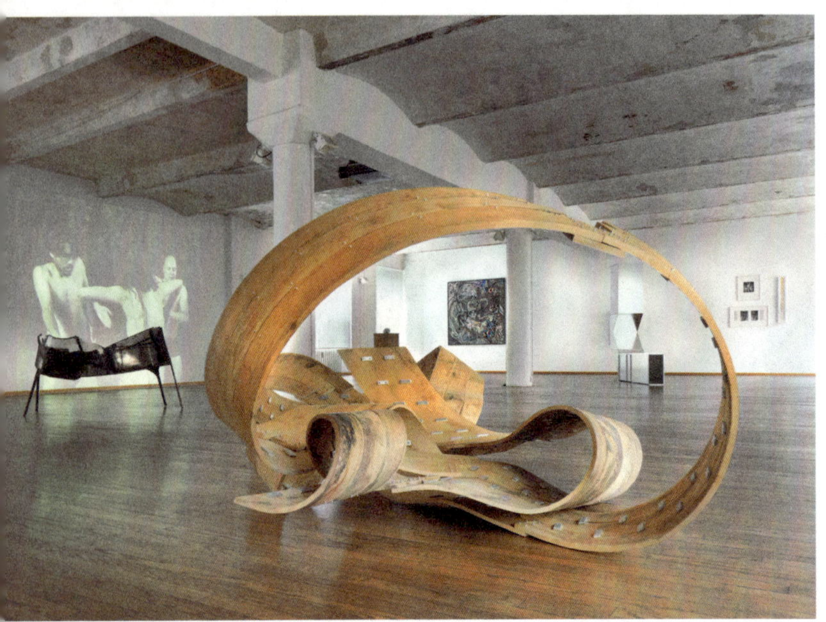

SAMMLUNG HOFFMANN

International contemporary art in a collector's private residence

Collectors:
Erika & Rolf Hoffmann

Address:
Sophie-Gips-Höfe, Staircase C
Sophienstrasse 21
10178 Berlin
Germany
Tel +49 30 28499120
info@sammlung-hoffmann.de
www.sammlung-hoffmann.de

Only guided tours with prior registration, every Saturday from 11am–4pm.
Closed through August and between Christmas and New Year.

They were among the first to head to Berlin after the Fall of the Wall to make their personal collection of art available to the public. Erika and Rolf Hoffmann, from Mönchengladbach, had been collecting German and American artists such as Günther Uecker, Frank Stella, or Bruce Nauman for some time. When they moved to Berlin, in the mid-1990s, they had long since sold their textile company. They acquired a former sewing-machine factory in Berlin's Mitte district, entirely renovated it, and then moved into two of its floors. And now they have created something of a ritual in the German capital: every Saturday small groups of visitors in gray felt slippers push through the spacious private rooms, led by young, laidback guides. Once a year the rooms are switched out with new works. Fresh acquisitions from Poland, Japan, or China have shifted the collection's focus ever more eastward. Since her husband's death, in 2001, Erika Hoffmann has been actively leading the project herself.

KIENZLE ART FOUNDATION

Exciting rediscoveries far from the mainstream

Collector:
Jochen Kienzle

Address:
Bleibtreustrasse 54
10623 Berlin
Germany
Tel +49 30 89627605
office@kienzleartfoundation.de
www.kienzleartfoundation.de

Opening Hours:
Thurs–Fri: 2–7pm
Sat: 11am–4pm
And by appointment.

Even in the Berlin art scene he is seen as an individualist, which says a lot. Jochen Kienzle collects and displays non-mainstream works of art, like those by painter Klaus Merkel, who in the 1980s worked exclusively in a limited gray palette. Or work by Josef Kramhöller, a painter and performance artist who committed suicide in 2000, at age thirty-one. Acknowledged as a talent by fellow artists, Kramhöller was pretty much ignored by the art market. With Jack Goldstein and Franz Erhard Walther, the collection also includes well-known names. Kienzle's parents collected modernist works; as a high-school student he purchased his first work at Art Basel, and went on to study art history. In 2010 the former gallerist opened the Kienzle Art Foundation, and his engagement in the Berlin scene has earned him much credit. The Kienzle Art Foundation works closely with curators organizing exhibitions, film screenings, and discussion forums.

KÖNIG FAMILY COLLECTION

Contemporary conceptual art in a converted church tower

Collector:
König Family

Address:
Belltower Apartment
St. Agnes Church
Alexandrinenstrasse 118
10969 Berlin
Germany
Tel +49 30 26103080
turm@st-agnes.net

Visitation with overnight stay.
By appointment only.

Johann König is one of those Berlin gallery owners who embodies the city's spirit in the most prominent of ways—at home and at international art fairs, where he mainly presents artists who work conceptually. This also suits König and Berlin: he commissioned architect Arno Brandlhuber to convert the former 1960s-era St. Agnes Church into a spectacular gallery—with roughly 800 square meters of exhibition space. But König reserved the square tower for his own collection. Here things are a bit cozier; 100 square meters of furnished space, spread over six levels, feature a rotating presentation of art that personally inspires him and his family—including artists such as Franz West, David Lamelas, Shannon Ebner, and Jorinde Voigt. Another highlight: the collection can only be viewed if you've made a reservation to stay there overnight.

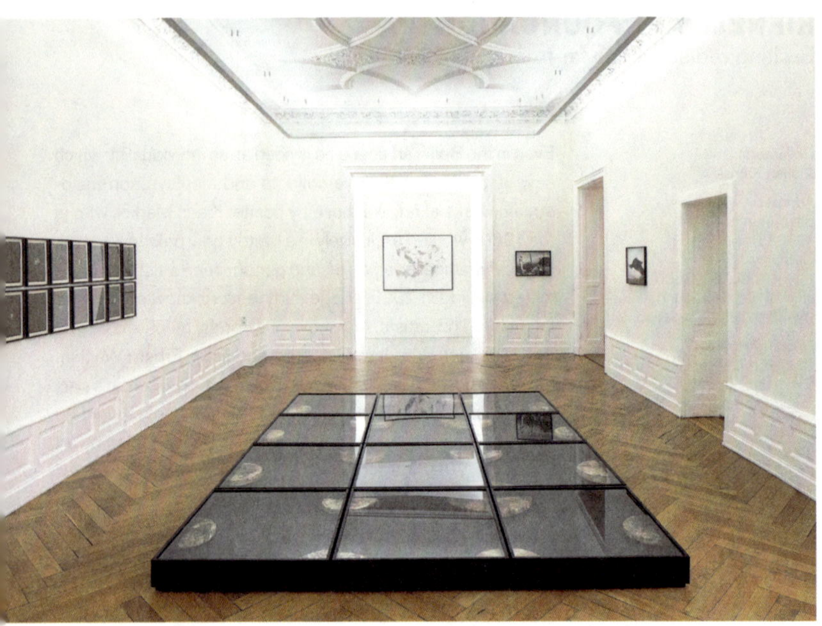

KUNSTSAELE BERLIN

An exciting private collection on a bel étage in Berlin's Schöneberg district

Collector:
Geraldine Michalke

Address:
Bülowstrasse 90
10783 Berlin
Germany
Tel +49 30 81801868
info@kunstsaele.de
www.kunstsaele.de

Opening Hours:
Wed–Sat: 11am–6pm
And by appointment.

This elegant flat on Bülowstrasse with lavishly ornamented ceilings has hosted works from the Bergmeier collection since 2010. Halle-native Geraldine Michalke, whose maiden name is Bergmeier, has assembled her collection over more than thirty years. The broad spectrum encompasses German Informel, including artists such as Gerhard Hoehme or Emil Schumacher, and young Leipzig photographers like Ricarda Roggan and Matthias Hoch. Recently acquired works, for instance by Michael Müller, Meuser, Ian Kiaer, or Art & Language, are indicative of an increasing shift towards sculptural and installative positions. Young curators are regularly invited to conceive exhibitions with works from the collection. The program is augmented by free-form projects including the "Zu Gast" format. Launched several years ago, this guest series invites fellow collectors like Herford-based entrepreneur Heiner Wemhöner to present works from their own collection.

THE LIBRARY BERLIN

A private library where world affairs, arts, and music come together

Collector:
Christian Kaspar Schwarm

Address:
Berlin, Germany
scsz@scsz.eu

Visitation permitted only occasionally. Please inquire by e-mail.

Beginning in 1900, the Klub der Kommenden—an interdisciplinary group of artists, authors, and scholars with an eye for the new—would meet not far from Nollendorfplatz. Inspired by this idea, strategic developer Christian Kaspar Schwarm initiated a library in the same neighborhood as a creative melting pot: the centerpiece is more than 5 000 artist publications and non-fiction books, nearly all published in the twenty-first century—supplemented by rotating works of concept-based and political art from Schwarm's collection, by Slavs & Tatars and others. A permanent sound installation by Bertrand Fleuret is based on the tradition of Japanese "jazz kissaten" (jazz clubs), where, after 1945, Western music was introduced to the Land of the Rising Sun and played through elaborate, lively loudspeaker systems. It's one of many examples that reflect the library's philosophy: "Innovation often comes from skillfully combining existing phenomena."

ME COLLECTORS ROOM BERLIN/ STIFTUNG OLBRICHT

A cabinet of existentially themed curiosities from the Renaissance to now

Collector:
Thomas Olbricht

Address:
Auguststrasse 68
10117 Berlin
Germany
Tel +49 30 86008510
info@me-berlin.com
www.me-berlin.com

Opening Hours:
Wed–Mon: 12–6pm

The body, eros, and the transitory are existential topics at the center of the collection owned by Thomas Olbricht, a physician and heir to the Wella hair-care fortune. Olbricht was influenced by his great-uncle Karl Ströher's passion for collecting. Moreover, he loves extremes: Cindy Sherman meets the grand-style painter Jonas Burgert; Marlene Dumas meets Andres Serrano. Since 2010 the collection has been on display at a Düttmann & Kleymann-designed building on Auguststrasse in Berlin-Mitte. The ground floor houses a café, a shop, and a lounge; the remaining 1 300 square meters are reserved for exhibition space. The core of Olbricht's subjective *Wunderkammer* is formed by over 200 objects, dating back to the Renaissance and Baroque periods. The ME Collectors Room quickly became a space for dialogue with other collections and discourse on art in general. The "ME," by the way, is an acronym for "moving energies."

COLLECTION REGARD

Overlooked photography of the twentieth century with a focus on Berlin

Collector:
Marc Barbey

Address:
Steinstrasse 12
10119 Berlin
Germany
Tel +49 30 84711947
info@collectionregard.com
www.collectionregard.com

Opening Hours:
Fri: 2–6pm
And by appointment.

It all began with a fortuitous discovery: a few years ago French photography collector Marc Barbey found a collection of negatives by the German artist Hein Gorny. Since then he has administered the estate of the underappreciated photojournalist and commercial photographer. In 2011 Barbey showed the first part of the collection, Gorny's images of war-ravaged Berlin, accompanied by art-historical research. Connoisseurs were impressed. The software entrepreneur Barbey has been focused on growing Collection Regard since 2005. He is endowed with a sharp instinct for other overlooked twentieth-century talents. Stylish vintage furniture from Scandinavia provides for a relaxed atmosphere in his Berlin-Mitte apartment, where not only exhibitions take place but also regular artist talks, guided tours, and movie screenings.

ROCCA STIFTUNG

A thematically structured collection of contemporary art in a villa

Collectors:
Joëlle & Eric Romba

Address:
Berlin, Germany
Tel +49 30 89398917
info@rocca-stiftung.de
www.rocca-stiftung.de

Visitation permitted only occasionally. Please inquire by e-mail.

Joëlle Romba brings the best possible conditions to building her own art collection. The art historian, curator, and collection consultant garnered experience in a Berlin gallery and as the Berlin representative of the auction house Sotheby's. For the past ten years Romba and her husband, Eric, a lawyer, have acquired around 150 works of contemporary art, ranging from Gregor Hildebrandt, Thilo Heinzmann, Eberhard Havekost, Joep van Lieflande, Kristine Roepstorff, and Wolfgang Tillmans, to Matti Braun and Charlotte Posenenske. The thematic foci of the collection—photorealistic painting, architecture in art, and the rethinking of art historical models—lends the collection structure and conceptual clarity. The Rombas present their treasures in a villa dating back to the turn of the century in Berlin-Schlachtensee. Visitors are welcome by appointment.

SØR RUSCHE SAMMLUNG

A traditional collection of Old Masters meets contemporary art

Collector:
Thomas Rusche

Address:
Berlin, Germany
m.kuehn@kleidungskultur-soer.de
www.kleidungskultur-soer.de

Visitation permitted only occasionally. Please inquire by e-mail.

Thomas Rusche is a fourth-generation collector. The textile entrepreneur's great-grandfather drove a horse and carriage through the Münster region buying antiques from farmers. His grandfather collected old paintings, and his father focused on Old Masters of the seventeenth century. His father also took his son to auctions and museums, and at age fourteen Rusche acquired his first work of art. Today, the collection boasts over 2 500 works from over 500 artists, located at the family estate in the Westphalian city of Oelde, and, at a second location, in an Art Nouveau apartment in Berlin-Charlottenburg. The focus of the collection is now on contemporary painting, with works by Marlene Dumas, Norbert Bisky, Daniel Richter, Matthias Weischer, Martin Eder, or Ruprecht von Kaufmann, among others. Rusche bought their works early and before the artists were well-known—a fact of which he remains proud.

SAMMLUNG SCHÜRMANN

Art and antagonism in a collection growing since 1972

Collectors:
Gaby & Wilhelm Schürmann

Address:
Berlin, Germany
visit@schuermann-berlin.de

Visitation permitted only occasionally. Please inquire by e-mail.

Gaby and Wilhelm Schürmann's collection has been part of their lives for four decades. Wilhelm Schürmann, a photographer, describes the moment of confronting a new artwork as being like "sudden enlightenment." For the collector couple, this is where the value of art truly lies: in asking us to continuously modify our own set of values. They find this kind of edginess in the works of renowned artists like Martin Kippenberger or Heimo Zobernig, as well as in the unsettling works of Monika Baer or Michael E. Smith. Continuously expanding since 1972, the Schürmanns' collection is housed in a private Berlin apartment and shown to interested parties occasionally upon request.

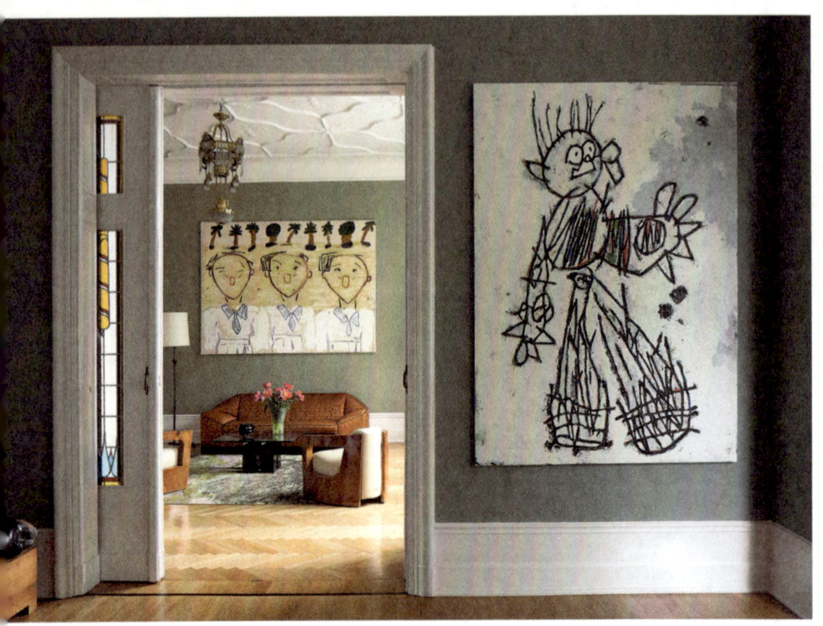

SAMMLUNG GNYP SPRINGMEIER

International contemporary art on one story of a Berlin building

Collectors:
Marta Gnyp &
Giovanni Springmeier

Address:
Berlin, Germany
homecollection@springmeier.eu
www.springmeier.eu

Visitation permitted only occasionally. Please inquire by e-mail.

Marta Gnyp and Giovanni Springmeier live with their collection. Springmeier, a doctor, has been acquiring work since the 1990s, from Phyllida Barlow to Liam Gillick, to Michael Kunze and Leidy Churchman. Gnyp, an art advisor and author, is adept at picking out the relevant and promising artists of our time, often before their big breakthroughs, as was the case with Raúl de Nieves, Orion Martin, Zachary Armstrong, Wojciech Fangor, and Rose Wylie. A few years ago, they combined their collections together in one apartment. When they occasionally open up their private space to visitors, you immediately get a sense of their enthusiasm for artistic positions and for the elaborate staging of their comprehensive collection of all media, which can be summed up under the general theme of "man and his complexities." What makes this experience unique is the holy alliance between art and life, where international art goes hand-in-hand with select design objects.

BERLIN

In Berlin, it is still possible to find undiscovered spaces with provisional charm. An ever-popular trend: converting former factory buildings into exciting locations for art. In April 2017, the Reinbeckhallen opened its doors in the city's southeastern district of Oberschöneweide—in a former transformer factory featuring 5000 square meters of space for exhibitions, workshops, and artist studios. The German and Swiss couple Burkhard Varnholt and Salome Grisard run the Kindl—Zentrum für zeitgenössische Kunst inside a former brewery in Neukölln. A pulsating international art scene gathers at openings in the galleries of Mitte, Tiergarten, Charlottenburg, or Kreuzberg, where the architectural dimensions also make more of an impression than in other locations around Germany: König Galerie presents exhibitions in the roughly 800-square-meter space of a former church, Sprüth Magers occupies a former dance hall, and Blain/Southern the old *Der Tagesspiegel* printing plant. The Martin-Gropius-Bau always attracts visitors with prestigious exhibitions of artists like Ed Atkins or Philippe Parreno. And C/O Berlin dedicates exhibitions to world famous photographers such as Sebastião Salgado or Irving Penn in the former Amerika Haus, just across from the Bahnhof Zoo train station. Since 1998, the Berlin Biennale has instigated contemporary discourse with new artistic positions. But new impulses can always be found: almost every evening, art enthusiasts can take part in intellectually stimulating events—artist talks, performances, or video screenings. And the art market? Gallery Weekend, which takes place around May 1, attracts hundreds of international collectors to the city. Via VIP shuttle or bike, visitors can hit about fifty galleries. At the start of the fall art season, in September, there is the fair Art Berlin, the centerpiece of Berlin Art Week, which every year offers an explosive array of openings, performances, and talks. This much is clear: a regular visit to Berlin is mandatory for all art fans.

SAMMLUNG IVO WESSEL

Profound and humorous German and international video and concept art

Collector:
Ivo Wessel

Address:
Berlin, Germany
email@ivo-wessel.de

Visitation permitted only occasionally. Please inquire by e-mail.

Ivo Wessel is a fixture of the Berlin art scene. He's a frequent guest at podium discussions, a favorite interview partner when the topic is private collections, and, together with fellow collector Olaf Stüber, an organizer of the successful monthly filmscreening series *Videoart at Midnight,* at Kino Babylon. This all makes sense, as the main focus of the software developer's collection is video art. Wessel owns work by artists of his generation, such as Bjørn Melhus, Stefan Panhans, or Tracey Moffatt, all of which lean toward the dreamily surreal. He also collects works of concept art by the likes of Karin Sander, Via Lewandowsky, or Sven Johne. For Wessel, how the work is shown is not important. His private rooms, located on a former military property, have more of a "warehouse feel than exhibit space." If you want to visit, arrange a personal tour with the collector himself.

WURLITZER—BERLIN-PIED-À-TERRE COLLECTION

An intimate view on emerging and established European artists

Collectors:
Gudrun & Bernd Wurlitzer

Address:
Berlin, Germany
gudrun.wurlitzer@artitious.com
www.wurlitzercollection.com

Visitation permitted only occasionally. Please inquire by e-mail.

Gudrun and Bernd Wurlitzer fell into collecting somewhat by chance. While the couple has actively purchased works from artist-friends for several decades, it wasn't until a more recent move to Berlin that they began collecting in earnest. Faced with numerous empty walls as new Berliners, Gudrun and Bernd Wurlitzer turned to old friends and new acquaintances to help fill the "gaps." The collection now includes works by Jürgen Drescher, Gregor Hildebrandt, Axel Kasseböhmer, Alicja Kwade, Wolfgang Tillmans, Raphaela Vogel, and others. In the process, the collection's private character has remained intact: architect Gudrun Wurlitzer and her art-advisor husband invite art enthusiasts on a by-appointment basis to their Berlin pied-à-terre, where they have gradually assembled the collection. For a short time, they have also been running a showroom where positions from the collection are exhibited together with artists from Artitious, their online platform.

KARIN & UWE HOLLWEG STIFTUNG

Fluxus, Informel, and Pop live in discreet Hanseatic ambience

Collectors:
Karin & Uwe Hollweg

Address:
Altenwall 6
28195 Bremen
Germany
office@hollweg-stiftung.de

By e-mail appointment only.

Businessman Uwe Hollweg and his wife, Karin, a painter, have been collectors since the early 1970s. They are known in Bremen as patrons and supporters of the local Kunsthalle. That the private collectors only sometimes open their collection to visitors is a bit of Hanseatic understatement. But whoever does manage to nab one of the very rare appointments will discover a fine collection in a historic trading house not far from the Kunsthalle. The collection bears the strong imprint of the collector couple's eclectic tastes, with works ranging from British Pop Art pioneer Richard Hamilton to those by Dieter Roth and Wols and the melancholic paintings of Bremen's local art hero, Norbert Schwontkowski. The couple also owns an impressive collection of artists' books. Chairs and sofas add to the cozy ambience. "I find it very important that our guests have the opportunity to sit down and be comfortable," says Karin Hollweg.

SAMMLUNG FAMILIE BECKER

Modern masterpieces and Cologne local color

Collector:
Becker Family

Address:
Cologne, Germany
mkomeyer.hgn@carbo.de

Visitation permitted only occasionally. Please inquire by e-mail.

Art is the great passion of Johannes Becker, Gaffel partner and owner of the Carbo Group. Gaffel's Kölsch beer might be one of Germany's most traditional brands, but Becker's private art collection is one of the country's most multifaceted. Having acquired works by renowned artists like Joseph Beuys, Dieter Roth, Anne Imhof, or Tracey Emin, Becker and his family have already proven their intuitive touch. As active members of the Cologne art scene, they have also been supporting local artists for many years. The fact that the native Rhinelander has assembled his collection not only with the help of a finely honed eye but also thanks to his humorous nature, is evidenced by works such as *Worldcup Again,* a football made of concrete by Sarah Lucas. Of course, Becker's professional theme—beer—also has a place in the collection that is installed in the private residence: a collage of flattened Gaffel cans by French artist César.

SAMMLUNG KÖSER

Younger generation art from the US and Europe

Collectors:
Laetitia & Alexander Köser

Address:
Cologne, Germany
koeser.art@gmail.com

Visitation permitted only occasionally. Please inquire by e-mail.

Alexander Köser's family introduced him to collecting. At eighteen he began buying art himself, starting with a work by Friedrich Kunath. Since then, he has focused on his own generation—artists born after 1974. Köser stresses he doesn't take a systematic approach to collecting but follows his heart. Personal contact with the artists is therefore particularly important to him. Only in hindsight has a focus revealed itself, for example on painting and sculpture. In order to make the artists' working methods and ideas visible, the Cologne-based, property management executive and his wife Laetitia typically don't collect individual works but follow artists over a longer period. On view in their home are works by L.A. artists Ivan Morley and Max Hooper Schneider as well as New Yorkers Rashid Johnson and Avery K Singer, among others. But numerous European painters and sculptors are also represented—such as Anne Imhof, David Shrigley, and Anna Uddenberg.

FÜRSTENBERG ZEITGENÖSSISCH

Innovative young art infiltrates princely pomp

Collectors:
Christian & Jeannette zu Fürstenberg

Address:
Am Karlsplatz 7
78166 Donaueschingen
Germany
Tel +49 771 229677563
info@fuerstenbergzeitgenoessisch.com
www.fuerstenbergzeitgenoessisch.com

Opening Hours:
April–November
Tues–Sat: 10am–1pm, 2–5pm
Sundays and public holidays: 10am–5pm

Christian and Jeannette zu Fürstenberg are incessantly on the lookout for "young, emerging artists who have distinguished themselves in recent years by new formal languages and concepts, and in so doing have influenced the international discourse." And not just for their collection since the hereditary couple also supports three artists annually with fellowships followed by an exhibition. Shooting stars like Julian Göthe, Kai Althoff, Juliette Blightman, Kasia Fudakowski, or Andreas Slominski are already represented with their own, distinct and modern artist spaces and site-specific interventions. Since its opening in 2011, works of contemporary art have gradually started to fill a number of display cabinets once dominated by hunting trophies and uniforms. Temporary exhibitions are also regularly presented of established artists such as Paloma Varga Weisz or Victor Man.

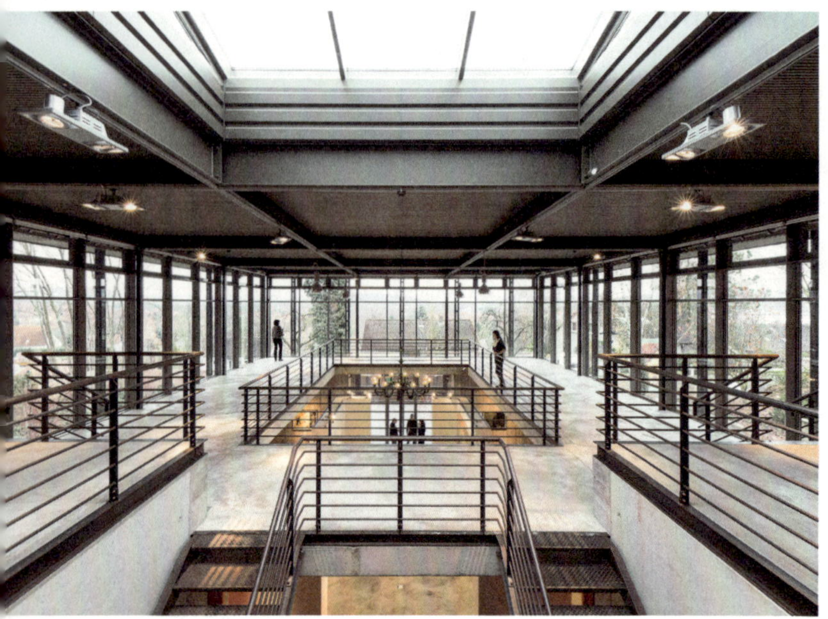

KUNSTHALLE HGN

With the gaze of a globetrotter: figurative painting, sculpture, and photography in Duderstadt

Collector:
Hans Georg Näder

Address:
Karl-Wüstefeld-Weg
37115 Duderstadt
Germany
info@kunsthallehgn.de
www.kunsthallehgn.de

Opening hours vary depending on exhibition. Please check the website for the most current information.

"I rediscover myself in the works—collecting is a reflection of my own development," says Hans Georg Näder, head of a medical technology company headquartered in Duderstadt, in Lower Saxony. During the many business trips he takes around the world, Näder consistently visits exhibitions and galleries—and especially likes to acquire non-European art. Twenty years ago, he began building his ever-growing collection, focusing on figurative painting, sculpture, and photography. Today, works by artists ranging from Norbert Bisky to Dan Flavin to Sylvie Fleury are represented. Exhibitions are occasionally shown in the 650-square-meter Kunsthalle HGN, opened in Duderstadt in 2011. The building's five staggered levels convey the character of an open workshop. Näder also shows parts of his collection at the local Hotel zum Löwen, including works by Neo Rauch, Annie Leibovitz, Arnold Newman, and others.

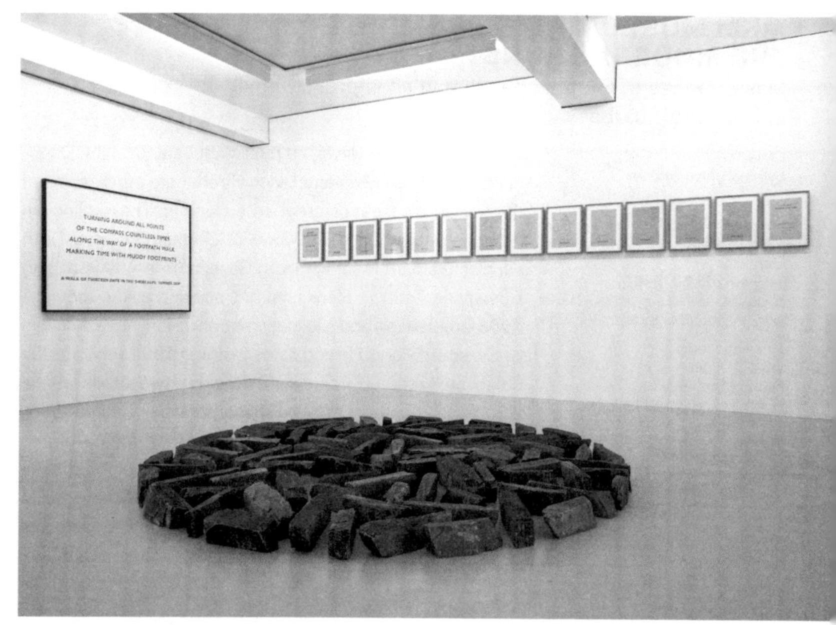

MUSEUM DKM

An eclectic collection from antiquity to the present

Collectors:
Dirk Krämer & Klaus Maas

Address:
Güntherstrasse 13–15
47051 Duisburg
Germany
Tel +49 203 93555470
mail@museum-dkm.de
www.museum-dkm.de

Opening Hours:
Sat–Sun: 12–6pm
Every first Friday of the month from 12–6pm.
And by appointment.

Germany is becoming a nation of nonprofits, with over 350 new foundations established each year. Dirk Krämer and Klaus Maas see their own Museum DKM as part of this trend. The two collectors have been involved with art for over twenty years, along the way encouraging the responsible behavior of private collectors vis-à-vis the public. They established their foundation in 1999, and ten years later they opened a private museum designed by Swiss architect Hans Rohr. Their collection covers a wide array of areas: from ancient art through classical photography to contemporary art—particularly abstract and conceptual positions like Blinky Palermo or Ai Weiwei. Krämer and Maas also administer the estate of the German sculptor Ernst Hermanns, an important representative of Concrete Art.

MKM MUSEUM KÜPPERSMÜHLE FÜR MODERNE KUNST

Masterpieces of German painting in an impressive mill in Duisburg's harbor

Collectors:
Sylvia & Ulrich Ströher

Address:
Philosophenweg 55
47051 Duisburg
Germany
Tel +49 203 30194811
office@museum-kueppersmuehle.de
www.museum-kueppersmuehle.de

Opening Hours:
Wed: 2–6pm
Thurs: 11am–6pm
Sundays and public holidays:
11am–6pm

No photos, no interviews, no public appearances: the Darmstadt collectors Sylvia and Ulrich Ströher are surely some of the Republic's most discreet art collectors. Their collection includes over 1 500 major works of German art since 1945 such as Gerhard Richter, Georg Baselitz, Anselm Kiefer, and Rosemarie Trockel. Here abstract painting is the focus. A 1908-erected mill and silo complex converted into a museum by Swiss architects Herzog & de Meuron in 1999 serves as the fitting architectural framework. Roughly two-thirds of the 3 600-square-meter exhibition space, spread over three floors, is reserved for the collection. The remaining area provides space for the three or four temporary exhibitions per year. Centrally situated in Duisburg's inland harbor, the MKM Museum Küppersmühle is one of the largest private museums in Germany.

SAMMLUNG PHILARA

Spectacular private museum in Düsseldorf's Flingern district

Collector:
Gil Bronner

Address:
Birkenstrasse 47
40233 Düsseldorf
Germany
info@philara.de
www.philara.de

Opening hours vary depending on exhibition. Please check the website for the most current information.

The Philara collection, founded in 2007, was previously housed in a former factory on the outskirts of Düsseldorf. In summer 2016, Gil Bronner moved everything to a centrally located, old industrial glass manufacturing plant in Flingern, a district popular with galleries. The new museum building features nearly 1 800-square-meters of exhibition space, a café, and a spacious rooftop sculpture garden. The busy real-estate developer from Düsseldorf feels bound to art on several levels. He not only owns a building with seventy artists' studios—the largest in the city—he also organizes exhibitions four times a year, endows artist stipends, and adds works to his collection, seemingly without pause. Bronner buys works that speak to him emotionally and aesthetically. Installations by Monika Sosnowska, Tobias Rehberger, Alicja Kwade, or Tomás Saraceno can be found as well as works of artists from the so-called New Leipzig School, such as Tilo Baumgärtel.

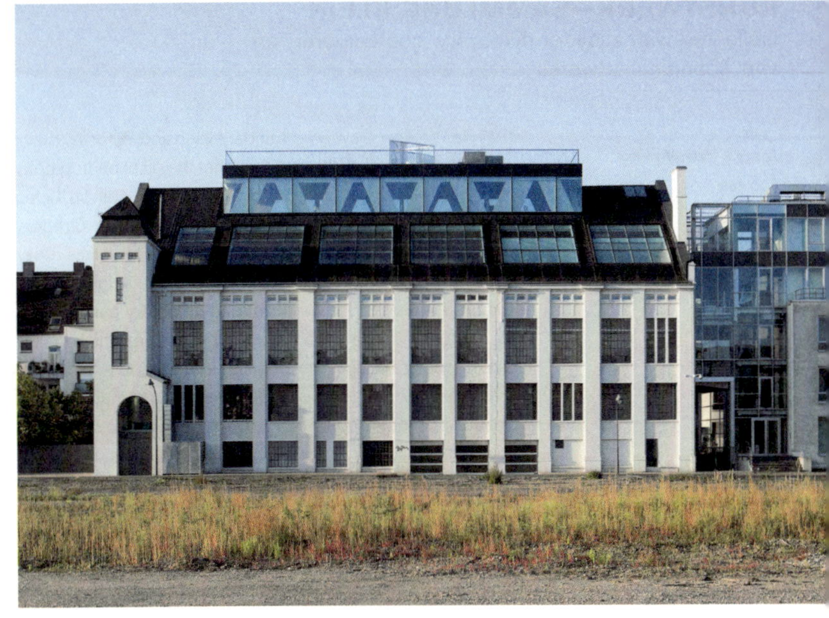

JULIA STOSCHEK COLLECTION

An ambitious young collector zeroed in on media art

Collector:
Julia Stoschek

Addresses:
Schanzenstrasse 54
40549 Düsseldorf
Germany
Tel +49 211 5858840
info@julia-stoschek-collection.net
www.julia-stoschek-collection.net

Berlin:
Leipziger Strasse 60
10117 Berlin
Germany
Tel +49 30 921062460
info@jsc.berlin
www.jsc.berlin

Please check the website for the most current information on opening hours.

For Julia Stoschek, opening a private museum in 2007 was a highlight of her rapid collecting career: one day while taking a walk, the heiress, who was born in 1975, came across an historic landmark factory building. Today it holds one of the most extensive private collections of media art in Germany. After undergoing complex modifications by the Berlin-based architecture firm Kuehn Malvezzi, the reinforced-concrete building shows videos, installations, and photographs spread across its multiple floors. The 2 500 square meters represent a veritable Who's Who of the international media-art scene, with annual exhibits featuring artists ranging from Douglas Gordon to Thomas Demand, to Pipilotti Rist or Andreas Gursky. The young collector is also devoted to up-and-coming stars, like the Frenchman Cyprien Gaillard. Since 2016, parts of the collection can also be seen in Berlin; the former spaces of the Czech Cultural Institute were redesigned for this purpose.

KUNSTWERK—SAMMLUNG KLEIN

Collected with a joy for discovery: contemporary art and Aboriginal artworks

Collectors:
Alison & Peter W. Klein

Address:
Siemensstrasse 40
71735 Eberdingen-Nussdorf
Germany
Tel +49 7042 3769566
kunstwerk@sammlung-klein.de
www.sammlung-klein.de

Opening Hours:
Wed–Fri: 11am–5pm
Sun: 11am–5pm

They don't follow art-market trends. Alison and Peter W. Klein, who live just outside Stuttgart, buy what they like: photography of the Helsinki School, paintings by Karin Kneffel, Anselm Kiefer, Sean Scully, works of the American photo-artist Gregory Crewdson, but also works by younger, emerging artists. Over the past thirty years, the Swabian and his American wife have amassed around 2000 works of contemporary painting and photography. They regularly travel to Australia, which is why contemporary Aboriginal art constitutes a second pillar of their collection. In 2007, Klein sold his company, a manufacturer of clutch systems, and opened this spacious, 1000-square-meter private museum not far from former company headquarters in Nussdorf—the town where Klein was once the largest employer.

SAMMLUNG VON KELTERBORN

Art about the social conflicts of our time

Collectors:
Julia & Mario von Kelterborn

Address:
Taunustor 3
60311 Frankfurt
Germany
info@kelterborn-collection.com
www.kelterborn-collection.com

By e-mail appointment only.

The collection of Julia and Mario von Kelterborn revolves around politically charged or philosophically minded works reflecting on current social issues and conflicts. The couple—she's a communications expert and he's an entrepreneur—launched The Good News App for "the best good news" in 2016. As collectors, they focus on photo and video works, such as *The Enclave,* a multi-part video installation shot by Irish artist Richard Mosse in Congo and exhibited at the 2013 Venice Biennale. Examples of the collection's other emphasis—concept- and language-based art—are shown in the couple's private residence and have previously been exhibited at the Weserburg Museum in Bremen and the Mönchehaus Museum Goslar. Included here are works by Jochen Gerz and Stuart Bird, as well as neon works by the artist collective Claire Fontaine—for example, a sculpture forming the words *Sell your debt,* conceived as an ironic commentary on the financial world.

FAIRS & BIENNIALS

How commercial may a biennial be? And how culturally engaged may an art fair be? Contemporary art fairs have become events that go far beyond their commercial function. Sections arranged by well-known curators, panel discussions, artists talks, and performances are all based on a model initiated by ArCo Madrid in the 1980s, and which Vincenzo de Bellis, the former artistic director of MiArt in Milan, has defined as "a process of biennializing the art fair." Biennials, on the other hand, have always claimed to be purely cultural events. Even mentioning "the art market" in this context can cause waves of outrage. Yet, it goes without saying that biennials have a significant effect on the career and market-value of the artists they exhibit. Though some people still idealize biennials as events free of business and commerce, it is worth remembering that until 1968 the Venice Biennale had a sales office, and it is no secret that, even today, gallerists make deals during opening days. What art fairs and biennials do have in common is the important role they play in proliferation at the global level; almost every single week, an art fair takes place somewhere in the world.

Participation in these fairs is fundamental to a gallery's business and reputation, even though it requires significant financial expenditure. Accordingly, biennials are sprouting up all over the globe. Some critics have complained about this increase, questioning the need for additional similar exhibition formats. Undoubtedly both developments must be considered a side effect of globalization and the concomitant growth of interest in contemporary art. By linking together local art scenes and bringing them to the international stage, biennials ultimately also contribute to building bridges between worlds and promoting intercultural dialogue.

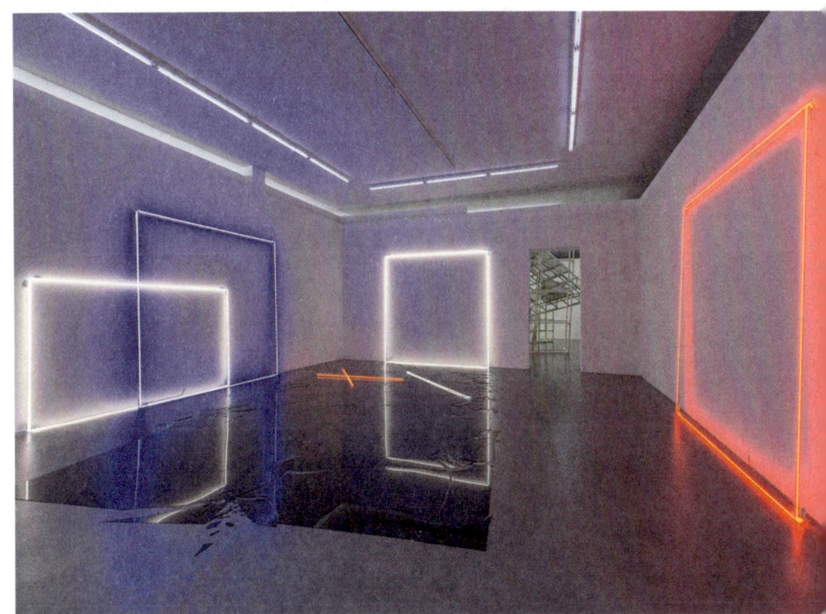

SAMMLUNG EGE—KUNST- UND KULTURSTIFTUNG IM KUNSTRAUM ALEXANDER BÜRKLE

Monochrome painting and Minimal art in dialogue with younger artists

Collectors:
Helga & Paul Ege

Address:
Robert-Bunsen-Strasse 5
79108 Freiburg
Germany
Tel +49 761 5106606
kunstraum@alexander-buerkle.de
www.kunstraum-alexander-buerkle.de

Opening Hours:
Tues–Fri: 11am–5pm
Sundays and public holidays:
11am–5pm

Established in 2004, the Kunstraum Alexander Bürkle is located in northern Freiburg on the premises of the electronics wholesale company Alexander Bürkle. The collector, Paul Ege, the third-generation head of the company, founded in 1900, has a clear guideline: "A collection should not be a mere accumulation. I think the strength of a collection lies in its unique focus." Based on this principle, three to four internationally staffed exhibitions are shown annually in the nearly 1 000-square-meter art space, which is committed to the neutrality of the white cube. Classics of Minimalism like Fred Sandback, Donald Judd, or—in the electronics industry, almost a must—light artist Dan Flavin, meet younger artists like the Swiss painter Adrian Schiess, known for his radical monochrome art.

MORAT-INSTITUT FÜR KUNST & KUNSTWISSENSCHAFT

An excellent print collection, African tribal art, and an extensive library

Collector:
Franz Armin Morat

Address:
Lörracher Strasse 31
79115 Freiburg
Germany
Tel +49 761 4765916
eva.morat@morat-institut.de
www.morat-institut.de

Opening Hours:
Sat: 11am–6pm
And by appointment.

At the Morat-Institut für Kunst und Kunstwissenschaft, in Freiburg, the focus is on research. The institute organizes symposiums, publishes catalogue raisonnés, and oversees a library with around 50 000 volumes. The institute boasts the largest collection of works by the Viennese painter Carl Schuch, and earns additional points with an extensive print collection featuring work by Giorgio Morandi, Max Beckmann, and Albrecht Dürer. Treasures like a complete set of prints by Francisco de Goya, or high-quality West African sculptures are often requested on loan by other museums. The foundation resides in a 1950s light-flooded shed-roof hall. Since early 2010 the institute has tried to streamline and decelerate, focusing exclusively on its own collection rather than cultivating special exhibitions.

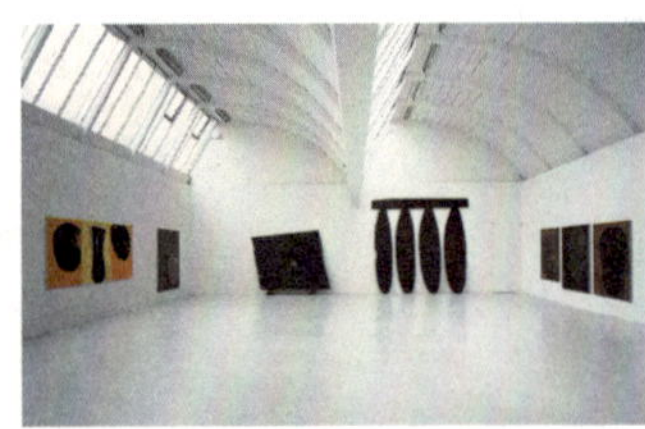

SAMMLUNG BLANKENBURG

Contemporary art in a charming historic building in Hamburg-Winterhude

Collectors:
Andrea & Markus von Goetz und Schwanenfliess

Address:
Hamburg, Germany
office@vgs-art.com

By e-mail appointment only.

Andrea and Markus von Goetz und Schwanenfliess live surrounded by art in a spacious apartment with Parisian charm. In 2006, Andrea von Goetz, a sociologist, asked for her first artwork as a birthday present: a large-scale watercolor by Hanna Nitsch. That was the starting point for the Blankenburg collection, named after the family farm in Lower Saxony. Meanwhile, the collection, which focuses on young contemporary art and, increasingly, on representatives of the 1980s, includes roughly one hundred works, from Rinus van de Velde, Ralf Ziervogel, Werner Büttner, and Georg Baselitz to Oda Jaune. In addition to her passion for collecting, Andrea von Goetz has also established herself as a curator and supporter of young art. In 2011, she initiated an international fellowship program, held annually as part of the Sommer.Frische.Kunst Festival in Bad Gastein, and the Collectors Room, which regularly hosts exhibitions of young and established artists in Hamburg.

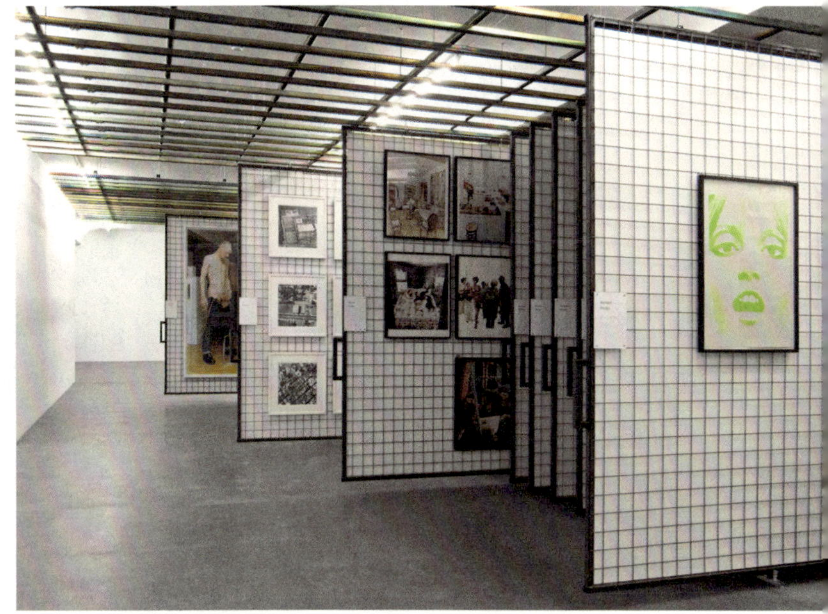

DEICHTORHALLEN HAMBURG—SAMMLUNG FALCKENBERG

Positions of social criticism in German and American contemporary art

Collector:
Harald Falckenberg

Address:
Phoenix-Hallen
Wilstorfer Strasse 71, Gate 2
21073 Hamburg
Germany
Tel +49 40 32506762
sammlungfalckenberg@deichtorhallen.de
www.deichtorhallen.de/sammlungfalckenberg

Please check the website for the most current information on opening hours.

Irony, social criticism, and the grotesque: Harald Falckenberg's art collection is essentially about resistance. Over the past twenty years, the Hamburg-based businessman has assembled around 2 000 works of art, mainly by German and American contemporary artists who use biting sarcasm to hold a mirror up to society's ills. Paul McCarthy, Andreas Slominski, Martin Kippenberger, and Paul Thek are just some of his favorites. Since 2001 Falckenberg has shown his collection in a 6 000-square-meter former rubber factory in Hamburg-Harburg, called the Phoenix Hallen, cleverly altered by the architect Roger Bundschuh. Unconventional temporary exhibitions and guest appearances by other private collections makes it one of the most important spaces for contemporary art. Since 2011 the Sammlung Falckenberg has cooperated closely with the Deichtorhallen Hamburg, which is now in charge of overall business operations.

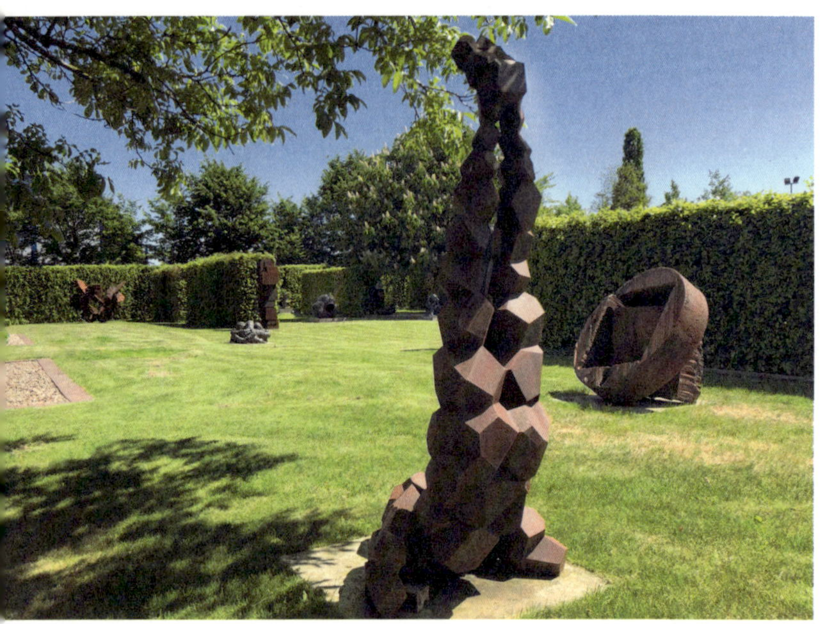

SAMMLUNG WEMHÖNER

Selected exhibits of an expansive collection in the East Westphalian city of Herford

Collector:
Heiner Wemhöner

Address:
Planckstrasse 7
32052 Herford
Germany
Tel +49 5221 770210
www.sammlung-wemhoener.com

By appointment only.

"The art I encounter and surround myself with improves my quality of life. It gives me strength and inspires me," says Heiner Wemhöner. In spring of 2014 the businessman from the East Westphalian city of Herford presented around 10 percent of his collection, compiled since the late 1990s, in Berlin's Osram-Höfe, the former home of one of Europe's largest lightbulb factories. This was the first time he exhibited his collection publicly—and apparently he enjoyed it. Now Heiner Wemhöner or his curator, Philipp Bollmann, guide interested art lovers through his company building in Herford, where around sixty works are on display: photographs by Isaac Julien, sculptures by Stephan Balkenhol, works on paper by Richard Serra, as well as works by Chinese artists, such as Zhou Tiehai or Yang Fudong. If there's time, the tour can be extended to Wemhöner's private sculpture park, with works by Antony Gormley and Tony Cragg.

HALL ART FOUNDATION/ SCHLOSS DERNEBURG MUSEUM

Impressive postwar art in a historic castle

Collectors:
Andrew & Christine Hall

Address:
Visitors Reception
Astenbeck 42
31188 Holle
Germany
Tel +49 5062 9640294
derneburg@hallartfoundation.org
www.hallartfoundation.org

Only guided tours with prior online registration.

Additional exhibition locations: Reading, United States of America, p. 254

At Schloss Derneburg you'll encounter works from an exquisite collection of American and European postwar art, set in a historic atmosphere. The castle, built in the thirteenth century as a convent, was home to Georg Baselitz from 1975 to 2006 until he sold it to Andrew and Christine Hall, a collector couple from the US. The Halls, who were looking for a second location to present their collection outside their main venue in Vermont, have now given the building a new lease on life after a ten-year renovation. A gigantic bronze sculpture by Julian Schnabel in the foyer instantly demonstrates that large-scale art is at home here. Seven exhibitions have been shown in parallel in the 10 000-square-meter space since 2017, by artists like Malcolm Morley, Isa Genzken, Hermann Nitsch, or Antony Gormley, whose steel sculptures exude an unexpected intensity here. Visualizing what places can do for art and vice-versa has never been easier to grasp.

STIFTUNG MUSEUM MODERN ART— SAMMLUNG JÜRGEN BLUM

Circa 3 000 works of Concrete, Constructivist, and Conceptual Art

Collector:
Jürgen Blum

Address:
Hersfelder Strasse 25
36088 Hünfeld
Germany
Tel +49 6652 72433
Tel +49 151 40470100
info@museum-modern-art.de
www.museum-modern-art.de

Opening Hours:
Tues–Sun: 3–6pm
And by appointment.

It's not an outpost of the Museum of Modern Art (MOMA) in New York City, but the Museum Modern Art Hünfeld is well worth the detour. Thanks to the German-Polish artist and collector Jürgen Blum, the small Hessian city near Fulda has a stellar private museum, with roughly 1 000 square meters of exhibition space, in a historic landmark building—a former gas plant. His collection brings together the East and the West, Concrete Art and conceptual thought, starkly reduced forms, and intellect. Along the way it highlights works by the Polish avant-garde. Now a foundation, the collection's exhibition administration has been taken over by the city of Hünfeld. Additionally, the artist Günter Liebau was appointed as external curator to organize temporary exhibitions of various contemporary art genres. A sculpture garden brings the presentation outdoors.

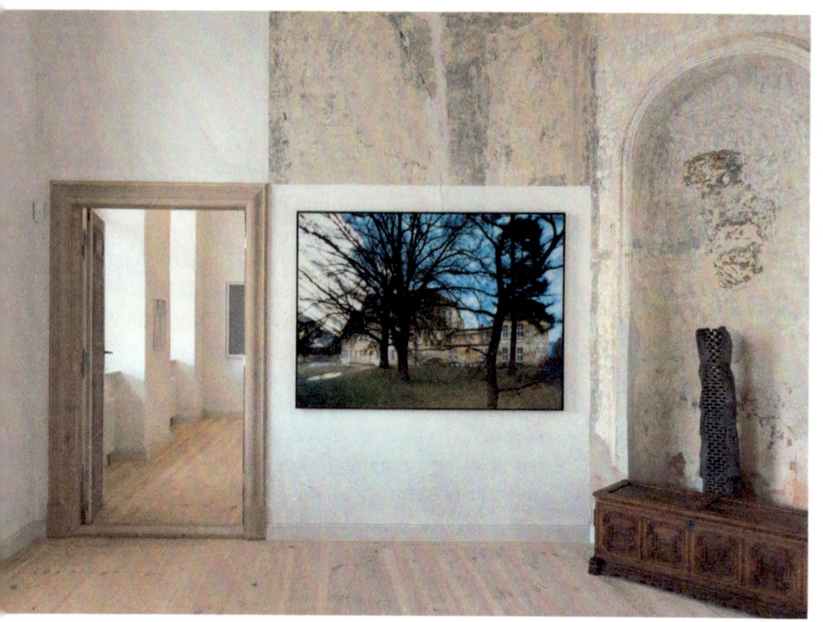

FOTOGRAFISCHE SAMMLUNG— SCHLOSS KUMMEROW

Top-notch photo collection in an exquisitely renovated castle

Collector:
Torsten Kunert

Address:
Dorfstrasse 114
17139 Kummerow
Germany
Tel +49 152 59868126
post@schloss-kummerow.de
www.schloss-kummerow.de

Please check the website for the most current information on opening hours.

In 2011, Torsten Kunert acquired Schloss Kummerow, a semi-derelict castle in Mecklenburg-Vorpommern, a two-and-a-half-hour drive from Berlin or Hamburg. The Berlin real-estate entrepreneur had the historic gem in the Mecklenburg Switzerland Nature Park meticulously renovated, and moved his photography collection there in 2016. The collector, who originally hails from eastern Germany, has roughly 2 000 works on display at the approximately 3 500-square-meter castle on Kummerow Lake, including many highlights of GDR photography. He is particularly interested in socially and politically relevant positions. Works by renowned East German photographers like Ute & Werner Mahler, Helga Paris, or Sibylle Bergemann are presented alongside international stars such as Marina Abramović, Thomas Struth, Wolfgang Tillmans, or Hiroshi Sugimoto. In the castle gardens, you'll encounter a sculpture by Matschinsky-Denninghoff.

SAMMLUNG WÜRTH

Art from the Middle Ages to the present at fifteen sites in Europe

Collector:
Reinhold Würth

Address:
Würth Museum
Reinhold-Würth-Strasse 15
74653 Künzelsau-Gaisbach
Germany
Tel +49 7940 152200
museum@wuerth.com
www.kunst.wuerth.com

Opening hours vary depending on exhibition. Please check the website for the most current information.

"Art at Würth should not take place in an ivory tower, but in everyday life; it should be experienced close to the work-place," says company president Reinhold Würth. Since the 1960s, the owner of a wholesale company for assembly and fastening materials has amassed a comprehensive collection of art—from the Middle Ages through the modern period to the present—comprised of roughly 16 000 works. In 1991 the Museum Würth opened at the company's headquarters, in Künzelsau. Then, in 2001, the Kunsthalle Würth was opened in Schwäbisch Hall. Today, fifteen exhibition spaces inside innovative architectural structures are located at various European locations of the Würth Group, from Norway to Spain. The temporary exhibitions shown here are drawn from the collection. Works from Pablo Picasso to Gerhard Richter, from Paul Gauguin to Alex Katz—and the largest compilation of works by Christo and Jeanne-Claude in central Europe—mark the impressive range of Würth's collection.

ARBEITSWOHNUNG FEDERKIEL

A former working-class apartment as a subtly ironic Gesamtkunstwerk

Collector:
Karsten Schmitz

Address:
Leipziger Baumwollspinnerei
Spinnereistrasse 7
04179 Leipzig
Germany
sammlung@federkiel.org
www.federkiel.org/sammlung

Visitation permitted only occasionally. Please inquire by e-mail.

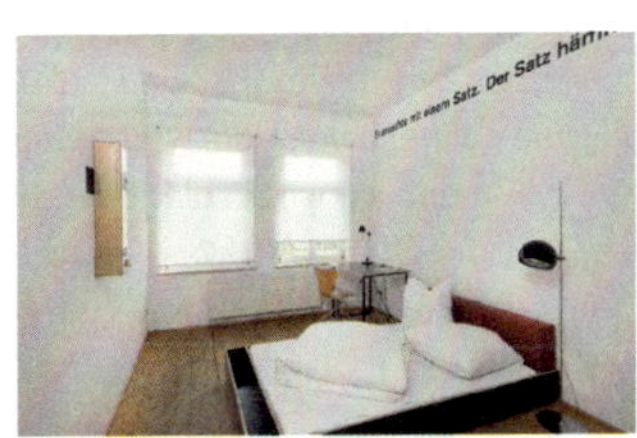

The Munich economist Karsten Schmitz is no stranger to the city of Leipzig. As an art collector and founder of the Stiftung Federkiel—whose mission is the preservation of Leipzig's Baumwollspinnerei as a location for galleries, studios, and institutional exhibition—Schmitz is among the most important private sponsors of this Leipzig art center. His own apartment, a former working-class home on the premises, is for the collector both a place to generate ideas and an exhibition space. But he also uses it regularly to accommodate collector friends, artists, or scholars. He invited the Leipzig artist-group Famed to use the apartment and its furniture as artistic material to create a permanent intervention. The result is an ironic narrative installation that runs through all of the rooms, providing a cheeky visual link between them.

G2 KUNSTHALLE

Large-scale paintings of the New Leipzig School in dialogue

Collector:
Steffen Hildebrand

Address:
Dittrichring 13
04109 Leipzig
Germany
Tel +49 341 35573793
info@g2-leipzig.de
www.g2-leipzig.de

Opening Hours:
Wed: 3–8pm
Thurs–Mon: Only guided tours with prior online registration.

Considering that the G2 Kunsthalle is located in the happening city of Leipzig, it is only fitting that the March 2015 inaugural exhibition focused on works by artists of the New Leipzig School. Most of these, including Neo Rauch, Matthias Weischer, and Tilo Baumgärtel, studied at the renowned local art school Hochschule für Grafik und Buchkunst Leipzig, and their figurative paintings have since achieved international prominence. Collector Steffen Hildebrand, a property investor based in the city, was an early supporter, and the artworks he has brought together are displayed in an expansive space in the center of Leipzig. The steadily growing collection also showcases other German and international artists such as Thomas Ruff, Alicja Kwade, Raymond Pettibon, or Judith Bernstein. Since 2017, a project space located on site features over one hundred square meters devoted exclusively to young and experimental art.

MUSEUM BRANDHORST

Art stars of the late twentieth century housed in a dazzling new space

Collectors:
Anette & Udo Brandhorst

Address:
Theresienstrasse 35 A
80333 Munich
Germany
Tel +49 89 238052286
presse@museum-brandhorst.de
www.museum-brandhorst.de

Opening Hours:
Tue–Wed: 10am–6pm
Thurs: 10am–8pm
Fri–Sun: 10am–6pm

The vibrant, shimmering façade of 36 000 ceramic rods in twenty-three colors has a magnetic effect on people. In its inaugural year, the Museum Brandhorst drew nearly 350 000 visitors. But perhaps it also owes its success to what's inside: here there are over one hundred pieces by Andy Warhol, more than anywhere else in Europe. Among other highlights are works by Gerhard Richter, Ed Ruscha, and Cy Twombly, to name just a few. Located in the heart of Munich's art quarter, this distinctive building—designed by Sauerbruch Hutton—quickly became one of Germany's most popular exhibition venues. The 700-work collection belongs to the late Henkel heiress Anette Brandhorst and her husband, Udo, who began acquiring art in the 1970s. They found a comfortable home for the collection in Munich, and the State of Bavaria covers building-maintenance costs. Financially well-endowed, the Brandhorsts' foundation guarantees the ability to purchase top-quality new work.

ART & ARCHITECTURE

Art and architecture often make harmonious and attractive allies, with many private collectors taking great pains to find the appropriate architectural framework for their art. Some of them commissioning the careful renovation of historical buildings; others erecting brand new ones. The documenta-tested, Berlin-based architect-trio Kuehn Malvezzi, for example, transformed a former picture-frame factory in Düsseldorf into a multifunctional enclosure for Julia Stoschek's media-art collection. On the other side of the Rhine, in the district of Flingern, Gil Bronner opened his new collector's museum, the Sammlung Philara, in summer 2016. Situated in the refined, converted old industrial halls of a former glazing factory, it also boasts a café and sculpture garden on the roof, making it the perfect environment for large-scale works by artists such as Tomás Saraceno or Tobias Rehberger. Some collectors even open their private homes and apartments by appointment. For visitors, it's interesting to see how the living environment engages in a dialogue with art. Munich-based Karsten Schmitz, of Stiftung Federkiel, commissioned the artist group Famed to transform his office apartment on the premises of the Leipziger Baumwollspinnerei, with minimal intervention, into a habitable Gesamtkunstwerk. Art collectors frequently have a clear preference for good design: Alexander Ramselaar lives with his art collection and avant-garde furniture in a historic townhouse in Rotterdam, where well-stocked bookshelves serve as a room divider. It is ideal, of course, when collectors are able to commission their favorite architects to create new spaces for their art. Another example is the Fondazione Prada in Milan. None other than the art-savvy, Rotterdam-based, star architect Rem Koolhaas was selected to convert a former distillery into a functioning ensemble of old and new. Here, he couldn't resist making an ironic gesture: in a free-form interpretation of the legend of King Midas, Koolhaas transformed the tallest building on site into a golden tower.

SAMMLUNG GOETZ

Impressive international art in a cube-shaped, elegant building

Collector:
Ingvild Goetz

Address:
Oberföhringer Strasse 103
81925 Munich
Germany
Tel +49 89 95939690
info@sammlung-goetz.de
www.sammlung-goetz.de

Opening Hours:
Thurs–Fri: 2–6pm
Sat: 11am–4pm
Online registration required.

Before she began concentrating on developing her own private collection in 1984, Ingvild Goetz had been a gallerist for fifteen years. With around 5 000 works by several hundred artists, she now ranks among the most important private collectors of contemporary art in Germany. She started out with Arte Povera. Then came works by American artists of the 1980s and the Young British Artists of the 1990s, as well as some German stars. Names like Richard Prince, Tracey Emin, or Rosemarie Trockel are prominently represented. Since 1993, the collection has been housed in a cube-shaped building constructed out of frosted glass and birch wood, designed by the Swiss architects Herzog & de Meuron. In 2014, Goetz donated 375 works of media art and her elegant private museum to the State of Bavaria. She nevertheless remains a passionate collector and honorary artistic director of the museum.

ALEXANDER TUTSEK-STIFTUNG

A location for contemporary glass and photography

Collectors:
Alexander Tutsek &
Eva-Maria Fahrner-Tutsek

Address:
Karl-Theodor-Strasse 27
80803 Munich
Germany
Tel +49 89 55273060
info@atstiftung.de
www.atstiftung.de

Opening Hours:
Tues–Fri: 2–6pm

Established in 2000 by entrepreneur Alexander Tutsek and his wife Eva-Maria Fahrner-Tutsek, the foundation is committed to showing the unique, the disregarded, and the overlooked. The internationally oriented collection and exhibition space focuses on contemporary photography from Asia and contemporary sculpture that makes use of glass in particular. Glass hasn't been recognized as a working material in art for very long. But it has received increasing interest in recent years, as the works of Tony Cragg, Mona Hatoum, or Kiki Smith attest. In a historically listed Art Nouveau villa in Schwabing—once home to sculptor Georg Albrechtsdorfer and today the foundation's headquarters—rotating exhibitions provide insight into the diverse applications of glass, presenting sculptures and installations in dialogue with photographic new discoveries.

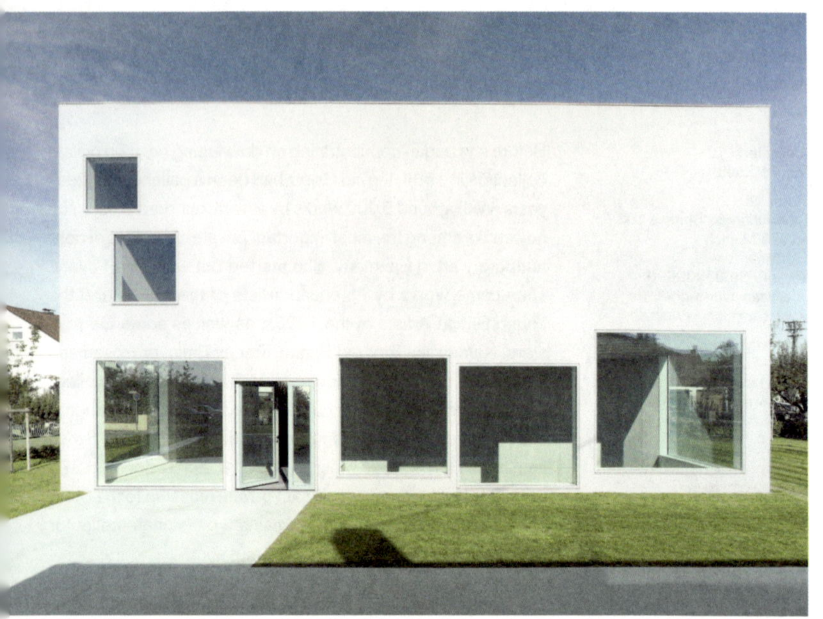

THE WALTHER COLLECTION

Discerning contemporary photographic art in the Swabian heartland

Collector:
Artur Walther

Address:
Reichenauer Strasse 21
89233 Neu-Ulm/Burlafingen
Germany
Tel +49 731 1769143
info@walthercollection.com
www.walthercollection.com

Opening Hours:
Thurs–Sun: 2–5pm

Additional exhibition locations:
New York, United States of America, p. 250

This is the tale of a man who went out to discover the world and ultimately returned to bestow a museum upon his hometown. Artur Walther worked as an investment banker on Wall Street. In 1994, the then forty-five-year-old decided to make a clean break and began focusing on art. More specifically, on photography. He embarked on African journeys with former Biennale director Okwui Enwezor in order to assemble an extensive collection of African photographic art. A large holding of Chinese and Japanese photography, nineteenth- and twentieth-century vernacular photography from America, as well as New Objectivity positions round out the collection. Walther had a bright white cube built on his parents' property featuring a 500-square-meter central gallery constructed below ground. Two regional-style houses also serve as exhibition spaces. The opening of the Neu-Ulm location was in 2010; an outpost in New York City was launched in 2011.

HERBERT-GERISCH-STIFTUNG

Contemporary sculpture in the park, modern and current art in the villa

Collectors:
Brigitte & Herbert Gerisch

Address:
Brachenfelder Strasse 69
24536 Neumünster
Germany
Tel +49 4321 555120
kontakt@gerisch-stiftung.de
www.herbert-gerisch-stiftung.de

Opening Hours:
Wed–Sun: 11am–6pm
Closed from January until beginning of March.

In the middle of Schleswig-Holstein lies Arcadia—this is how Brigitte and Herbert Gerisch describe their sculpture park in Neumünster. Here you'll find contemporary sculptures by Bogomir Ecker, Ian Hamilton Finlay, Markus Lüpertz, or Mimmo Paladino situated among intricate paths, water lily ponds, and fields of forget-me-nots. Established in 2001, the foundation transformed an overgrown historical Reform garden designed by Harry Maasz into a high-profile international sculpture garden. Brigitte Gerisch and her now-late husband, restored the run-down Villa Wachholtz inside the park to its original glory. In 2007, both the mansion and the park were opened to the public. Since then, exhibitions of modern and contemporary art by artists from Emil Nolde to Henry Moore, to Mark Dion and Carsten Höller, as well as young unknown talents, have been presented at Villa Wachholtz and the former swim hall of Villa Gerisch, located next door.

MUSEUM INSEL HOMBROICH

Two thousand years of art in harmony with nature and the landscape

Collector:
Karl-Heinrich Müller

Address:
Minkel 2
41472 Neuss
Germany
Tel +49 2182 8874000
museum@inselhombroich.de
www.inselhombroich.de

Opening Hours:
April–September
Mon–Sun: 10am–7pm
October–March
Mon–Sun: 10am–5pm

On your visit to Museum Insel Hombroich, you'll wander through meadows, the old park, and a terrace, and repeatedly encounter one of sculptor Erwin Heerich's brick pavilions. The museum was conceived as an ideal blend of museal space and landscape. Collector and patron Karl-Heinrich Müller (1936–2007) worked together with artists Gotthard Graubner, Erwin Heerich, Anatol Herzfeld, and landscape architect Bernhard Korte to develop a design to present his collection. Works by Hans Arp, Alexander Calder, Lovis Corinth, Jean Fautrier, Yves Klein, and Kurt Schwitters form the centerpiece of the collection, which also features East Asian art as well as an archaeological collection. Established in 1997, the Foundation Insel Hombroich comprises the Museum Insel Hombroich and the Kirkeby-Feld—showcasing architectural sculptures by the Danish artist—as well as the Raketenstation Hombroich, where exhibitions of visual art, photography, and architecture are staged.

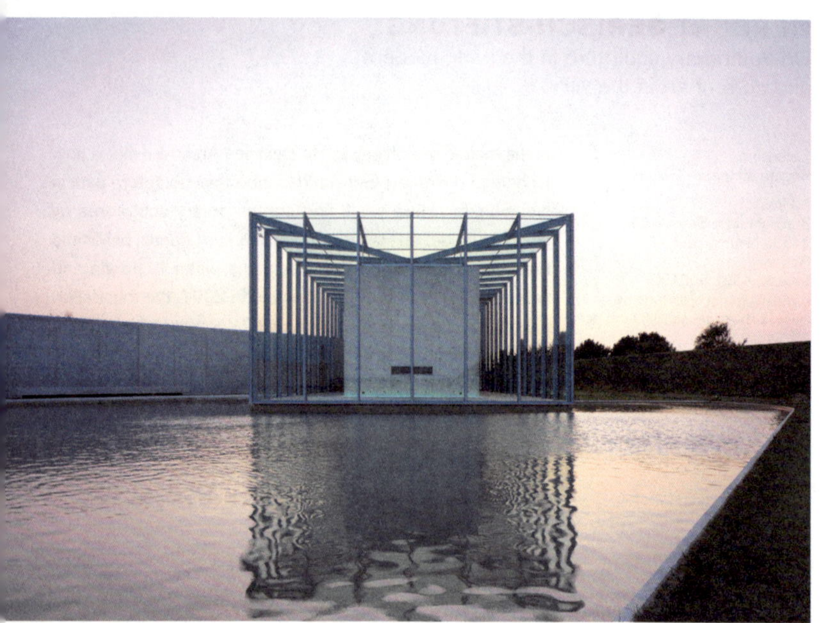

LANGEN FOUNDATION

European and Asian art presented in a fascinating building by Tadao Ando

Collectors:
Marianne & Viktor Langen

Address:
Raketenstation
Hombroich 1
41472 Neuss
Germany
Tel +49 2182 570115
info@langenfoundation.de
www.langenfoundation.de

Opening Hours:
Mon–Sun: 10am–6pm

A highlight for architecture fans: the Langen Foundation fits perfectly into the vastness of the Raketenstation Hombroich—a former NATO base—not far from the Museum Insel Hombroich. For founder Marianne Langen, who died in 2004, the minimalist building, made of exposed concrete by Japanese architect Tadao Ando, is the most important work of art she ever acquired. Together with her husband, Viktor Langen, she began to compile a collection of modernist work at the beginning of the 1950s, now numbering roughly 300 works of art ranging from Max Ernst and Paul Klee to Pablo Picasso. The second focus is on a collection of Japanese artworks quite unique to Europe: nearly 500 scrolls, Shoji screens, and sculptures spanning eight centuries. The collectors' motto: *Art is not luxury; it is necessity.* The 1 300-square-meter exhibition space is used to show contemporary art in dialogue with the permanent collection.

GRATIANUSSTIFTUNG

Plentiful space for artifacts from the Paleolithic to the present

Collectors:
Hanns-Gerhard Rösch &
Gabriele Straub

Address:
Gratianusstrasse 11
72766 Reutlingen
Germany
Tel +49 7121 490177
info@gratianusstiftung.de
www.gratianusstiftung.de

Opening Hours:
Mon: 2–6pm
Every first Thursday of the month from 6–8pm.
And by appointment.

A comprehensive view of the world: the Reutlingen-based collector couple Hanns-Gerhard Rösch and Gabriele Straub offer a concise overview of the world's art history in a modernized mansion from 1904. They mix epochs and genres in thirteen rooms on two floors. The spectrum runs from Paleolithic tools through African tribal art, and from Columbian shamanic figures to precious East Asian artifacts and works by modernists like Henri Matisse, Giorgio Morandi, or Paul Klee. The collectors are brave enough to leave their shows up for a longer duration. Their current exhibition, *Anziehungskraft Farbe, Geist und Erinnerung* (The Appeal of Color, Intellect, and Memory), is on display until 2021 and features works by a range of artists from various generations, including Hans Arp, Blinky Palermo, and Norbert Prangenberg. It is designed so that visitors "experience the art without first knowing or thinking about biographies or chronological reference points."

STIFTUNG FÜR KONKRETE KUNST

Concrete Art on three levels of a former factory building

Collector:
Manfred Wandel

Address:
Eberhardstrasse 14
72764 Reutlingen
Germany
Tel +49 7121 370328
skk.kuebler@t-online.de
www.stiftungkonkretekunst.de

Opening Hours:
Wed, Sat: 2–6pm
And by appointment.

At the Stiftung für konkrete Kunst, personalized art education is the core mission: each visitor is guided individually through the exhibition by the collector, Manfred Wandel, or his wife, Gabriele Kübler. Theo van Doesburg's 1924 definition of Concrete Art provides the collection its philosophical underpinnings: "There is nothing more concrete or more real than a line, a color, or plane." Wandel's collection features positions like Dadamaino or Bernard Aubertin, augmented by additional artwork holdings and archives. The plain and no-nonsense floors of the former wire-mesh factory exude industrial flair. In 2017, Wandel transferred ownership of the foundation's collection to the City of Reutlingen. The donation forms the basis of a new urban museum institution, which utilizes the building's second floor as the Sammlung für konkrete Kunst Reutlingen. The foundation continues its collecting, archiving, and exhibition activities on two other floors.

SAMMLUNG SIEGFRIED SEIZ

Figurative painting from the last decade of East Germany

Collector:
Siegfried Seiz

Address:
Reutlingen, Germany
info@sieger-seiz.de

Visitation permitted only occasionally. Please inquire by e-mail.

As soon you hear the phrase "painting from the GDR," Socialist Realism comes to mind—and with it all its stereotypes. But business executive Siegfried Seiz's Reutlingen-based collection shows that there was another, non-official kind of figurative painting in East Germany. Sixty-six primarily large-format paintings by twenty-three artists have found a comfortable home in his 600-square-meter exhibition space, built out of a former factory. The art historian Gisold Lammel pointed Seiz to artists' studios in Berlin, Dresden, Leipzig, and Halle, which he visited during the last decade of the GDR. Alongside early pictures by Neo Rauch, Seiz's collection holds unexpected works, like some wildly expressive paintings by Klaus Killisch, or the realist punk portraits by Clemens Gröszer.

MESSMER FOUNDATION/KUNSTHALLE MESSMER

Concrete and Constructivist Art, plus the estate of Swiss painter André Evard

Collector:
Jürgen A. Messmer

Address:
Grossherzog-Leopold-Platz 1
79359 Riegel am Kaiserstuhl
Germany
Tel +49 7642 9201620
info@kunsthallemessmer.de
www.kunsthallemessmer.de

Opening Hours:
Tues–Sun: 10am–5pm

His life is defined by art and design. In 2005 Jürgen A. Messmer, a former manufacturer of premium writing utensils, established the Messmer Foundation in memory of his deceased daughter, Petra. In 2009 he opened the Kunsthalle Messmer in a former brewery in Riegel am Kaiserstuhl. In a 900-square-meter space he exhibits works from his trove of 1 000 paintings and sculptures in thematic and monographic groupings in up to three shows a year: classics like Paul Klee and Otto Freundlich, inspiring figures of Concrete Art like Max Bill or Victor Vasarely, as well as numerous positions like Ai Weiwei, Günther Uecker, or François Morellet. Loans from other art institutions broaden the exhibitions' scope. Forming a central pillar of the Messmer collection is the main part of the estate of the Swiss painter André Evard, which Messmer acquired in 1979 and has shown regularly ever since.

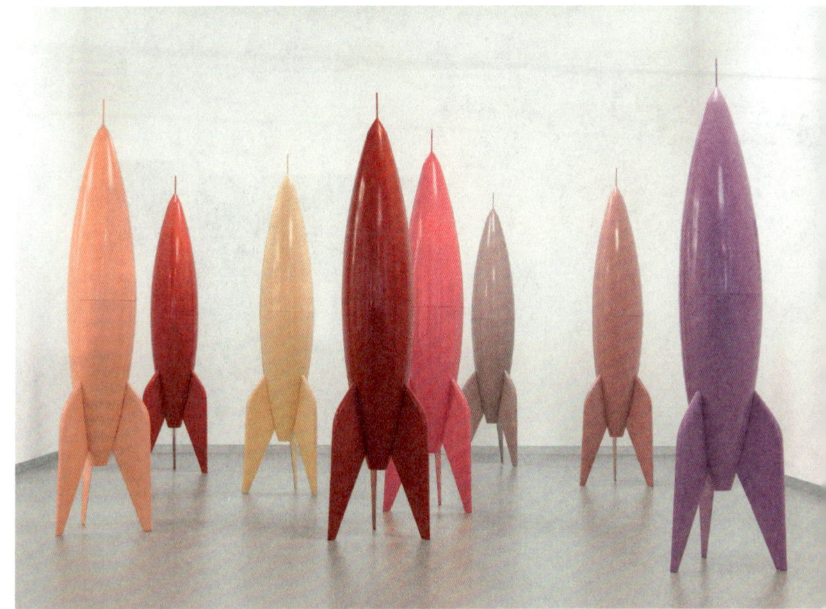

SCHAUWERK SINDELFINGEN

First-rate international contemporary art in a remodeled factory

Collectors:
Peter Schaufler &
Christiane Schaufler-Münch

Address:
Eschenbrünnlestrasse 15/1
71065 Sindelfingen
Germany
Tel +49 7031 9324900
contact@schauwerk-sindelfingen.de
www.schauwerk-sindelfingen.de

Opening Hours:
Sat–Sun: 11am–5pm
Tues, Thurs: 3–4:30pm

For the now-late Swabian businessman Peter Schaufler beauty had a lot to do with purity and the harmony of form and color. His company, a manufacturer of refrigerator compressors, is a global market leader. Schaufler and his wife, Christiane Schaufler-Münch, opened their private museum, Schauwerk Sindelfingen, in summer 2010. At that time, only a handful of people were even aware that they had started building their private collection in the late 1970s, considered one of the largest in Germany today. This made the surprise even more impressive: a 6 500-square-meter exhibition space where visitors can see top-quality works by artists like Donald Judd, Hanne Darboven, Frank Stella, Imi Knoebel, Katharina Grosse, John Armleder, Subodh Gupta, or Sylvie Fleury, and an equally impressive collection of photography, which boasts works by the most important of the Becher students, as well as international names like Nobuyoshi Araki or Vanessa Beecroft.

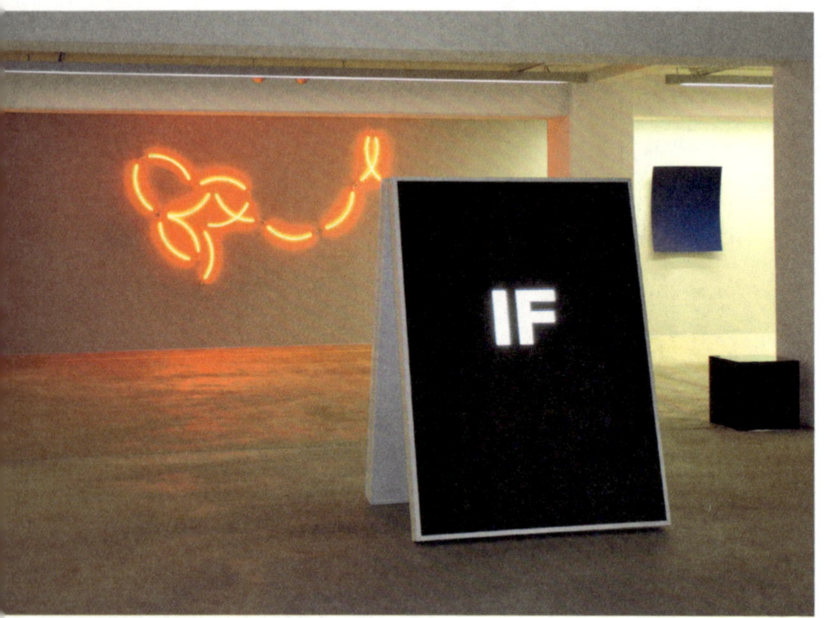

STIFTUNG KONZEPTUELLE KUNST MIT SAMMLUNG SCHROTH

Concrete and Minimalist Art at the Museum Wilhelm Morgner

Collector:
Carl-Jürgen Schroth

Address:
Thomästrasse 1
59494 Soest
Germany
Tel +49 2921 14177
info@skk-soest.de
www.skk-soest.de

Opening Hours:
Tues–Fri: 2pm–5pm
Sat–Sun: 11am–5pm
And by appointment.

Carl-Jürgen Schroth discovered his interest in Constructivism in art class. But first he got a degree in mechanical engineering and then focused on expanding the family business, in the city of Arnsberg, in Sauerland. Schroth devoted his entire professional career to the development of better safety belts, but in his free time he was drawn ever closer to art. He began building a collection in the 1980s, focusing on Concrete Art and Post-Minimalism, as well as on artists who were interested in scientific and mathematical investigations like light, space, and perception. Daniel Buren, François Morellet, or Victor Vasarely are featured prominently in addition to younger positions. Previously housed in private spaces, rotating themed exhibitions featuring works from the collection as well as external loans have been presented in the light-flooded Raum Schroth at the Museum Wilhelm Morgner since 2016.

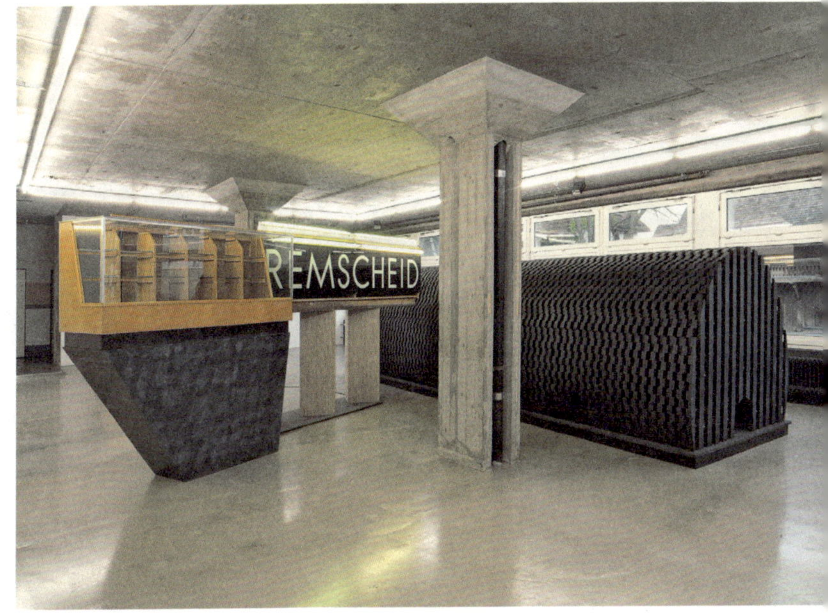

SAMMLUNG GRÄSSLIN— KUNSTRAUM GRÄSSLIN & RÄUME FÜR KUNST

An extraordinary collection with a Black Forest backdrop

Collector:
Grässlin Family

Address:
Museumstrasse 2
78112 St. Georgen
Germany
Tel +49 7724 9161805
info@sammlung-graesslin.eu
www.sammlung-graesslin.eu

By appointment only.

Ever since the Grässlin family established the Räume für Kunst, in 1995, the city of St. Georgen has become obsessed with art. Every weekend the art-going crowd courses through the vacant shops and factory floors erected to temporarily house artworks by figures like Albert Oehlen, Reinhard Mucha, Isa Genzken, or Cosima von Bonin. A tour of the impressive collection starts at the Kunstraum Grässlin, opened in 2006, and leads through the long-since-faded economic miracle of the 1960s, which is when the previous Grässlin generation began collecting Art Informel. Since the 1980s, their children have been adding contemporary works to the collection. Artist Martin Kippenberger also knew that St. Georgen breathed art, ever since he began coming to the Black Forest to recuperate from his excesses. Today, the Grässlins are among the largest holders of Kippenberger's works.

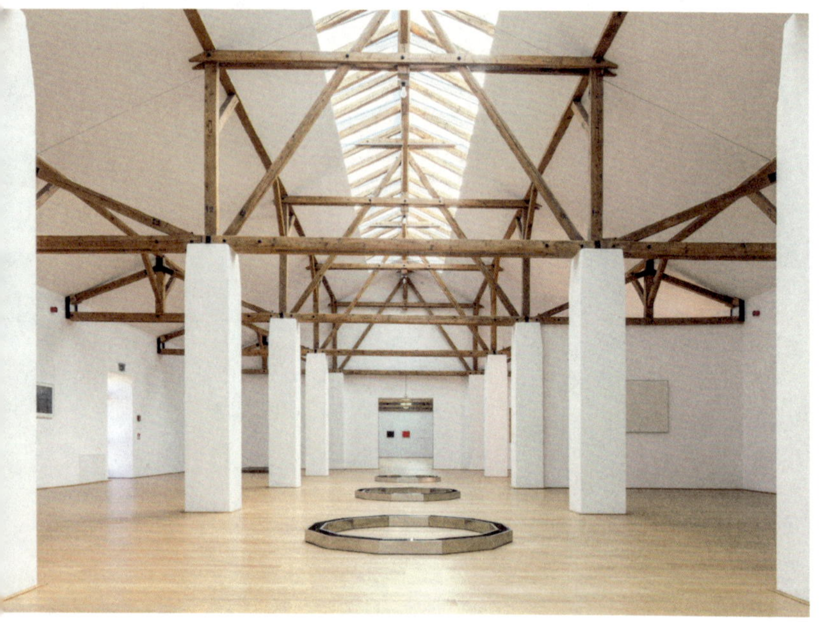

DASMAXIMUM—KUNSTGEGENWART

A rewarding permanent exhibition of four German and four American artists

Collector:
Heiner Friedrich

Address:
Fridtjof-Nansen-Strasse 16
83301 Traunreut
Germany
Tel +49 8669 1203713
mail@dasmaximum.com
www.dasmaximum.com

Opening Hours:
April-October
Sat–Sun: 12–6pm
November–March
Sat–Sun: 11am–4pm
And by appointment.
Closed in December.

"It was always important for me to be in a dialogue with artists," says Heiner Friedrich. The former gallerist, collector, patron, and international art networker, who has lived in New York City since 1971, is co-responsible for such important projects as the Dia Art Foundation and Walter De Maria's Land-Art icon *The Lightning Field*. With his private museum in Traunreut, in southern Bavaria, Friedrich brings top artists to the city of his youth. In a space measuring over 3000 square meters you'll find works by Andy Warhol, Georg Baselitz, John Chamberlain, Imi Knoebel, and Uwe Lausen. An entire hall is dedicated to an early work of light artist Dan Flavin; since 2016, another new, 800-square-meter hall presents works by Walter De Maria and Blinky Palermo. Typical for the pioneering Friedrich: the collection is permanently on display, but opening hours change according to the shifting seasonal light.

SAMMLUNG HALKE

Contemporary art in a cool, modernist house on Lake Constance

Collector:
Gunter Halke

Address:
Überlingen, Germany
halke@web.de

By e-mail appointment only

If they are convinced of an artist, they immediately buy entire work groups. For example, photo series by Tobias Zielony or Elad Lassry. The Überlingen-based orthodontist Gunter Halke and his wife passionately collect young art. And it may well raise political or social issues. A large showcase work of Josephine Meckseper is placed right in the entrance hall of their light-flooded house. "The criteria are a mixture of spontaneity, enthusiasm, and a certain training of the eye," they say. "We try to be stubborn and deaf and often find without searching. We are eager to see whether the collection still looks fresh and justifiable twenty years from now." If you want to get to know the collection, you'll receive an extensive tour of its various rooms, running across works by André Butzer, Keltie Ferris, Andy Hope 1930, Borden Capalino, Katja Novitskova, Franz Erhard Walther, or Günther Förg, among others.

SAMMLUNG FER COLLECTION

Minimal and Conceptual Art since the 1960s as an intellectual challenge

Collectors:
Friedrich E. Rentschler &
Maria Schlumberger-Rentschler

Address:
Magirus-Deutz-Strasse 16–18
89077 Ulm
Germany
Tel +49 731 3885478
maria.schlumberger@fer-collection.de
www.fer-collection.de

Only guided tours with prior online registration.

Friedrich E. Rentschler collects art that inspires thought, whether it's American Minimalism by Carl Andre or Sol LeWitt, Conceptual work by Robert Barry, or Italian Arte Povera by Giulio Paolini. Younger artists like Sylvie Fleury or Mathieu Mercier have also found their way into the collection of this pharmaceutical entrepreneur, which has been growing constantly since 1960. This Ulm-based collection could be characterized by its discerning selectivity and its collector's undeviating courage to acquire works early on. Since 2009 Rentschler has shown his treasures at the award-winning Ulmer Stadtregal, a former factory building turned into lofts, workshops, and cultural institutions in the western part of the city. With a little luck, you can catch a tour by Rentschler himself, who will explain why he doesn't just collect with his eye but also with his intellect.

KUNSTHALLE WEISHAUPT

Geometric American and European art since the 1960s

Collectors:
Siegfried & Jutta Weishaupt

Address:
Hans-und-Sophie-Scholl-Platz 1
89073 Ulm
Germany
Tel +49 731 1614360
info@kunsthalle-weishaupt.de
www.kunsthalle-weishaupt.de

Opening Hours:
Tue–Wed: 11am–5pm
Thurs: 11am–8pm
Fri–Sun: 11am–5pm

Siegfried Weishaupt likes to point out that he collects by instinct. His father, Max, had good contacts in the Ulm School of Design. Like his father, Siegfried was inspired by director Max Bill and interested in the connections between aesthetics and mathematics. In his early acquisitions, in the mid-1960s, the young engineer focused on Concrete and Geometric Art by professors at the Ulm School, such as Josef Albers. Later, travels to America opened his eyes to Color Field Painting, like the works of Mark Rothko. Under the guidance of his daughter, the art historian Kathrin Weishaupt-Theopold, the Kunsthalle Weishaupt has acquired some more contemporary positions, like Markus Oehlen, Robert Longo, or Liam Gillick. Works from the collection are regularly shown in a transparent glass building in the center of Ulm.

MUSEUM RITTER—
SAMMLUNG MARLI HOPPE-RITTER

Geometric abstraction focusing on the square from the twentieth and twenty-first century

Collector:
Marli Hoppe-Ritter

Address:
Alfred-Ritter-Strasse 27
71111 Waldenbuch
Germany
Tel +49 7157 535110
besucherservice@museum-ritter.de
www.museum-ritter.de

Opening Hours:
Tues–Sun: 11am–6pm

Almost everyone knows the infamous square-shaped Ritter Sport chocolate bar. Marli Hoppe-Ritter, the grandchild of the company's founder, took this basic form as the starting point for her art collection. Kazimir Malevich defined the square in 1915 as "the first step of pure creation in art"; a small drawing by the Russian Constructivist forms the basis of the collection. Constructivist, geometric works from Joseph Albers, Johannes Itten, and the Zurich Concrete artists to the Zero Group form the collection's inner core. Add to this a few younger artists like Gerold Miller or Paola Pivi, and the consistent 900-work collection progresses further into the present. Swiss architect Max Dudler constructed a modernistic limestone cube on the chocolate company's Waldenbuch property. Since its inauguration, in 2005, the Museum Ritter has staged three to four exhibitions annually, derived from the collection.

AUCTIONS

It can be difficult to acquire works by promising and in-demand artists in galleries, particularly if gallery owners prefer to place them exclusively in prestigious collections. Auctions, however, are a more democratic affair: anyone—with sufficient financial means—can bid. Typically, works are offered that have one or more previous owners, which means the secondary market is not necessarily the place to discover new artists. This is the task usually reserved for galleries, which often develop the careers of their protégés over long periods. But if and when a certain price level and corresponding popularity are attained, auction houses enter the picture, taking on the works of these artists and increasing their value. Phillips, an auction house specializing in contemporary art, regularly brings new names into the game. At Christie's, young artists are introduced to the auction market in First Open auctions. These have been held since 2014 not only in New York but also in London, Hong Kong, and online. Similarly, Sotheby's has introduced promising talents for several years under the auction title Contemporary Curated. If the hammer price far exceeds the estimate in the catalogue, or if demand is very high, these artists might also appear in the high-priced and media-intensive evening sales. But auction houses have become more wary of creating short-term price bubbles for young shooting stars, whose price levels can heat up too quickly in the auction room, as was the case a few years ago with the so-called Zombie Formalists Jacob Kassay, Lucien Smith, or Christian Rosa. Investing in young artists whose prices have rapidly crossed the 100 000-dollar mark with an eye to future returns is a risky financial endeavor. It is difficult to predict whether an artist will have the power and potential to build a compelling body of work in the decades ahead and to remain a permanent presence in the public eye.

WAI WOODS ART INSTITUTE— SAMMLUNG REINKING

Works that speak to viewers about existence

Collectors:
Anna-Julia & Rik Reinking

Address:
Golfstrasse 5
21465 Wentorf bei Hamburg
Germany
Tel +49 40 24895811
info@woodsartinstitute.com
www.woodsartinstitute.com

Online registration required.

He purchased his first artwork at the age of sixteen, a self-portrait by Horst Janssen. Since that time, Rik Reinking's passion for art has never wavered. Today, the works assembled by the Hamburg art dealer, curator, and founder of an art endowment fund form one of Europe's most fascinating collections. Reinking focuses on pieces that confront viewers with their memories and emotions. Whether classical positions such as Jimmie Durham and Edward & Nancy Reddin Kienholz, or contributions by younger artists like Ulla von Brandenburg and Terence Koh—Reinking is invariably interested in works that examine and call into question human existence and identity and which deal with nature and the elements. Starting in 2019, he presents his collection in a building complex just beyond Hamburg's gates in the center of a spacious English-style park with a café and multiple artists' studios—a place where art and nature can communicate in an ideal fashion.

SKULPTURENPARK WALDFRIEDEN

World-class sculpture in harmony with nature

Collector:
Tony Cragg

Address:
Hirschstrasse 12
42285 Wuppertal
Germany
Tel +49 202 47898120
mail@skulpturenpark-waldfrieden.de
www.skulpturenpark-waldfrieden.de

Opening Hours:
March–October
Tues–Sun: 10am–7pm
November–February
Fri–Sun: 10am–5pm

Skulpturenpark Waldfrieden combines the experience of nature with sustainable architecture and world-class sculpture. In 2006, British sculptor and Wuppertal resident Tony Cragg acquired the fallow, fourteen-hectare site located in Bergisches Land. The elegant villa in anthroposophical style, erected by manufacturer Kurt Herberts shortly after the war, was then carefully renovated. When strolling through the extensive park and its wealth of native and exotic tree species, you encounter not only a selection of Cragg's own sculptures, but also an ever-growing collection of prominent works by sculptors including Richard Deacon, Erwin Wurm, Jaume Plensa, and Markus Lüpertz. Three large pavilions provide space for exhibitions of renowned artists and musical concerts. Film director Wim Wenders used one of these as a location for filming his homage to the late, Wuppertal-based choreographer Pina Bausch.

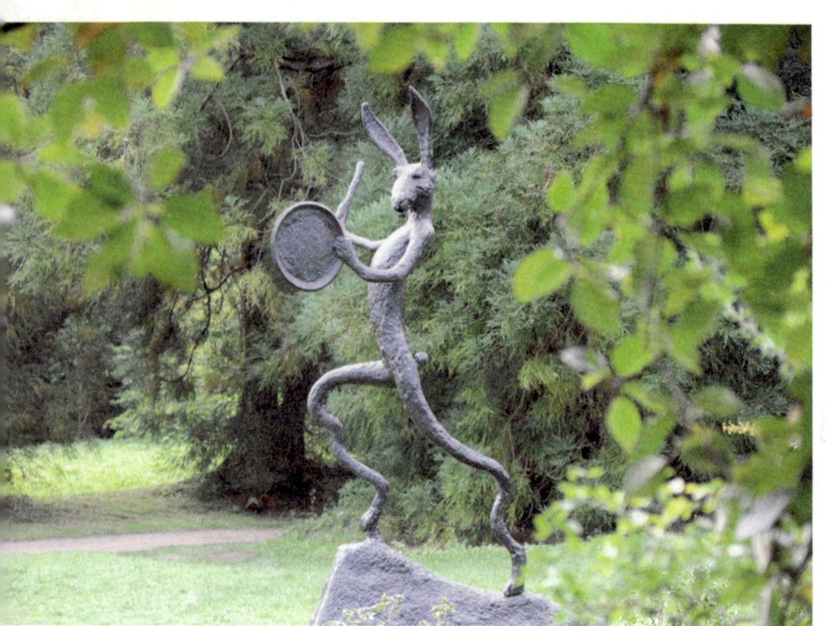

CHATSWORTH

A ducal collection facilitates art historical dialogue from antiquity to the present

Collectors:
The Duke & Duchess of Devonshire

Address:
Bakewell
Derbyshire DE45 1PP
Great Britain
Tel +44 1246 565300
www.chatsworth.org

Opening Hours:
March–December
Mon–Sun: 11am–5:30pm

The breathtaking landscape of the Peak District in Derbyshire and the palatial manor house may be the biggest attractions for visitors to the country estate of Chatsworth. Between ancient sculptures, valuable furniture pieces and aristocratic portraits of centuries past, the twenty-first century has also entered the collection. The 12th Duke of Devonshire, Peregrine Cavendish, passionately continues his family's 500-year-old collecting tradition, which over the generations has compiled one of the most important art collections in Europe. The Duke and his wife have carefully added works of contemporary art, design, and ceramics, by artists such as Allen Jones, Edmund de Waal, and Nicola Hicks. A small suite of rooms is entirely devoted to the contemporaries, and in the spacious garden, between the decorative hedges, one can find sculptures by Richard Long, Elisabeth Frink, and William Turnbull.

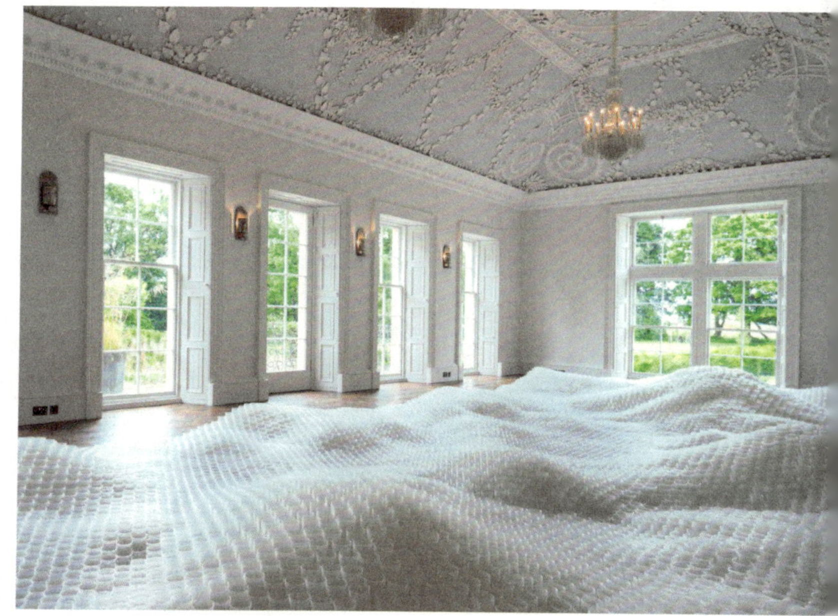

JUPITER ARTLAND

A sculpture garden where art is anything but parked and forgotten

Collectors:
Robert & Nicky Wilson

Address:
Bonnington House Steadings
Wilkieston
Edinburgh EH27 8BB
Great Britain
Tel +44 1506 889900
enquiries@jupiterartland.org
www.jupiterartland.org

Please check the website for most current information on opening hours.

In 1999 Robert and Nicky Wilson acquired the historic Bonnington House and its surrounding property. Since then, monstrous exotic flowers have begun to bloom, courtesy of *Love Bomb,* by Marc Quinn. And Charles Jenck's *Life Mounds* have transformed part of the grounds into wavy terraces. Such alterations have come about because the couple has engaged internationally acclaimed sculptors and installation artists—Anish Kapoor, Jim Lambie, or Antony Gormley—to create works specifically for their garden. The pieces fit seamlessly into the landscape; some, like Andy Goldsworthy's *Stone House,* spur an art double take. Jupiter Artland is closed during the winter. The lively dialogue the collectors demand of their art garden cannot flourish when the garden is barren of natural life.

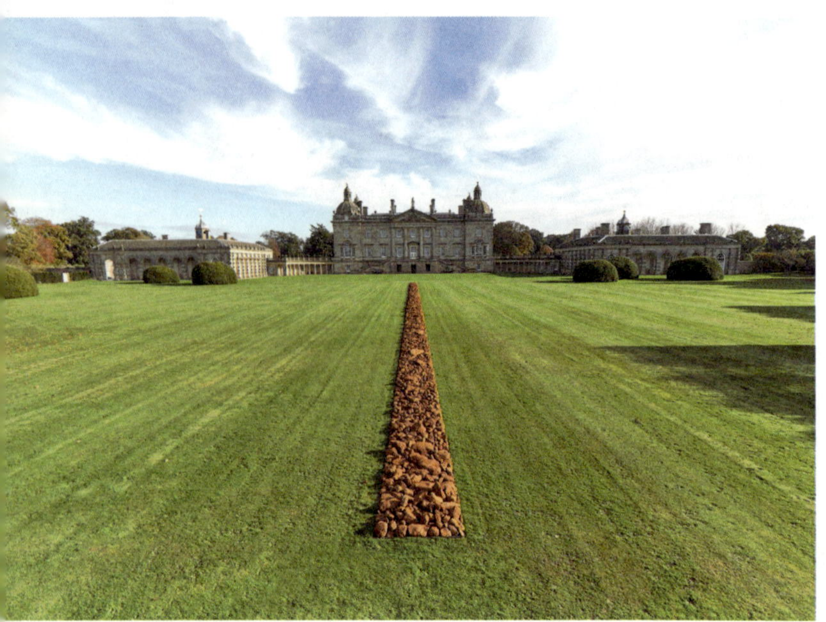

HOUGHTON HALL

Lavish eighteenth-century interiors juxtaposed with contemporary outdoor sculpture

Collectors:
Rose & David Cholmondeley

Address:
King's Lynn
Norfolk PE31 6UE
Great Britain
Tel +44 1485 528569
info@houghtonhall.com
www.houghtonhall.com

Please check the website for the most current information on opening hours.

When exploring the sprawling, landscaped grounds of Houghton Hall, one of England's finest Palladian houses, stumbling across a contemporary sculpture feels like a happy accident. The imposing house was built in the 1720s for Great Britain's first prime minister, Sir Robert Walpole, who assembled one of the country's greatest collections of European art. Later, however, his indebted grandson had to sell the collection's paintings to Catherine the Great of Russia. The current owner, Lord David Cholmondeley, continues in the collecting tradition, this time with a focus on contemporary outdoor sculpture. The first commission was *Skyspace* by James Turrell in 2000; works by Anya Gallacio, Zhan Wang, Stephen Cox, Jeppe Hein, Rachel Whiteread, and Phillip King were added later. In 2017, British sculptor and Turner Prize winner Richard Long created a remarkable series of stone and slate pieces as part of a major exhibition of his work.

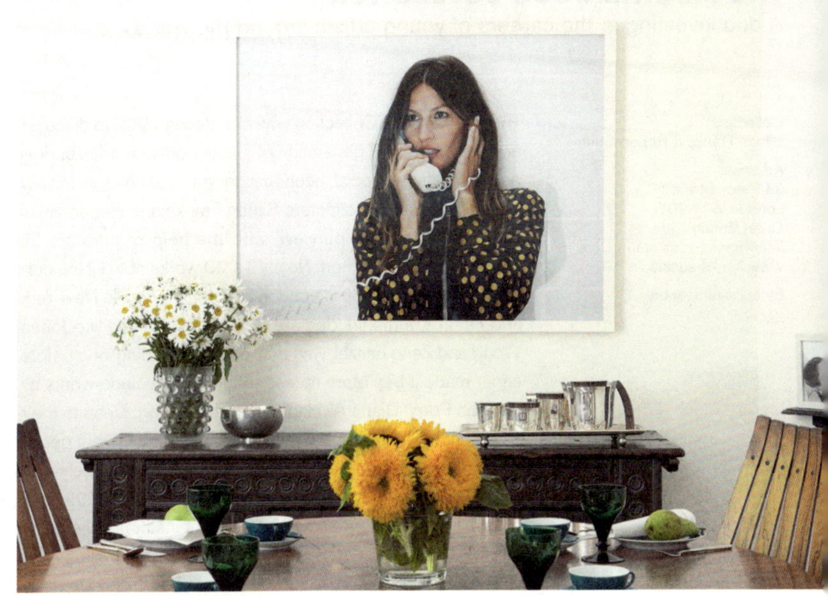

CRANFORD COLLECTION

One of Europe's most important collections with renowned contemporaries in Regent's Park

Collectors:
Muriel & Freddy Salem

Address:
London, Great Britain
Tel +44 20 78130916
office@cranfordarts.org
www.cranfordarts.org

By e-mail appointment only.

For over forty years London has been the home of collectors Muriel and Freddy Salem, a place where they acquired their first works of art in the 1990s. First it was the Young British Artists, then other European and American artists were added to their collection. Their elegant home, designed by John Nash in Regency style, is only a stone's throw away from Frieze London, the annual contemporary art fair held in Regent's Park. The number-one criterion: being able to live with the artworks in order to confront and experiment with them in their daily life. The collection is rotated approximately every eighteen months and today comprises over 500 works. A large number of these are by women artists including Rebecca Warren, Bridget Riley, and Carla Accardi. Distributed over four floors are large-format works by Christopher Wool or Albert Oehlen, alongside works by young stars like Emily Sundblad and Fredrik Værslev.

THE FRANKS-SUSS COLLECTION

A duo investing in the careers of young artists around the world

Collectors:
Simon Franks & Robert Suss

Address:
34 Percy Street
London W1T 2DG
Great Britain
info@franks-suss.com
www.franks-suss.com

By appointment only.

The Franks-Suss Collection was founded in 2002 to discover and support a new generation of artists from countries undergoing significant social, economic, or political change. Initially focused on China, collectors Simon Franks and Robert Suss soon widened their purview, with the help of curators Eli Zagury and Tamar Arnon. Nearly 1 000 works now fill the collection's main location in London and its outposts in New York and Hong Kong. Included are established names like Jonas Wood and Zeng Fanzhi, who they began collecting long before either made it big. More recent acquisitions include works by Hannah Perry, Diana Al-Hadid, and Zhai Liang. Despite their prescient track record, the two have collected in direct opposition to the art-as-an-asset-class trend, working closely with the artists on shows or at their residences, like the 2009 exhibition at Franks's Hampstead home, or at institutional spaces like the Saatchi Gallery.

THE NAPOLEONE COLLECTION

A dedicated collector with a clear mission

Collector:
Valeria Napoleone

Address:
London, Great Britain
pa@valerianapoleone.com

By e-mail appointment only.

Valeria Napoleone purchased her first work of art in New York, before moving to her adopted home of London. That was almost twenty years ago. What sets her collection apart is that the Italian-born collector actively seeks out underrepresented positions and therefore only acquires works by women artists whose career Napoleone has followed and supported for many years—such as Margherita Manzelli, Lily van der Stokker, Ghada Amer, and Lisa Yuskavage, among others. The philanthropist lives for and with art—and the works that hang on her walls or fill up her home are constantly in flux. New works are often added, or others that have been in the collection for a long time are brought out again. In the spring of 2019, Napoleone and her family are moving into a new, multi-story house in Kensington, where her exquisite collection, which has grown to several hundred works, will receive the space it duly deserves.

LONDON

The exclusive center, the elegant West, the hip East, or the up-and-coming South: in London contemporary art has developed its own urban coordinates around which you can plan your art walks. In the West, long distances must be traversed between institutions, such as the Serpentine Galleries, the Institute of Contemporary Arts (ICA), and the Saatchi Gallery. But in Mayfair—within the vicinity of the Royal Academy of Arts (RA)—the most prominent auction houses and galleries, such as Pace, Hauser & Wirth, David Zwirner, Sprüth Magers, or Blain/Southern are huddled between designer boutiques and grand hotels offering high tea. Super-dealer Larry Gagosian maintains his exhibition hall near King's Cross Station, in addition to his two galleries in Mayfair. From there it's just a stone's throw away to Golden Square, where Marianne Goodman has set up shop next to the Frith Street Gallery. North of Oxford Street, around Eastcastle Street, you can find another hotspot for contemporaries including the Alison Jacques Gallery and Carroll/Fletcher. The East End of London is not solely a hipster and media hub: from the Old Street Roundabout, near where Victoria

Miro and Modern Art are located, additional galleries and scores of artists' studios stretch from Shoreditch to Hackney Wick. Any visit to the East should include the Whitechapel Gallery, whose exhibitions are always well worth seeing. Located off the beaten path, in the Southeast, are Jay Jopling's gallery White Cube, on Bermondsey Street, as well as Damien Hirst's exhibition hall: Newport Street Gallery. Also situated south of the Thames, next to the perennially crowd-pleasing Tate Modern, are the art schools Camberwell College of Arts and Goldsmiths, which present graduate shows once a year. The non-commercial South London Gallery can also be found here. Following a visit you can round off a fine summer evening at Frank's Bar, surrounded by art students, on the roof terrace of a parking garage in Peckham, overlooking the annual sculpture exhibition *Bold Tendencies*—and the London skyline.

THE PERIMETER

Famous contemporaries and Victorian industrial architecture in Bloomsbury

Collector:
Alexander Petalas

Address:
20 Brownlow Mews
London WC1N 2LE
Great Britain
Tel +44 20 74043313
info@theperimeter.co.uk
www.theperimeter.co.uk

Only guided tours with prior online registration.

You probably wouldn't expect exhibition spaces for contemporary art to be nestled between densely packed, eighteenth-century coachman's houses on a quiet side street, just behind the traditional townhouse in Bloomsbury where Charles Dickens once lived. But this is precisely where Alexander Petalas had a former three-story Victorian warehouse completely gutted and constructed expansive spaces for his art collection. Winding from cellar to ceiling is a newly installed staircase featuring a shiny nickel silver railing designed by Petalas himself. Represented in the collection, which has steadily grown in size since 2009, are works by both established names as well as emerging artists. Included here is the American Christopher Williams and many British and German artists such as Sarah Lucas, Wolfgang Tillmans, Tomma Abts, Rebecca Warren, or the young Turner Prize winner Helen Marten. The Perimeter presents them in changing exhibitions.

SAATCHI GALLERY

A collector and gallerist, who puts Young British Artists first

Collector:
Charles Saatchi

Address:
Duke of York's HQ
King's Road
London SW3 4RY
Great Britain
www.saatchigallery.com

Opening Hours:
Mon–Sun: 10am–6pm

Charles Saatchi is known as a man who makes artists' careers. Born in Iraq, he's been collecting for over forty years. The Young British Artists have him to thank for jumpstarting their stratospheric rise in the 1990s. The founder of the Saatchi & Saatchi advertising agency has a second passion as a gallerist. In the beginning, he was interested in artists like Andy Warhol or Donald Judd, whose work has been in Saatchi's private London museum since 1985. A few years later he acquired a cornucopia of works by Damien Hirst, Tracey Emin, or Jake & Dinos Chapman, making the graduates of Goldsmiths College a flourishing brand name. His collection, which since 2008 has been housed in a classically restored building by the architecture firm Alford Hall Monaghan Morris, counts among the world's largest. This remains true, even though he donated part of it to the British government, and over 140 works were destroyed in a 2004 fire.

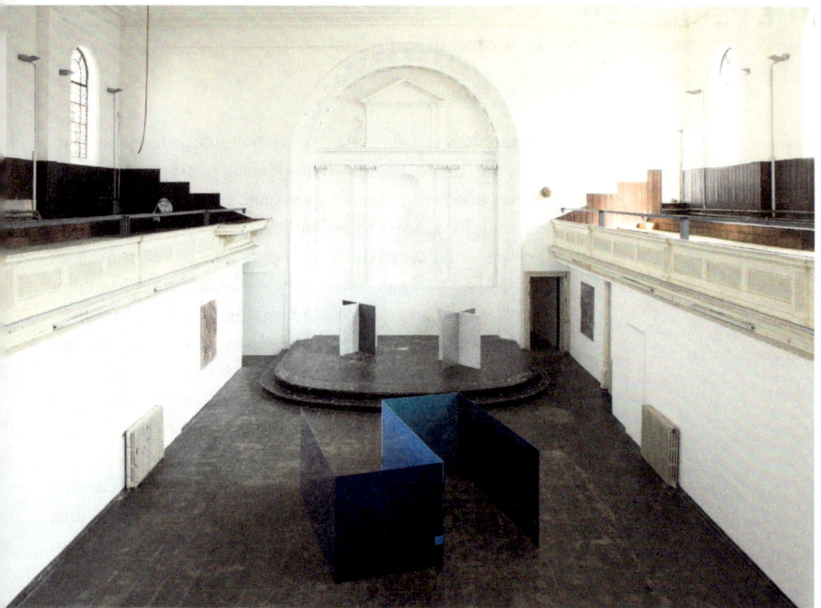

ZABLUDOWICZ COLLECTION

A collection in the unconventional ambiance of a church

Collectors:
Anita & Poju Zabludowicz

Address:
176 Prince of Wales Road
London NW5 3PT
Great Britain
info@zabludowiczcollection.com
www.zabludowiczcollection.com

Opening Hours:
Thurs–Sun: 12–6pm
And by appointment.

After studying art, Anita Zabludowicz began, in 1994, to amass a private collection, placing young, international, untested positions at the center. Her husband, Poju Zabludowicz, the Finnish financier, preferred to collect more established names. Given this combination, one finds in the couple's 3000-work collection of videos, photographs, drawings, and installations stars like Vanessa Beecroft or the Swiss duo Fischli/Weiss—as well as artists like Tom Burr or Ryan Gander, whose thematically complex works are less prevalent. The main exhibition space in London is located in a nineteenth-century Methodist church, where large parts of the collections have been shown since 2007. The second site, on the Finnish island Sarvisalo, is reserved exclusively for artist residencies, but once a year visitors can admire works by leading artists created in situ.

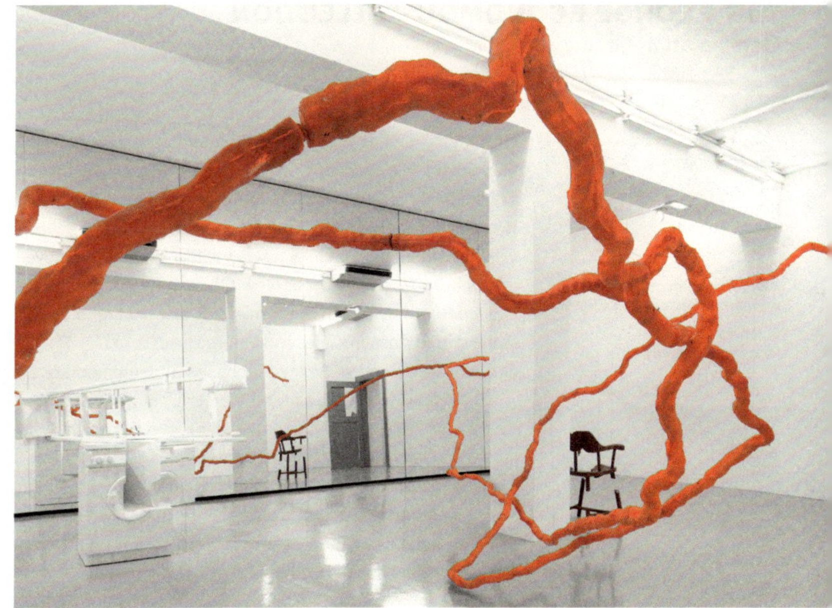

DESTE FOUNDATION FOR CONTEMPORARY ART

A renowned collection with a flair for color and provocation

Collector:
Dakis Joannou

Address:
Filellinon 11, Nea Ionia
14234 Athens
Greece
Tel +30 210 2758490
info@deste.gr
www.deste.gr

Opening hours vary depending on exhibition. Please check the website for the most current information.

While walking through New York's East Village in the 1980s, Greek Cypriot industrialist Dakis Joannou passed by the International With Monument gallery, saw Jeff Koons's *One Ball Total Equilibrium Tank,* and bought it. This, anyway, is the legendary tale of how Joannou began his collection of contemporary art, today acknowledged as one of the most important in the world and shown in museums like the Palais de Tokyo, in Paris, and the New Museum, in New York. Joannou's Deste Foundation, established in 1983, aims to be a "container for culture," an idea suggested by the design of the foundation's main entrance: a giant wooden crate similar to those used to transport works of art. Since 1999 the foundation has been supporting young artists through the biannual, 10 000-euro Deste prize, whose recipients include Anastasia Douka and Eirene Efstathiou.

THE GEORGE ECONOMOU COLLECTION

German art in Greece

Collector:
George Economou

Address:
Kifissias Avenue 80, Marousi
15125 Athens
Greece
Tel +30 210 8090519
info@economoucollection.com
www.thegeorgeeconomoucollection.com

Opening Hours:
Mon–Fri: 10am–6pm

Greek ship-owner George Economou has a penchant for German art. His collection, which has been expanding rapidly since the late 1990s—at a rate of roughly one new work every two days according to *The Economist*—offers in-depth insights into modern art in Germany, with a focus on art movements like Expressionism or New Objectivity. But the coverage does not end with modernism; it also includes artists ranging from Anselm Kiefer and Georg Baselitz, to Neo Rauch and Andreas Gursky. "All my purchases of contemporary art have a strong historic element," says Economou. Alongside his interest in artists like Ellsworth Kelly, Cady Noland, Dan Flavin, Jenny Saville, Mark Bradford, or Agnes Martin, the collector is also drawn to postwar Conceptual Art. Since 2011, two to three exhibitions have been organized annually in his exhibition space in Athens.

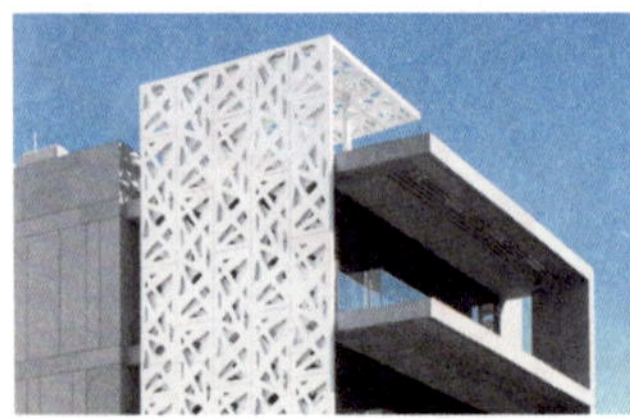

FRISSIRAS MUSEUM

3 500 contemporary figurative paintings

Collector:
Vlassis Frissiras

Address:
Monis Asteriou 3 & 7, Plaka
10558 Athens
Greece
Tel +30 210 3234678
info@frissirasmuseum.com
www.frissirasmuseum.com

Opening Hours:
Wed–Fri: 11am–6pm
Sat–Sun: 11am–5pm

"In our age, art has a right to pure madness. Assuming a defensive position against the prevailing artistic atmosphere, I made my personal aesthetic choices and embraced contemporary painting with an anthropocentric slant." With his bold statement, Greek lawyer and passionate collector Vlassis Frissiras explains how he became the proud owner of over 3 500 contemporary paintings of the human figure. "Anything else leaves me indifferent," he told *Athens News,* explaining the emotional nature of his connection to his paintings, adding: "I decided right away that I wanted the paintings to be anthropocentric. That's my character—it is monomaniacal and very focused." The Frissiras Museum includes, of course, a number of Greek artists, such as Yannis Moralis and Diamantis Diamantopoulos, as well as other established names like David Hockney and Frank Auerbach.

HERAKLEIDON—EXPERIENCE IN VISUAL ARTS

The perfect place for mathematicians with an eye for art

Collectors:
Paul & Anna-Belinda Firos

Address:
Herakleidon 16, Thissio
11851 Athens
Greece
Tel +30 210 3461981
info@herakleidon-art.gr
www.herakleidon-art.gr

Please check the website for the most current information on opening hours.

Few visual motifs have found the commercial success of Dutch graphic artist M. C. Escher's interlocking patterns of nature and geometry, mathematics and architecture. The consequence of Escher's ubiquity is that almost anyone, no matter how unversed in art, can recognize his work when they see it. Lesser known, however, is exactly where to do so. That one of the largest collections of Escher's work is located in Athens, Greece, in a neoclassical building next to the Acropolis, may come as a surprise. Yet Paul and Anna-Belinda Firos's collection, aside from the impressive gathering of Escher prints, shows a general predilection for mathematical and geometrical patterns: Op Art pioneer Victor Vasarely and American engraver Carol Wax are both extensively represented. The institution also organizes exhibitions of earlier modernists like Edgar Degas, Edvard Munch, and Henri de Toulouse-Lautrec.

PORTALAKIS COLLECTION

International art in the heart of the business district

Collector:
Zacharias Portalakis

Address:
Pesmazoglou 8, 8th Floor
10559 Athens
Greece
Tel +30 210 3318933
info@portalakiscollection.gr
www.portalakiscollection.gr

Opening Hours:
Wed: 12–8pm
Sat: 11am–3pm
And by appointment.

The typical art lover might not go to the business district to look for art, but, then again, the eighth floor of Zacharias Portalakis's brokerage company, located directly across from the former location of the Athens Exchange, is not your typical location. A self-made broker, Portalakis once told the *National Herald*, "All of the money I made is now colors." He started buying Greek artists at the end of the 1980s and then moved on to expatriated Greeks, such as Jannis Kounellis and Theodoros Stamos, the latter of whom he is the world's foremost collector. It has not always been like this: when Portalakis first met Stamos, the baffled collector says he did not understand the work. Instead, he let his then eight-year-old daughter choose a painting for her father's burgeoning collection, which today counts such international stars as Lucio Fontana, Christopher Wool, and Richard Prince among its highlights.

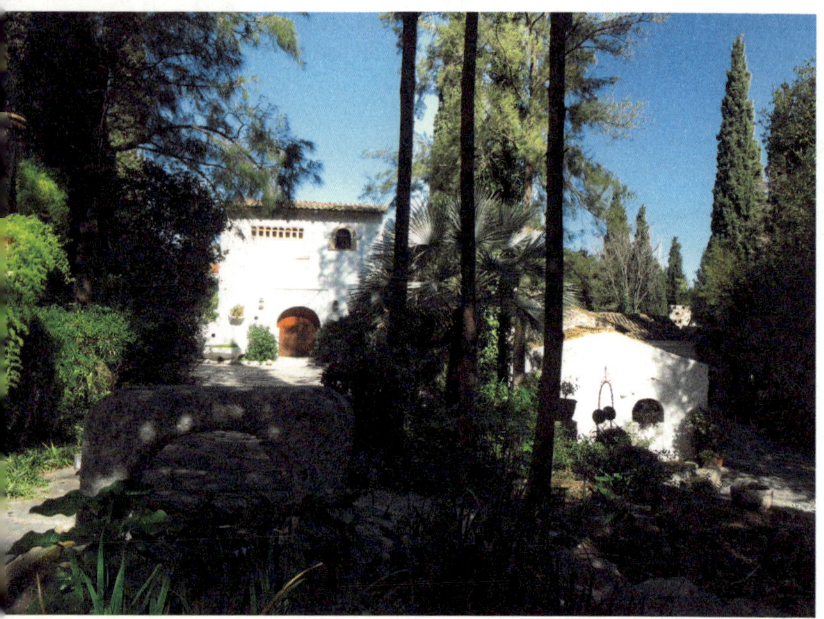

VORRES MUSEUM

3 000 years of Greek history and postwar Greek art

Collector:
Ian Vorres

Address:
Diadochou Konstantinou 1
19002 Paiania
Greece
Tel +30 210 6642520
mvorres@otenet.gr
www.vorresmuseum.gr

Opening Hours:
Sat–Sun: 10am–2pm
And by appointment.
Closed in August.

In the small town of Paiania, just east of Athens, the Vorres Museum strives to preserve Greek national heritage by covering 3 000 years of the nation's history. The nearly 6 000 works in the collection are divided into two sections: an impressive folk art collection, exhibited in four reconstructed village houses, and a museum of contemporary art, featuring paintings and sculptures by Greek artists from the second half of the twentieth century, including Lucas Samaras and Vlassis Caniaris. The sheer diversity of the collection reflects the personality of its owner, Ian Vorres, who died in 2015. During his lifetime, the Greek expatriate lived in Canada and made a name for himself as an art critic. He also served as a liaison between Canada and Greece, authored a biography of Russian grand duchess Olga Alexandrovna, and was even mayor of Paiania. Since 2016, the museum also temporarily houses the estate of Greek painter Jannis Spyropoulos.

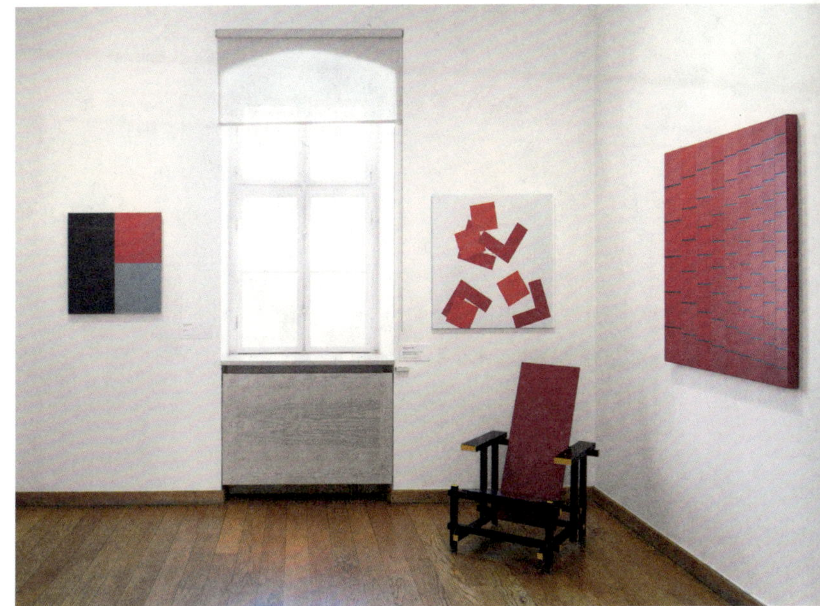

VASS COLLECTION

Hungarian and international abstraction, Constructivist and Concrete Art

Collector:
László Vass

Address:
Vár Utca 3–7
8200 Veszprém
Hungary
Tel +36 88 561310
info@vasscollection.hu
www.vasscollection.hu

Opening Hours:
May–October
Mon–Sat: 10am–6pm
November–April
Mon–Sat: 10am–5pm

In keeping with the Budapest cordwainer tradition, the name László Vass is known as a hallmark of quality and elegance in men's handmade leather shoes. Less well known—but no less refined—is the Vass Collection, preserved in the castle district of Veszprém, a small town of history and lore located 100 kilometers from Budapest. Incidentally, Veszprém is also known as "the city of queens": for centuries, Hungary's female royals were crowned by the local bishop. Vass began collecting contemporary Hungarian art in the 1970s and, influenced by an encounter with artist Jenő Barcsay, initially focused on native Constructivist Art and abstraction. He then turned to the same positions on an international level, assembling a collection of roughly 600 works by artists like Max Bill, Josef Albers, Manfred Mohr, Sean Scully, and Günther Uecker.

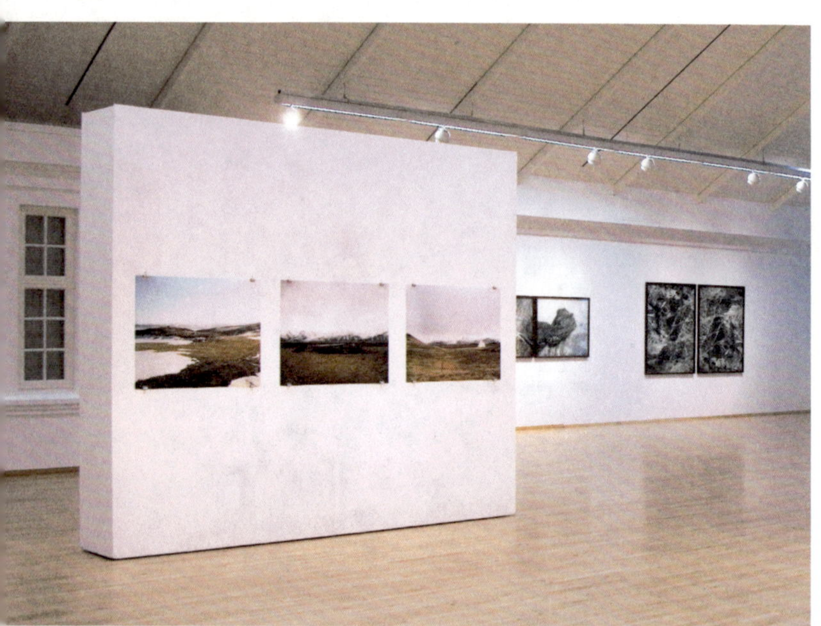

HAFNARBORG—THE HAFNARFJÖRÐUR CENTRE OF CULTURE AND FINE ART

Icelandic art of the twentieth century

Collectors:
Sverrir Magnússon &
Ingibjörg Sigurjónsdóttir

Address:
Strandgata 34
220 Hafnarfjörður
Iceland
Tel +354 585 5790
hafnarborg@hafnarfjordur.is
www.hafnarborg.is

Opening Hours:
Fri–Mon: 12–5pm

No matter if it's in Berlin, New York, or Venice, Icelandic art has great appeal. And whoever wishes to trace Icelandic art to the homeland of elves and mountain trolls should start with the Hafnarborg—The Hafnarfjörður Centre of Culture & Fine Art. In 1983 the pharmacist couple Sverrir Magnússon and Ingibjörg Sigurjónsdóttir donated their extensive collection of Icelandic modern art, and their private home, to the small town near Reykjavík. An extensive cultural center was developed around the building and opened in 1988. Almost every month there is a new special exhibition focusing mainly on Icelandic art. Today the ever-expanding collection includes 1 400 works. Icelandic artists living outside their home country, such as Ragnar Kjartansson, Egill Sæbjörnsson, or Ólafur Elíasson, have all had exhibitions there. Elíasson has the home-town advantage: he grew up in Hafnarfjörður.

DEVI ART FOUNDATION

The spectrum of Indian contemporary art
in one family collection

Collectors:
Lekha & Anupam Poddar

Address:
Sirpur House, Plot 39
Sector 44, Gurgaon
India
Tel +91 124 4888177
info@deviartfoundation.org
www.deviartfoundation.org

Please check the website for the most current information on opening hours.

Businesswomen Lekha Poddar began collecting art in the 1970s, concentrating on work that highlighted domestic Indian art. Her son Anupam Poddar has since broadened the scope of the family collection by harnessing work from the Asian sub-continent: Pakistan, Bangladesh, and Sri Lanka, as well as from Afghanistan, Tibet, and the Middle East. His main interest is in experimental artists of his own generation whose genre-bending artworks mirror the vision of India. Examples range from Sudarshan Shetty, Bharti Kher, Alwar Balasubramaniam through Subodh Gupta, Mithu Sen or Jagannath Panda, all the way to Sakshi Gupta. Also represented are the Iranian Golnaz Fathi and Kuwaiti Hamra Abbas. The Devi Art Foundation, in Gurgaon, near New Delhi, displays a large part of its collection in the family's company building, completed in 2008.

THE KIRAN NADAR MUSEUM OF ART (KNMA)

150 years of Indian art

Collector:
Kiran Nadar

Address:
145, DLF South Court Mall, Saket
New Delhi 110017
India
roobina.karode@hcl.in
www.knma.in

Opening Hours:
Tues–Sun: 10:30am–6:30pm

One of the first private museums in India was opened in New Delhi in 2010. Kiran Nadar not only aims to make her twenty-year-old collection publicly accessible, but to increase the quality of India's museum culture while doing so. A large part of Nadar's program is dedicated to education for schoolchildren and university students. 90 percent of the roughly 450 artworks are from India, while the remainder comes primarily from Pakistanis and from Indian artists who live abroad. In the museum's 1 600 square meters, visitors find key works by well-known Indian modernists, such as Raja Ravi Varma or Maqbool Fida Husain, the "Picasso of India." Alongside these are works by a pioneering group of Bombay artists who worked together in the 1940s, as well as art by contemporaries like Anish Kapoor, Bharti Kher, or Raqib Shaw.

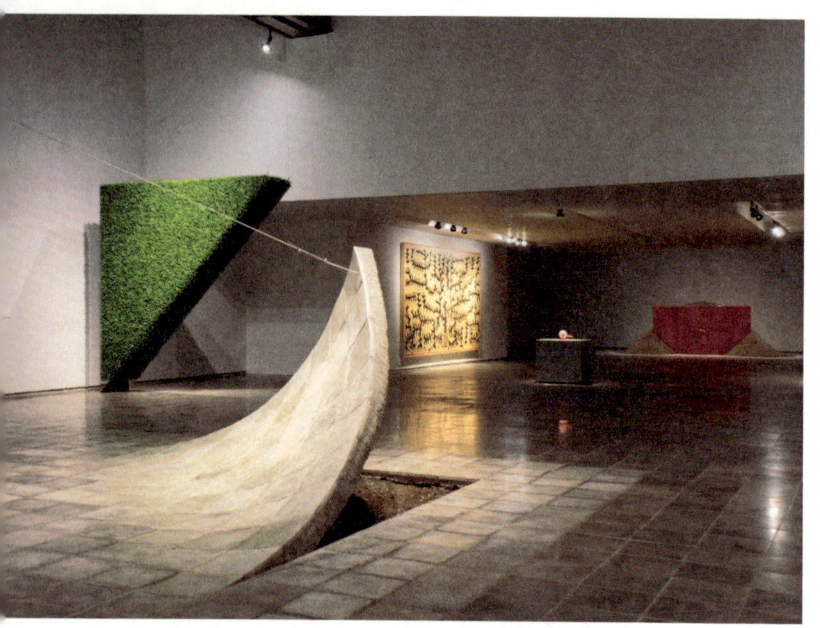

OHD MUSEUM OF MODERN & CONTEMPORARY INDONESIAN ART

A private collection with museum-level Indonesian art

Collector:
Oei Hong Djien

Address:
Jl. Jenggolo 14
Magelang 56122
Central Java
Indonesia
Tel +62 293 362444
info@ohdmuseum.com
www.ohdmuseum.com

Opening Hours:
Wed–Mon: 10am–5pm

Quite an accomplishment: since the 1980s former physician Oei Hong Djien has assembled roughly 3 000 works of Indonesian art. The result is a stellar overview of abstract and figurative painting, print, sculpture, photography, installation, and video art. The collection spans from the European-educated Prince Raden Saleh (1811–1880) to pioneer artists of the twentieth century, such as Affandi, S. Sudjojono, Hendra Gunawan, Haji Widayat, and Soedibio. Notable are European artists like Rudolf Bonnet or Walter Spies, both of whom played important roles in Balinese modern art. Roughly half of the collection consists of contemporary artists, among them Entang Wiharso, Heri Dono, Nasirun, Nyoman Masriadi, and Rudi Mantofani. For some of them, the culture of the Wayang, or "shadow play," has been an important factor in their works. The collection is housed in three beautiful two-story buildings in the city of Magelang.

TEL AVIV

Tel Aviv is an acclaimed place not only for art fans, but also for architecture enthusiasts: roughly 4 000 buildings are built in the Bauhaus or International Style. An audio tour of the White City—appointed a UNESCO World Heritage Site in 2003—and a visit to the Bauhaus Center Tel Aviv should also be on everyone's agenda. The Tel Aviv Museum of Art (TAM), founded in 1932, presents art of all periods, from the Old Masters to contemporary, in its historic building, erected in the 1970s, and in the geometrically designed Herta and Paul Amir Building, which opened in 2011. Also part of the major city museums, but run virtually independently, is the Helena Rubinstein Pavilion for Contemporary Art, which specializes in innovative exhibition formats of Israeli and international art. The Herzliya Museum of Contemporary Art concentrates on art with a social and political dimension, often by Arab and Palestinian artists. Established in 1998 as a nonprofit space, the Center for Contemporary Art (CCA), with its two exhibition spaces and an auditorium, offers a platform for all those interested in video art, experimental film, and performance. The Sommer Contemporary Art gallery, opened in

1999 and located in a 1920s building at the top of the Rothschild Boulevard, shows internationally renowned Israeli artists like Yael Bartana and Yehudit Sasportas. Other members of Sommer's program like Tom Burr and Saâdane Afif make the gallery an equally important showcase for international artists as well. This is much the same at Dvir Gallery, in the hipster neighborhood Florentin, whose program includes Claire Fontaine and Jonathan Monk as well as Israeli artists like Omer Fast and Ariel Schlesinger. The Chelouche Gallery for Contemporary Art, which moved into the west wing of the city's famed historic Twin Houses, in 2010, shows Michelangelo Pistoletto and William Kentridge, among other greats. The final amazing thing about Tel Aviv: from nearly every nook of the city the beach is just a few blocks away.

IGAL AHOUVI ART COLLECTION

An international collection emphasizing contemporary art's pluralistic aspects

Collector:
Igal Ahouvi

Address:
Tel Aviv, Israel
Tel +972 3 64025005
info@igalahouviartcollection.com
www.igalahouviartcollection.com

By appointment only.

With around 1 500 works, Igal Ahouvi owns one of the largest private collections of art in Israel. It includes some 750 pieces by international artists, from Andy Warhol, Anselm Kiefer, Bruce Nauman, Cindy Sherman, and Christopher Williams, to Marlene Dumas and David Hammons. Another focus of the collection is on Israeli contemporary art, including 750 works by artists such as Sigalit Landau, Elad Lassry, Moshe Gershuni, and Igael Tumarkin. The collection is committed to reflecting the diverse nature of art and strives to incorporate a broad range of works by artists working in a variety of techniques. Businessman Ahouvi is closely involved in the local art scene and actively supports local artists and galleries through acquisitions, in addition to sponsoring exhibitions in Israeli museums. Works from the collection have been featured in a number of exhibitions in recent years, making a lasting impression on public audiences in Israel.

GIVON ART FORUM

The Tel Aviv collection where art runs in the family and ideas come first

Collector:
Noemi Givon

Address:
Alroi 3, Neve Tzedek
Tel Aviv 6514905
Israel
Tel +972 3 9490999
givonartforum@gmail.com
www.givonartforum.com

Opening Hours:
Fri–Sat: 11am–3pm
And by appointment.

Launched in 2012 in Tel Aviv's oldest and most exclusive neighborhood, Neve Tzedek, the Givon Art Forum presents the private collection of Tel Aviv-based gallerist and collector Noemi Givon, as well as showing and caring for the collection of her father, the late Sam Givon. She opened the Forum in the belief that—in order to generate new ideas— there needed to be an exhibition space freed of the commercial constraints of a gallery and the structural limitations of a museum. The Forum's first exhibition, *Accelerating towards Apocalypse,* featured the collection of Israeli businessman Doron Sebbag—and Givon hopes to invite other collectors to exhibit in the future. Additional programming at the Givon Art Forum has drawn from her own holdings, with shows ranging from solo presentations of Aviva Uri, Gabriel Klasmer, and Israel Kabala to thoughtfully curated group exhibitions such as *Who Is Content and Lives?* focusing on artists of the 1980s.

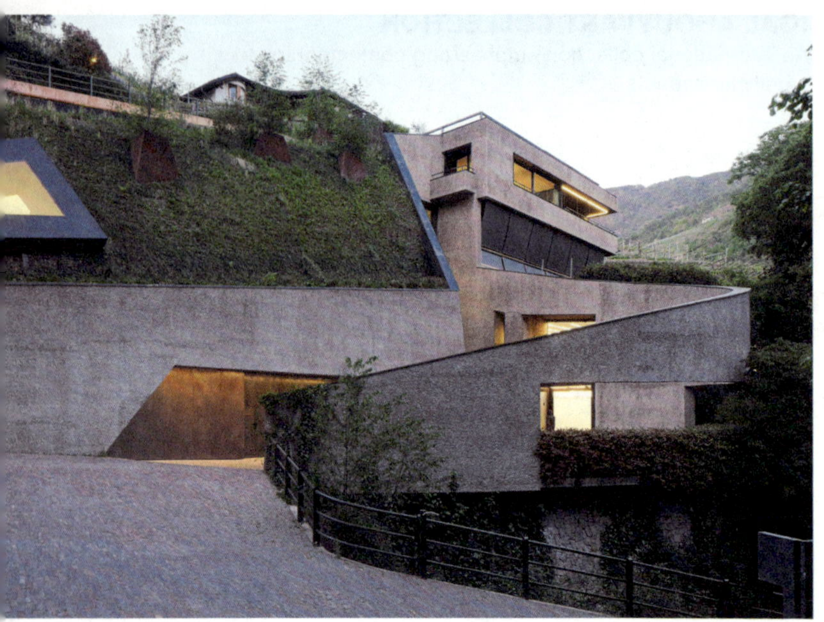

ANTONIO DALLE NOGARE FOUNDATION

Contemporary art and architecture in the vineyards of South Tyrol

Collector:
Antonio Dalle Nogare

Address:
Via Rafenstein 19
39100 Bolzano
Italy
Tel +39 0471 971626
info@adncollection.it
www.adncollection.it

Please check the website for the most current information on opening hours.

Invigorating landscape and distinctive architecture make a visit to the Antonio Dalle Nogare Foundation already worthwhile. Surrounded by vineyards, the building is home to both the collection and the private residence of Antonio Dalle Nogare. A mountain was hollowed out for its construction and the pink porphyry stone excavated there was reused as building material, allowing local architects Walter Angonese and Andrea Marastoni to insert the structure harmoniously into the landscape. Dalle Nogare, who began collecting thirty years ago, focuses on Minimal and Conceptual Art. In his collection, positions of the 1960s and 1970s stand in dialogue with younger contemporary artists. The foundation, which he established in 2017, not only organizes temporary exhibitions but is also engaged in the region culturally, for example, by supporting local art production.

ROSSINI ART SITE (RAS)

Large-scale sculptures in a landscaped park

Collector:
Alberto Rossini

Address:
Via Col del Frejus 3
20836 Briosco
Italy
Tel +39 335 5378472
info@rossiniartsite.com
www.rossiniartsite.com

Please check the website for the most current information on opening hours.

Just north of Milan is a park that fuses modern and contemporary sculpture, architecture, and landscape. It is, in fact, an open-air museum, founded in 2010 by the now-late entrepreneur Alberto Rossini and his wife, Luisa, in memory of their son Pietro. Alberto Rossini's interest in art began in the 1950s. Several large sculptures are located in the park, some of them developed as site-specific projects. Among the artists are important Italian names of the postwar period, including Fausto Melotti, Pietro Consagra, or Giulio Turcato, as well as international names such as Dennis Oppenheim, César, Erik Dietman, Daniel Spoerri, Franz Staehler, David Fried, Jean Tinguely, or Hidetoshi Nagasawa. A pavilion in the park used for exhibitions was designed by James Wines of the New York architecture office Site—one of the largest firms in the field of green architecture.

COLLEZIONE LA GAIA

Minimal Art, Conceptual Art, and Arte Povera in Piedmont

Collectors:
Bruna Girodengo &
Matteo Viglietta

Address:
Strada Monte Gaudio 13
12022 Busca
Italy
Tel +39 0171 946000
info@collezionelagaia.it
www.collezionelagaia.it

Visitation permitted only occasionally. Please inquire by e-mail.

When Bruna Girodengo and Matteo Viglietta began collecting art at the end of the 1970s, they did so "on tiptoe and with a big desire to learn." Initially the pair bought modernist works—their first acquisition a 1918 collage by Giacomo Balla—but they soon turned their attention to art from the 1960s to the present. Today the collection boasts nearly 1 200 pieces, including a significant group by Arte Povera artists like Alighiero Boetti, Giuseppe Penone, and Michelangelo Pistoletto, which are placed in a "conversation" with more contemporary works by the likes of Bill Viola, Anish Kapoor, and Tony Cragg. Among Girodengo and Viglietta's recent acquisitions, always based on their personal preferences, are works by Bas Jan Ader, David Hammons, Sanja Iveković, Robert Gober, Roman Ondák, and Christian Rosa.

FONDAZIONE PIER LUIGI E NATALINA REMOTTI

A marriage in the name of art, and a collection in a former church

Collectors:
Pier Luigi & Natalina Remotti

Address:
Via Castagneto 52
16032 Camogli
Italy
Tel +39 0185 772137
info@fondazioneremotti.it
www.fondazioneremotti.it

Please check the website for the most current information on opening hours.

Since their wedding nuptials at the end of the 1960s, Pier Luigi and Natalina Remotti have been collecting contemporary art. "We have always looked for artists who are experimenting with a new language but who do not yet command exorbitant prices," says Natalina Remotti. "A collector must recognize an artist before the market does." Their collection includes works by Francesco Vezzoli, Vanessa Beecroft, and Nico Vascellari and has a special slant toward photography. Their foundation was opened in 2008 in a former church renovated by the artist Alberto Garutti. There they present their collection and organize exhibitions with additional artists they appreciate. "Our collection has grown quite nicely because my husband and I agree on things," Natalina Remotti says. "It's often happened that I've shown him a work of art at a fair and he says, 'I just bought that.'"

FONDAZIONE BRODBECK

Contemporary art in a post-industrial complex—in the shadow of a volcano

Collector:
Paolo Brodbeck

Address:
Via Gramignani 93
95121 Catania
Italy
Tel +39 095 7233111
info@fondazionebrodbeck.it
www.fondazionebrodbeck.it

By appointment only.

The 6 000-square-meter industrial complex in the neighborhood of San Cristoforo, in Catania, used to be a factory for producing licorice and processing nuts. It has also served as a garrison, a storage facility, and joinery. Now it is home to Fondazione Brodbeck, founded by industrialist Paolo Brodbeck in 2007, which aims to transform the region into an international art nexus. So far the commitment has entailed the renovation of a section of the industrial area and a chance to rethink the entire neighborhood. Brodbeck's collecting is equally sweeping: Arte Povera and Gruppo Forma, as well as international artists like Louise Bourgeois, Tony Cragg, and Julian Opie. With an eye to the future, Brodbeck supports young artists through a residency program. So far, it has hosted artists such as João Maria Gusmão + Pedro Paiva, whose works have found their way into Brodbeck's esteemed compendium.

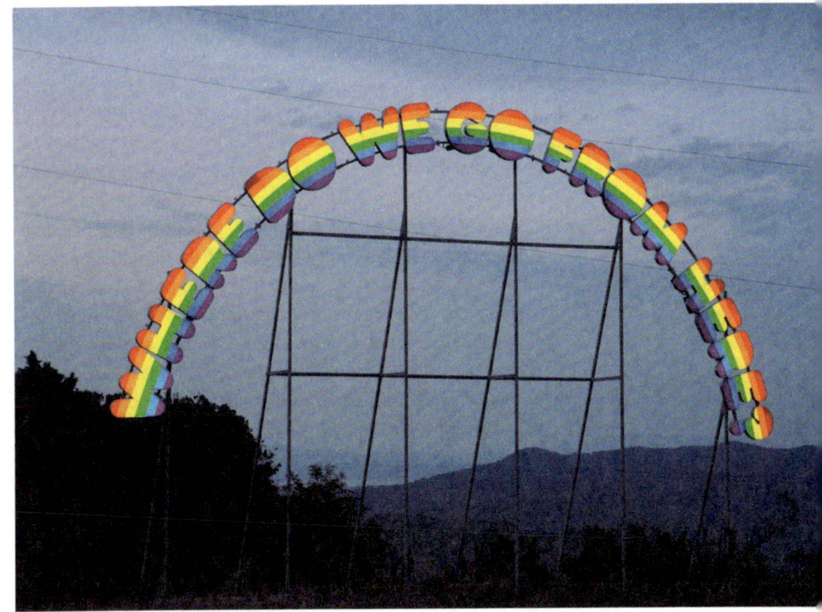

IL GIARDINO DEI LAURI

Contemporary blue chips in the Umbrian countryside

Collectors:
Massimo & Angela Lauro

Address:
Località San Litardo
ss Umbro Casentinese km 79
06062 Città della Pieve
Italy
Tel +39 333 81099572
elda@ilgiardinodeilauri.it
www.ilgiardinodeilauri.it

Opening Hours:
Fri–Sat: 10am–1pm,
3:30–6:30pm
And by appointment.

Born into a family of art collectors, Massimo Lauro came in contact with art at a young age. He was love-struck by his parents' enthusiasm and eventually began collecting on his own. Knowing he could not compete with his parents' stately compilation, he began, in the 1990s, garnering the work of a younger generation. Today the collection that Massimo Lauro and his wife, Angela, have amassed in their Umbrian countryside residence boasts more than 300 works of established contemporary artists like Urs Fischer, Jeff Koons, Allora & Calzadilla, Takashi Murakami, and Fischli/Weiss. Some sculptures are installed in the garden: a hulking metallic hand by Piotr Uklański, and an unsettling sculpture of a hanged child by Maurizio Cattelan, which shocked some of Milan's residents in 2004. A neon rainbow by Ugo Rondinone glows over wandering garden visitors, asking, *Where Do We Go from Here?*

SENSUS—LUOGHI PER L'ARTE CONTEMPORANEA

Space as leitmotif in a 1960s building

Collector:
Claudio Cosma

Address:
Viale Gramsci 42
50132 Florence
Italy
info@sensusstorage.com
www.sensusstorage.com

By e-mail appointment only.

"Even as a child I was collecting things that triggered my imagination. I used them to create my own world." This is how insurance broker Claudio Cosma explains the motivation behind his passion of the last thirty years. "My greatest satisfaction," he says, "is being part of the creative process, exchanging ideas with artists." This approach is reflected in the name of Cosma's showroom in Florence, Sensus, a reference to perception. Opened in 2012, and spread over two levels of a 1960s-era building, the collection is focused on the relationship between art and its surrounding space. Featured are Italian artists like Angelo Barone and Maurizio Nannucci as well as Asian representatives like Maitree Siriboon or Yuki Ichihashi. In Florence, where the cultural heritage of the Renaissance still dominates, Sensus contributes to the positioning of contemporary art in important ways as a meeting place for international artists and art enthusiasts.

FONDAZIONE DINO ZOLI

Twentieth-century Italian art in a multifunctional museum

Collector:
Dino Zoli

Address:
Viale Bologna 288
47100 Forlì
Italy
Tel +39 0543 755770
info@fondazionedinozoli.com
www.fondazionedinozoli.com

Opening Hours:
Tues–Thurs: 9:30am–12:30pm
Fri–Sun: 9:30am–12:30pm, 4–7pm
And by appointment.

The Fondazione Dino Zoli, located in the city of Forlì, in the central-north region of Emilia-Romagna, calls itself a "dynamic museum." Rightly so: opened by local industrialist Dino Zoli in 2007, the foundation not only houses his exquisite collection of modern art, but also hosts a vibrant series of talks, music events, fashion shows, and book launches, with a regional focus. The foundation's connection to the surrounding locale is also evidenced by exhibitions of paintings by Mattia Moreni, an artist from Emilia-Romagna. The collection as a whole functions as a visual excursus of twentieth-century Italian art, featuring established names like Alberto Magnelli, Mimmo Paladino, and Fabrizio Plessi, as well as those lesser-known internationally but beloved in Italy: Salvatore Fiume and Emilio Scanavino.

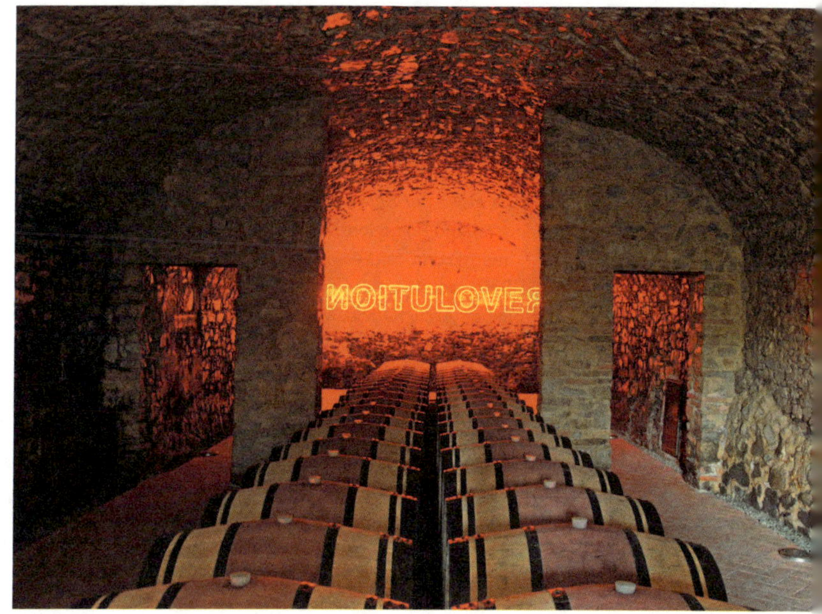

CASTELLO DI AMA PER L'ARTE CONTEMPORANEA

Site-specific installations for a dual passion: art and wine

Collectors:
Marco & Lorenza Pallanti

Address:
Località Ama
53013 Gaiole in Chianti
Italy
Tel +39 0577 746031
info@castellodiama.com
arte@castellodiama.com

By e-mail appointment only.

One thing is essential for the vintner couple Marco and Lorenza Pallanti: the uniqueness of place. This is true of their wines, of course, whose uniqueness is owed to the soil's inherent qualities, but also of their art collection, which consists exclusively of site-specific installations. Since 2000 they have invited artists once a year to install work on their vineyard estate. The project was created in collaboration with Lorenzo Fiaschi of the Galleria Continua in San Gimignano. The first artist was Michelangelo Pistoletto, who set up a four-meter-high tree with a mirror hidden inside of it—a trademark of the artist—in the basement of the Villa Pianigiani. After Pistoletto, many other well-known artists, such as Daniel Buren or Ilya & Emilia Kabakov, came and dealt with this unique space in their own striking way.

COLLEZIONE NUNZIA E VITTORIO GADDI

International contemporary art in the city and country

Collectors:
Nunzia & Vittorio Gaddi

Address:
Viale Carducci 627
55100 Lucca
Italy
Tel +39 0583 587748
info@collezionegaddi.com
www.collezionegaddi.com

By appointment only.

Tuscan notary Vittorio Gaddi has been collecting contemporary art since the early 1990s. His first work was the sculpture *La Figlia del Sole* (The Daughter of the Sun) by the Italian artist Giò Pomodoro. After this, his attention shifted to more international and emerging art. Today, Gaddi owns around 350 works by artists such as Tatiana Trouvé, Kader Attia, Anne Imhof, Alicja Kwade, Mario Garcia Torres, Michael E. Smith, Nairy Baghramian, Simon Denny, or Jonathas de Andrade. His interest is triggered less by a specific style or medium than by an artist's contemporaneity. From the very outset Gaddi wanted his collection to be publicly accessible. Today it is divided among a 1920s Art Nouveau mansion, in the city of Lucca, and two old farmhouses nestled in the countryside. One of these adjacent houses was intended as a country chalet but was gradually taken over by art. The other was renovated for the collection in summer 2012.

LA CASABIANCA

Graphic art from the 1960s to the 1990s

Collector:
Giobatta Meneguzzo

Address:
Largo Morandi 1
36034 Malo
Italy
Tel +39 0445 602474
info@museocasabianca.com
www.museocasabianca.com

Opening Hours:
Sun: 10am–12:30pm, 3–6pm
And by appointment.

Aspiring collectors with insufficiently deep pockets can always turn to works on paper for beauty and value. Giobatta Meneguzzo turned to exactly such work in the 1970s, and his decisions have paid off. Today he possesses a distinguished collection of more than 1 200 works by 700 international artists spanning from the 1960s to the 1990s. His collection, replete with a library, is housed in a seventeenth-century palace—La Casabianca—in a small town in the Veneto region. The collection's artworks are grouped together by movement and, all told, evidence a tight spectrum: Minimalism and Pop, Conceptual Art and Transavanguardia. All the works are hung salon style—and without labels—so that visitors approach the works with an unbiased eye.

DIGITALIZATION OF THE ART MARKET

While these days it may be commonplace in virtually every industry for goods to be bought and sold with a click more often than with a handshake, the art market has remained more conservative in adopting digital technologies. This is changing. The online art market has grown at breakneck pace in recent years. According to figures compiled by the Hiscox Online Art Trade Report 2017, 3.75 billion US dollars of art was traded online in 2016, equaling 8.4 percent of the global art market. Most sales still occur at the low end of the spectrum, between 1000 and 5000 US dollars, with prints, photography, and painting the most popular mediums. But many art market players are still betting on that changing as well. The space is a competitive one, with legacy innovators like Artnet, the nearly thirty-year-old price database and online auction house, which has a leg up on more recent entrants like Artsy and Paddle8. The platforms vary in their strategy when it comes to presenting art online. Artsy invests in a more tech-minded marketplace approach, providing a platform for museums, galleries, and auction houses to display (and in the latter two cases sell) art. Paddle8 procures and sells its own inventory. All are banking on the fact that the online art market will continue to expand beyond its traditional centers. As the art market is increasingly democratized, buyers of all stripes peruse the available inventory of works by their favored artists with the scroll of a mouse rather than on foot. In large part, art dealing still remains a personal affair, conducted in the back rooms of galleries, across tables at art fairs, and in the salesrooms of major auction houses. There will be a significant contingent of collectors for whom the online art buying experience can never replace the opening day at Art Basel or the thrill of the salesroom floor. But especially as more young art lovers follow suit, in particular via social networks like Instagram, the ease of access to new artists online will certainly see the sector grow.

FONDAZIONE OPERA

Contemporary art meets toys and antiques

Collectors:
Guido Galimberti &
Donatella Picenelli

Address:
Piazza San Marco 1
20121 Milan
Italy
info@operadv.com

By e-mail appointment only.

If you're the son of a passionate collector who was already purchasing works by Lucio Fontana and Piero Manzoni in the 1960s, chances are that you would fall in love with art at an early age. This is precisely what happened with Guido Galimberti. He was twenty years old when he acquired his first work of art: *Flowers,* by Andy Warhol, which he paid for in installments. For years he had worked as a financial consultant but considered art his passion. In 2007 he transformed his hobby into his profession and became an art consultant. Galimberti's handling of art is playful and provocative, combining works of contemporary artists like Nedko Solakov and Pascale Marthine Tayou with Asian antiques or toys. You will find, for example, a top hat by Giulio Paolini next to a Japanese samurai helmet, or a cube by Stuart Arends next to an antique Chinese vase.

FONDAZIONE MORRA GRECO

International contemporary art in the historic heart of Naples

Collector:
Maurizio Morra Greco

Address:
Largo Avellino 17
80138 Naples
Italy
Tel +39 081 210690
info@fondazionemorragreco.com
www.fondazionemorragreco.com

Please check the website for the most current information on opening hours.

The Neapolitan palace that houses the foundation of dentist Maurizio Morra Greco has contained art for centuries. It was used in the seventeenth century as an exhibition hall by the House of Caracciolo, the royal family of Avellino. Today, works by Italian artists such as Roberto Cuoghi and Diego Perrone are represented, as are those of international names such as Mark Dion or Manfred Pernice. "I started to buy antiques at the age of fourteen," says Morra Greco. "Then I understood that contemporary art is an expression of my time." The artists of Morra Greco's collection not only draw the zeitgeist to Naples, they also provide a connection to the city: the foundation regularly invites artists to create site-specific works. One of the most spectacular was an installation by the German artist Gregor Schneider, who transformed the basement of the palace into a shadowy labyrinth.

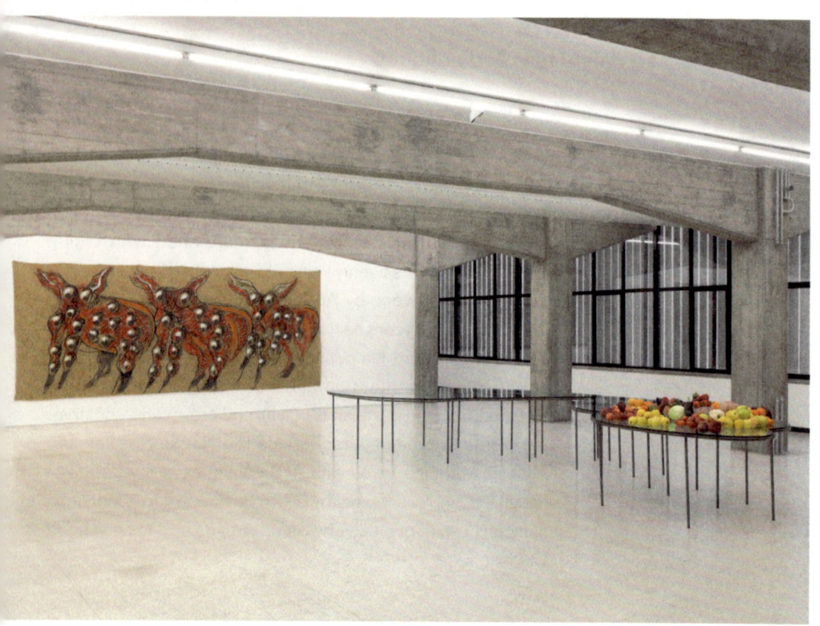

COLLEZIONE MARAMOTTI

From prêt-à-porter to contemporary art

Collector:
Maramotti Family

Address:
Via Fratelli Cervi 66
42124 Reggio Emilia
Italy
Tel +39 0522 382484
info@collezionemaramotti.org
www.collezionemaramotti.org

Please check the website for the most current information on opening hours.

Achille Maramotti, founder of fashion group Max Mara, was not only the inventor of prêt-à-porter in postwar Italy, he was also an enthusiastic collector of art. His focus was on painting—above all, Transavanguardia—but he also assembled works by international stars such as Julian Schnabel and Alex Katz, of whom he was the first European collector. Sharing Maramotti's collection with the public dates back thirty years: initially it hung in the corridors of the Max Mara factory. When production was moved to accommodate company's expansion, the factory was turned into a museum that exhibited 200 of Maramotti's 1 000 collected works. Though he passed away in 2005, Maramotti's three children have continued to buy and commission works by young artists for their family's collection, such as those by Jacob Kassay, Claudia Losi, and Krištof Kintera.

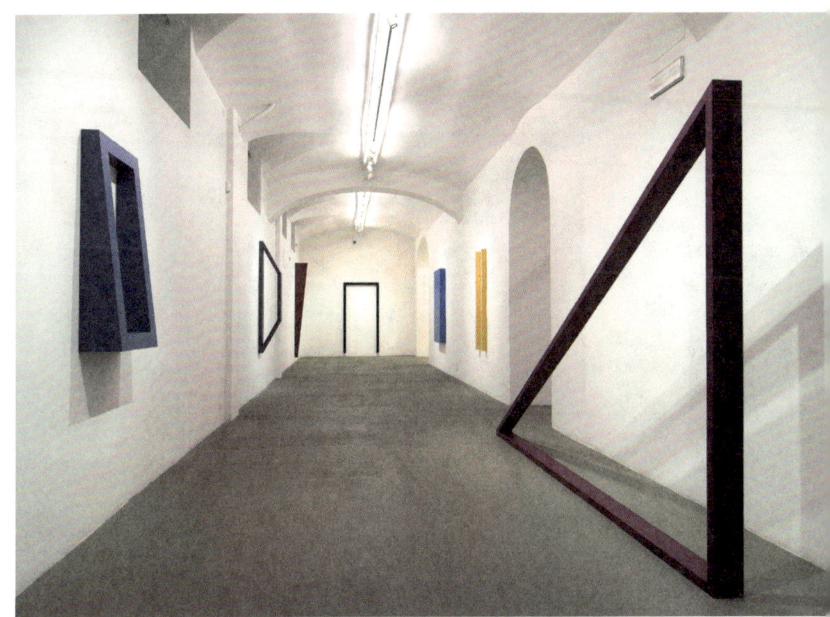

FONDAZIONE GIULIANI

Contemporary flair with blue-collar neighbors

Collectors:
Giovanni & Valeria Giuliani

Address:
Via Gustavo Bianchi 1
00153 Rome
Italy
Tel +39 06 57301091
info@fondazionegiuliani.org
www.fondazionegiuliani.org

Opening Hours:
Tues–Sat: 3–7:30pm
And by appointment.

Over the past few years, Rome's contemporary art scene has boomed—not least because of the opening of the Museo Nazionale Delle Arti Del XXI Secolo (MAXXI). Giovanni Giuliani and his wife, Valeria, have also played a part here by opening their impressive private exhibition space in 2010—a white cube in the basement of a housing project in the neighborhood of Testaccio. The area alone is worth a visit: a working-class district with strong character that offers an attractive nightlife. The Giulianis, who began collecting at the end of the 1980s, now maintain nearly 400 works, primarily sculptures and installations by artists including Cyprien Gaillard, Mona Hatoum, Alicja Kwade, and Nedko Solakov, as well as works by figures of Arte Povera and Conceptual Art. The exhibition space has regular opening hours, but the collection—at times also integrated into the foundation's exhibition program—can be toured by request only.

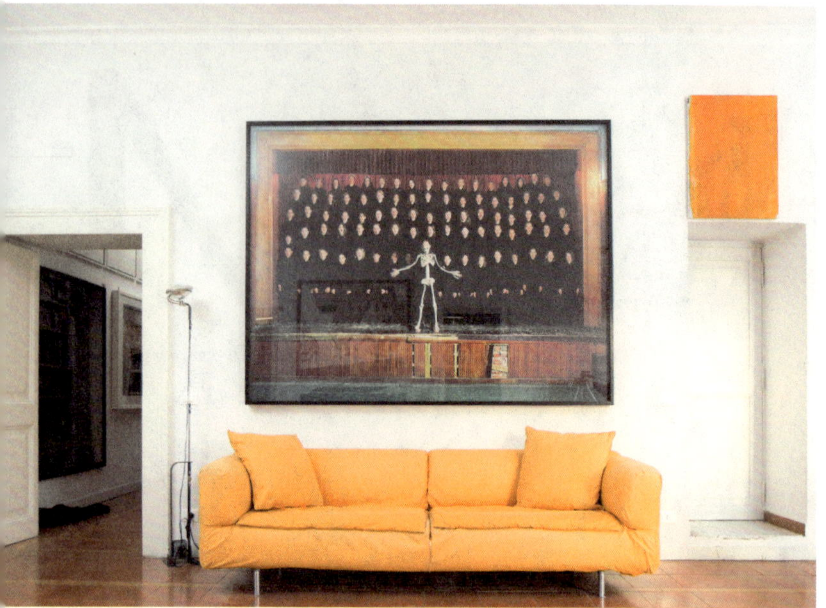

CASA MUSUMECI GRECO

An historic apartment for contemporary art in central Rome

Collectors:
Ines & Giuliano Musumeci Greco

Address:
Piazza dell'Orologio 7
00186 Rome
Italy
inesmusumeci@hotmail.com

By e-mail appointment only.

Visiting the Roman home of Ines Musumeci Greco—a former art writer and gallerist—you'll find a collection of works by contemporary Italian and international artists like Alighiero Boetti, Marina Abramović, Mario Schifano, Pascale Marthine Tayou, or Chen Zhen. But you're also entering a private apartment where life meets art, and modernity encounters history. Greco's apartment is located inside Palazzo Bennicelli, a stately seventeenth-century building in the heart of the historic center, designed in 1660 by the famous Baroque architect Francesco Borromini, and renovated in the nineteenth century by Gaetano Koch, with an eye toward the idiosyncrasies of a location steeped in history. Artists' talks and lectures are regularly hosted at the apartment, attesting to Greco's preference for direct, daily interaction with artists and their work, and special projects beyond the collection are also promoted in institutional and private spaces around the world.

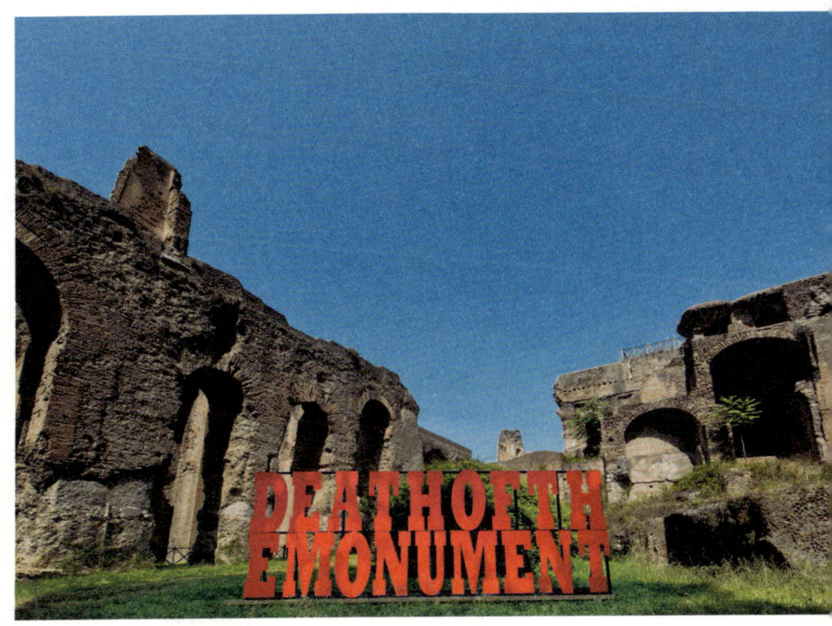

NOMAS FOUNDATION

Nomadism and otherness against the force of homogeneity

Collectors:
Raffaella & Stefano Sciarretta

Address:
Viale Somalia 33
00199 Rome
Italy
Tel +39 06 86398381
info@nomasfoundation.com
www.nomasfoundation.com

Opening Hours:
Tues–Fri: 2:30–7pm
And by appointment.

The word *nomas* is Latin for "nomad." This is how the Romans described the Saharan Berbers, who spoke neither Latin nor Greek and opposed any foreign attempt to suppress their culture and identity. The Rome-based collectors Raffaella and Stefano Sciarretta were inspired by this concept of nomadism and otherness when they opened their foundation in 2008. Here they present their expansive collection, complemented by exhibitions, talks, and seminars. One of their goals is to offer residencies to support young artists with their projects. The Sciarrettas began to collect in the 1990s—at first Italian Pop Art, and then international contemporary works. Today they own about 700 artworks by 300 artists, among them Rossella Biscotti, Alexandre Singh, and Ryan Gander.

COLLEZIONE GORI—FATTORIA DI CELLE

Site-specific and land-based art nestled in the Tuscan hillside

Collector:
Giuliano Gori

Address:
Via Montalese 7
51030 Santomato di Pistoia
Italy
info@goricoll.it
www.goricoll.it

By appointment only.
Please inquire via website.

The beauty of the Tuscan countryside is known the world over. And at Fattoria di Celle, near Pistoia, the region's natural beauty is complemented by the profundity of art. It is here that Giuliano Gori, since the 1980s, has been inviting international stars like Robert Morris, Sol LeWitt, Richard Serra, or Daniel Buren to create site-specific works in the park surrounding his majestic residence. Each artist chose a location after carefully sizing up the local elements and conditions and allowing the local charm and history of the Tuscan region—birthplace of the Renaissance—to win them over. When you visit the Collezione Gori, be sure to bring the right shoes and time: more than thirty years of collecting have amassed an extensive variety of works that can take several hours to experience.

COLLEZIONE DE IORIO

Art about beauty and infirmity

Collector:
Mauro De Iorio

Address:
Trento, Italy
Tel +39 347 0110774
info@collezionedeiorio.art
www.collezionedeiorio.art

By appointment only.

As a radiologist, Mauro De Iorio has a unique view and understanding of the human body. In his profession, beauty and infirmity are closely interconnected. No wonder that both aspects are centrally featured in his collection. De Iorio acquired his first work of art—Giulio Paolini's *Orfeo* from 1976—in 2002. Numerous other pieces followed. In scouting for new works, he doesn't pay much heed to the art market or critical reviews. For him, collecting ultimately comes down to whether a work is capable of moving him emotionally or whether it has a symbolic dimension. Examples here include Ettore Spalletti's monochromatic light-blue canvases, with colors you can lose yourself in, or Andra Ursuta's *Broken Obelisk,* a deeply melancholic object that sits in a blue chair. The works can be seen in three different locations in Trento: in an apartment in a centrally located historic building, a modestly maintained showroom, and at De Iorio's medical center.

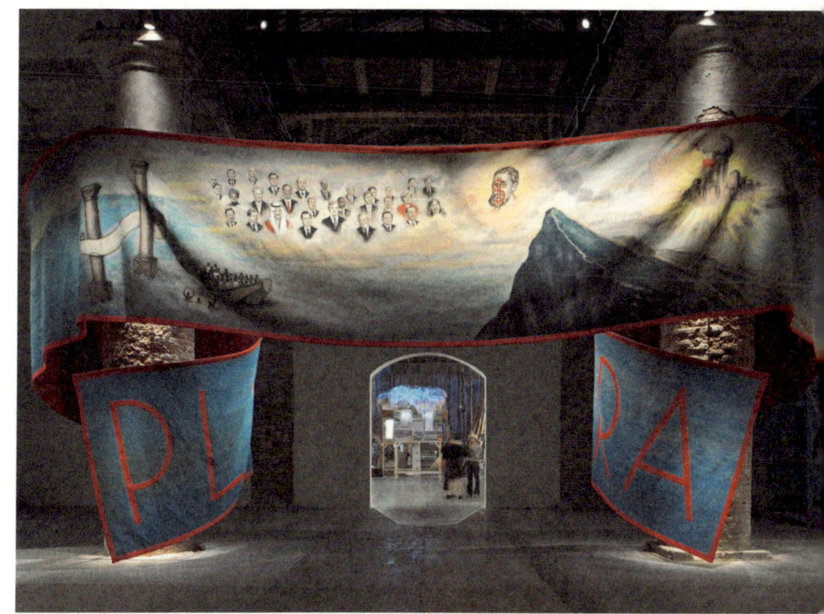

FONDAZIONE SANDRETTO RE REBAUDENGO

Not just a collection—a foundation to promote the new

Collector:
Patrizia Sandretto Re Rebaudengo

Address:
Via Modane 16
10141 Turin
Italy
Tel +39 011 3797600
info@fsrr.org
www.fsrr.org

Opening Hours:
Thurs: 8–11pm
Fri–Sun: 12–7pm

Thanks to a mix of institutional and private initiatives, the region of Piedmont has become an important hub for contemporary art in Italy. And among all the private ventures, perhaps the most well-known is Fondazione Sandretto Re Rebaudengo, which was established in 1995 by the Italian grande dame of contemporary collecting, Patrizia Sandretto Re Rebaudengo. The foundation prides itself on recognizing early on talented artists who have achieved international acclaim since the 1990s, like Californian multimedia artist Doug Aitken. Among Sandretto Re Rebaudengo's more recent acquisitions are works by Tauba Auerbach and João Onofre, among others. But because the main aim of the foundation is to promote the work of young artists, it not only shows works from the collection, it also organizes thematic exhibitions and supports the production of work by artists just entering the fray. In 2019, the collection will open an additional venue in Madrid.

VIDEOINSIGHT FOUNDATION

Art and psychotherapy—a healing combination

Collector:
Rebecca Russo

Address:
Via Ferdinando Bonsignore 7
10131 Turin
Italy
Tel +39 331 3093959
videoinsight@videoinsight.it
www.fasv.it

By e-mail appointment only.

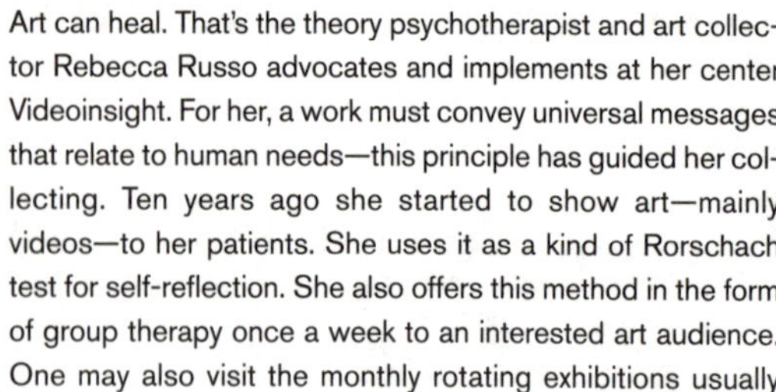

Art can heal. That's the theory psychotherapist and art collector Rebecca Russo advocates and implements at her center Videoinsight. For her, a work must convey universal messages that relate to human needs—this principle has guided her collecting. Ten years ago she started to show art—mainly videos—to her patients. She uses it as a kind of Rorschach test for self-reflection. She also offers this method in the form of group therapy once a week to an interested art audience. One may also visit the monthly rotating exhibitions usually devoted to one artist. The collection includes, among others, Joseph Kosuth, Santiago Sierra, Natalie Djurberg, Yael Bartana, Marinella Senatore, Ragnar Kjartansson, Eva Kot'átková, and Franceso Vezzoli, as well as many artists from Asia, such as Japanese Koki Tanaka or Indonesian Etang Wiharso.

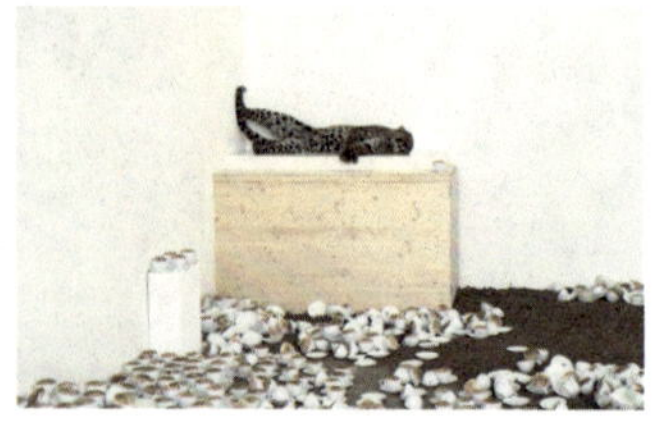

VILLA E COLLEZIONE PANZA/ FONDO AMBIENTE ITALIANO (FAI)

Minimal Art in a neoclassical villa in dialogue with antique furniture and African art

Collector:
Giuseppe Panza di Biumo

Address:
Piazza Litta 1
21100 Varese
Italy
Tel +39 0332 283960
faibiumo@fondoambiente.it
www.villapanza.it

Opening Hours:
Tues–Sun: 10am–6pm

When Giuseppe Panza di Biumo passed away in 2010, the *Los Angeles Times* described him as "a Milanese businessman who was the first great international collector of postwar American art." In the mid-1950s, after a trip to America, Panza di Biumo began acquiring art super-stars like Mark Rothko, Bruce Nauman, and Richard Serra. His collection holds a few Europeans but consists mostly of American Abstract Expressionist, Pop, Minimal, and Conceptual Art. Large parts of the trove are now in museums like the Guggenheim in New York, and the Museum of Contemporary Art, Los Angeles (MOCA). But an important group of works is still maintained in his neoclassical villa near Varese. One wing boasts light installations by Dan Flavin and James Turrell, and Minimal Art and monochromes sit next to Renaissance furniture and African and pre-Columbian art, arrangements decided upon by Panza di Biumo's own keen eye.

VENICE

Venice is known the world over for its extraordinary beauty and legendary canals, but in the context of art there is another reason for its fame: the Biennale. Every two years the art world gathers in the Giardini and at the adjacent Arsenale for the oldest and most prestigious art biennial in the world. Founded in 1895, the Venice Biennale has lost none of its appeal and significance. But contemporary art doesn't simply stop here with this big event. The Fondazione Bevilacqua La Masa promotes exhibitions of well-known international artists such as Peter Doig and Sebastião Salgado, and also fosters emerging artists with a residency program. The Fondazione Giorgio Cini, which is committed to the promotion of Italian twentieth-century glass art, also hosts exhibitions of contemporary art when the Biennale is in town. Furthermore, there is the Fondazione Querini Stampalia, which owns a collection of Old Masters but also integrates current positions into its exhibition program. Since 2011, the Venetian art scene has been graced by the addition of Fondazione Prada at Ca' Corner della Regina. Established by fashion designer and art collector

Miuccia Prada and her husband Patrizio Bertelli, the foundation has already presented a number of trailblazing exhibitions. In Dorsoduro, another private foundation can be found next to the Peggy Guggenheim Collection and the exhibition spaces of collector François Pinault: the Moscow-based V-A-C Foundation of Russian collector Leonid Mikhelson opened its Venice outpost in 2017 in a palazzo, and offers exhibitions in addition to residencies for artists and curators. And even if Venice is not an important center for the art market, there are some interesting galleries to discover, such as Caterina Tognon, Galleria Michela Rizzo, and Victoria Miro, a gallery from London, has occupied the former spaces of the long-standing Galleria Il Capricorno since 2017, which is now closed. All these attest to Venice being much more than "just" the Biennale.

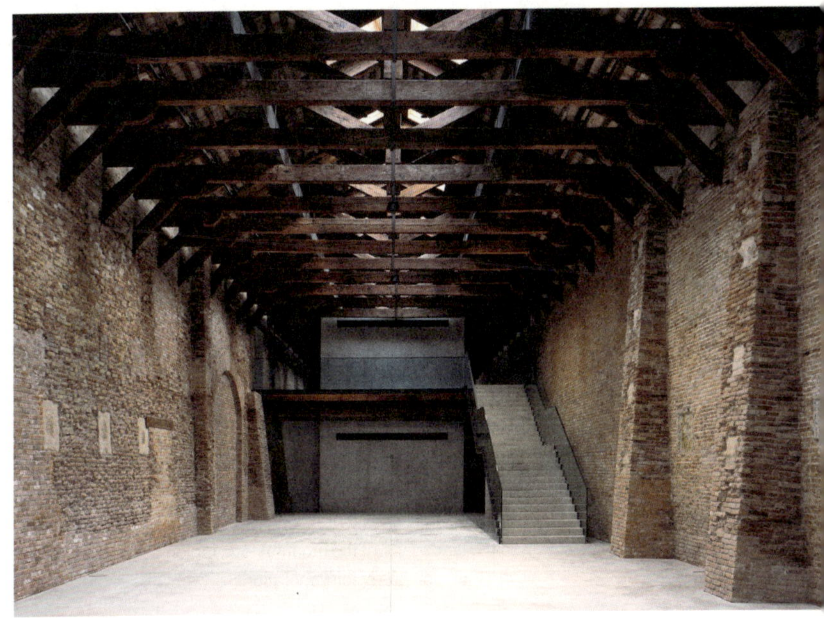

FRANÇOIS PINAULT FOUNDATION/ PALAZZO GRASSI & PUNTA DELLA DOGANA

High art with an even higher profile

Collector:
François Pinault

Addresses:
Campo San Samuele 3231
30124 Venice
Italy
Tel +39 041 2719031
www.palazzograssi.it

Punta della Dogana:
Sestiere Dorsoduro 2
30123 Venice
Italy

Opening Hours:
Wed–Mon: 10am–7pm

Luxury-goods magnate François Pinault is not only famous in the fashion world, he's also famed in the art world, as the owner of the auction house Christie's and as a collector of contemporary art. Since 2006 the fruits of his passion can be admired in Venice. Here, Pinault commissioned the Japanese architect Tadao Ando, first to modify the Palazzo Grassi and then, in 2009, the historic customs building Punta della Dogana, which is situated at the eastern tip of the Dorsoduro district. In both places he presents his collection in curated temporary exhibitions. Among the artists shown are Martial Raysse, Wade Guyton, Danh Vo, and Philippe Parreno. Pinault's hope is that "his collection can be appreciated by as many people as possible, especially by the younger generation," he says in summing up his mission as a collector. "It opened me up. With a bit of luck, it might change their lives too."

PRATO D'ARTE COLLEZIONE MARZONA

Land Art without borders: installations in the Carnia Alps

Collector:
Egidio Marzona

Address:
Villa di Verzegnis
33020 Verzegnis
Italy
Tel +39 0433 487779
carnia.musei@cmcarnia.regione.fvg.it

The park is open at all times.

It's a truism that many great ideas are conceived in conversation over a glass of wine with good friends on a midsummer's eve. This was surely the case with Prato d'Arte, a sculpture garden founded in the late 1980s in Verzegnis, a town of 400 residents in northeastern Italy. The two friends were German art dealer Konrad Fischer—an early supporter of American Minimal and Conceptual artists who was responsible for bringing many of them to Europe—and Egidio Marzona, one of the world's most important collectors of Conceptual, Minimal, Land Art, and Arte Povera, who donated a large part of his collection to Berlin's Hamburger Bahnhof museum in 2002. The sprawling Prato d'Arte Collezione Marzona contains thirteen sculptures by the likes of Bruce Nauman, Richard Long, Dan Graham, and Lawrence Weiner, among others, all nestled in the landscape of the mountainous region of Carnia, home to the Marzona family for generations.

AMC COLLEZIONE COPPOLA

A curious collector acquiring art to broaden his understanding of the world

Collector:
Antonio Michele Coppola

Addresses:
Via Zamenhof 615
36100 Vicenza
Italy

Fondazione Coppola:
Corso Palladio 1
36100 Vicenza
Italy

Tel +39 0444 913410
info@collezionecoppola.it

Opening Hours:
AMC Collezione Coppola:
Mon–Fri: 10am–12pm, 2:30–4:30pm
Sat: by appointment only
Fondazione Coppola:
Wed–Sun: 11am–5pm

Established in 2008, the AMC Collezione Coppola comprises the private collection of Antonio Michele Coppola, founder of Italian medical supply firm Biomax. Coppola's sizable holdings of works by artists such as Nathalie Djurberg, Nicola Samorì, Marcel Dzama, Neo Rauch, Nina Canell, Ruprecht von Kaufmann, and Uri Aran attest to the collector's abiding effort to better understand, interpret, or simply experience the world around him. Figurative painting and installations play central roles here, but video works also feature in the collection. In 2017, Coppola acquired a stately medieval tower at the entrance to Vicenza's historical city center, close to Piazza dei Signori. As a sign of his civic allegiance, he then donated the building to the city. In public hands again for the first time in 500 years, the tower is now home to the recently founded Fondazione Coppola, which presents exhibitions of works from the private collection here since fall 2018.

TOKYO

Tokyo is a bona-fide challenge. Whether encountering traditional, high-tech, or garish amusements—there's much of everything to be found here. Even art lovers will feel put to the test, which is why it is advisable to initially limit yourself to the centrally located district of Roppongi. The bustling business and entertainment district has become a hotspot for already established contemporary art in recent years. Hardly surprising, therefore, that Emmanuel Perrotin opened one of his worldwide offshoots here in 2017. The spaces of the Parisian gallerist, who reportedly was pivotal in turning Takashi Murakami into a world-famous Japanese Pop Art star, are located in the Piramide Building. Opened in 2011, it is home to numerous first-rate galleries including Ota Fine Arts, one of the top addresses for Japanese art with blue-chip artists like Yayoi Kusama and newcomers such as Tsuyoshi Hisakado. At Wako Works of Art you'll find German stars like Gerhard Richter or Andreas Slominski, and, for those interested in film and photography, works by Nobuyoshi Araki or Thomas Demand at the Taka Ishii Gallery. Even outside the building, the range of cultural offerings in Roppongi is virtually limitless—ranging from the Nogi Jinja Shrine to the Snoopy Museum. In Tokyo Midtown, a building complex with the city's tallest skyscraper, the Suntory Museum of Art is home to a superb arts and crafts collection. On the fifty-second floor of the nearby Roppongi Hills Mori Tower, the Mori Art Museum showcases contemporary artists from around the world and also features a spectacular multi-story observation deck. The National Art Center Tokyo (NACT), also opened in 2007, is just a stone's throw away. The gigantic wave-shaped building designed by Kishō Kurokawa, the founder of Metabolism, is the largest museum in Japan, with 14 000 square meters of exhibition space. From here you can enjoy a view of Mount Fuji in good weather. While the mythical mountain radiates something enduring, Tokyo's art scene, experience teaches, may soon be expanding into the next trendy district.

DREAM HOUSE

High-quality Asian and international art in an extravagant building

Collector:
Daisuke Miyatsu

Address:
3-3-17 Wakamiya
Ichikawa
Chiba Prefecture 272-0812
Japan
Fax +81 47 3321141

Visitation permitted only occasionally. Please inquire by mail or fax.

A house made by an artist for art: installation artist Dominique Gonzalez-Foerster designed a colorful, structurally eye-catching house for the collector Daisuke Miyatsu. In and around the Dream House you'll find works by Asian and international contemporary artists like Yayoi Kusama, Yoshitomo Nara, Yang Jun, Lee Kit, or Ólafur Elíasson. Many of the works were designed particularly for the Dream House—where the telecommunications employee lives with his family. Media art is the main focus of this roughly 300-work collection, spanning from Yang Fudong or Cao Fei & Ou Ning, from China, through American Tony Oursler, to Nina Fischer & Maroan el Sani from Germany. Works from the video collection, which began in 1994, are screened upon request.

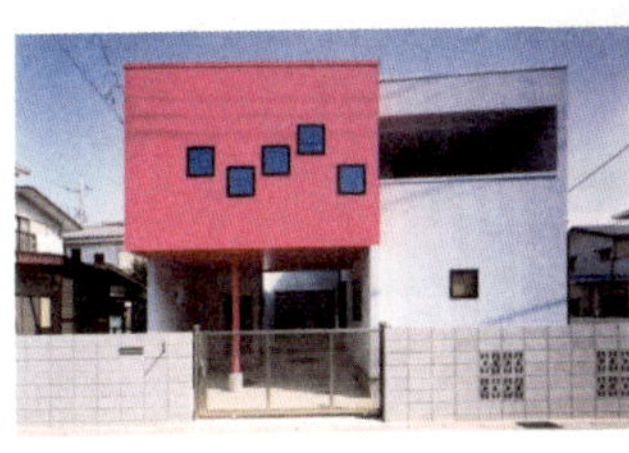

TAKAHASHI COLLECTION

One of the most important collections of contemporary Japanese art

Collector:
Ryutaro Takahashi

Address:
Tokyo, Japan
art@takahashiryutaro.com
www.takahashi-collection.com

Visitation permitted only occasionally. Please inquire by e-mail.

Psychiatrist Ryutaro Takahashi is regarded as one of the most important collectors of contemporary art in Japan today. It all began in 1997 when he visited an exhibition of the artist Yayoi Kusama in Tokyo, where works from her *Net Paintings* series in particular captured his eye. Since then, Takahashi has concentrated on collecting works mainly by contemporary Japanese artists—in addition to Yayoi Kusama this includes Yoshitomo Nara, Makoto Aida, and Kohei Nawa, and others. He now owns more than 2 500 works that he exhibits at his three clinics in Tokyo. Takahashi says that patients show great interest in the works and ask questions—especially when the hanging is changed. The opening of his own museum is planned for 2019. Until then, you can request to see approximately forty works at his private apartment and studio in Tokyo's Minato-ku district.

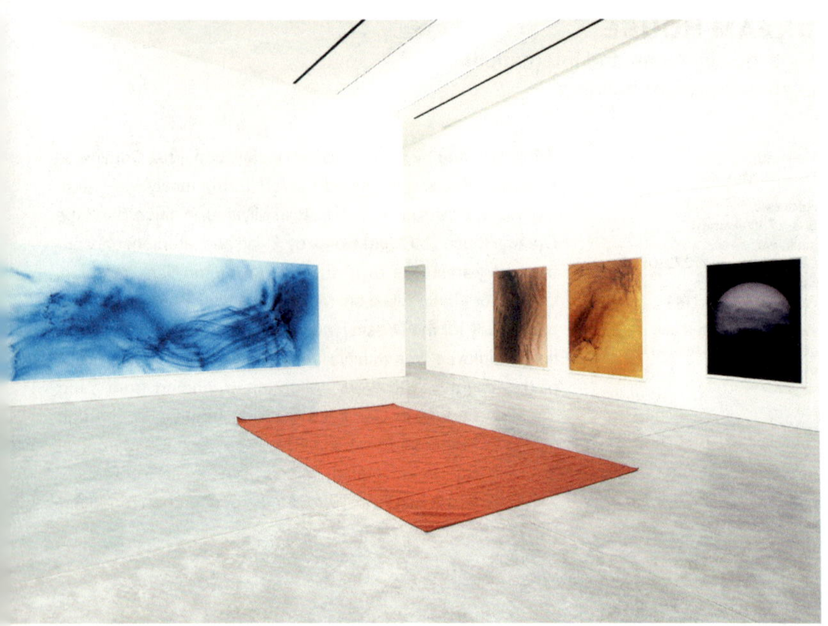

AÏSHTI FOUNDATION

A leading Lebanese contemporary art collection setting standards in the Middle East

Collector:
Tony Salamé

Address:
Aïshti by the Sea
Jal Eld Dib, Seaside Road
Beirut
Lebanon
Tel +961 4 717716
www.aishtifoundation.com

Opening Hours:
Wed–Sun: 11am–7pm
And by appointment.

Housed in a David Adjaye-designed shopping center, the Aïshti Foundation is dedicated to the collection of Tony Salamé, luxury retailer and owner of the Aïshti shopping mall empire. Opening to great fanfare in October 2015, it is the most significant collection of contemporary art in Lebanon. Jeffrey Deitch and other respected curators have served as advisors to the collection, helping Salamé assemble over 2500 artworks within eighteen years. The collection focuses mainly on international contemporary art from the 1960s onwards. Italian avant-garde positions from Piero Manzoni to Lucio Fontana serve as a fulcrum for newer positions from Willem de Rooij to Ryan Sullivan to Tauba Auerbach. Sterling Ruby, Wade Guyton, Seth Price, and Rudolf Stingel round out the list. It is the first time these artists have been presented in Lebanon, and the foundation thus offers Beirut residents unique access to the Western art scene.

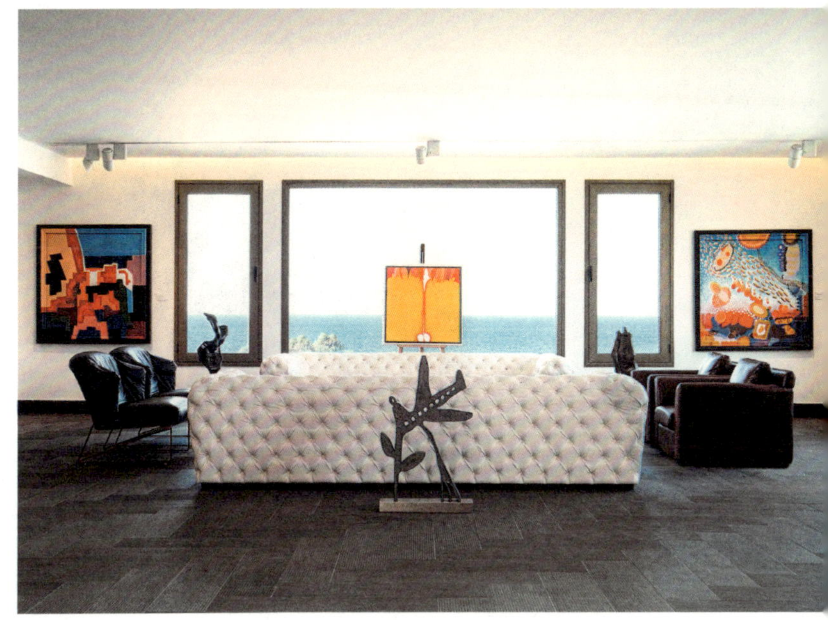

KA MODERN & CONTEMPORARY ART SPACE

900 square meters dedicated to Lebanon's most significant artists

Collectors:
Abraham Karabajakian &
Roger Akoury

Address:
Beirut, Lebanon
Tel +961 4 712711
mahfoudbettina@gmail.com

By appointment only.

Abraham Karabajakian has high hopes for Lebanon's art and culture. Together with his partner Roger Akoury, whose museum in Bucharest is also featured in this book, the Armenian-born insurance broker has assembled a collection over the past twenty years with works by nearly all of Lebanon's most important artists. But the collectors do not see their collection as art for art's sake. Instead, they want to use art to help bring people together in a country that has been shaken by civil war and crisis. The art space they founded in 2011 plays a pioneering role: before, hardly anyone was thinking about a museum for modern and contemporary Lebanese art, whereas now planning for a civic institution is in full swing. The Beirut Museum of Art (BeMA) will also showcase permanent loans from their private collection—meanwhile, works by artists such as Etel Adnan, Mona Hatoum, Nabil Nahas, or Akram Zaatari await visitors in Waterfront City.

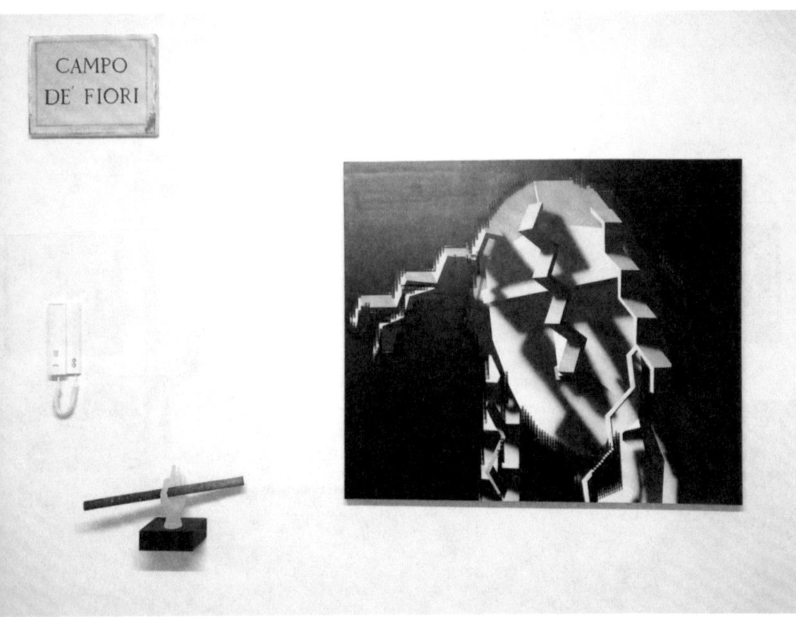

SAMMLUNG MAJERUS

Trenchant contemporary concept art with critical potential

Collector:
Patrick Majerus

Address:
Luxembourg City, Luxembourg
patrick.majerus@hotmail.com

Visitation permitted only occasionally. Please inquire by e-mail.

"Either you're a collector or you're not," says Patrick Majerus, perhaps the only officer in the Luxembourg army with a distinct interest in contemporary concept art, primarily from Berlin. His collection attained international attention in 2010, when it was shown at the Kunstsaele Berlin. Majerus collects entire groups of works from just a few select artists of his generation, convinced that it is more important to collect deeply than broadly. Around thirty artists, mostly between the ages of thirty and forty, including Tim Berresheim, Katja Novitskova, Dominik Sittig, Michael E. Smith, and Sven Johne, share the walls in Majerus's remodeled private home, which, as one might guess, does not keep fixed opening hours. Instead, he likes to personally guide art enthusiasts through his collection from time to time.

FUNDACIÓN JUMEX ARTE CONTEMPORÁNEO

Young Latin American and international contemporary art in two locations

Collector:
Eugenio López Alonso

Addresses:
Museum:
Miguel de Cervantes Saavedra 303
Col. Ampliación Granada
Mexico City C.P. 11529
Mexico

Galería Jumex:
Vía Morelos 272
Col. Santa María Tulpetlac
Ecatepec de Morelos C.P. 55400
Mexico

info@fundacionjumex.org
www.fundacionjumex.org

Please check the website for the most current information on opening hours.

Viva México! Since the end of 2013, when the Museo Jumex opened in the upscale district of Polanco, Mexico City has become even more firmly established on the international art map. With its roof in the shape of a saw blade, this building, designed by British star architect David Chipperfield, his first in Latin America, is already worth a visit. The new headquarters of the largest collection of contemporary Latin American and international art on the continent, with 2800 works, shows artists such as Francis Alÿs, Damián Ortega, Tacita Dean, or Danh Vo, in addition to international temporary exhibitions that travel to Mexico for the first time. Eugenio López Alonso, a colorful character and the sole heir of Jumex, the country's largest juice company, continues to present parts of his collection at the previous location, at Galería Jumex, on the company's premises outside the city.

COLECCIÓN CONTEMPORÁNEA

A global collection from a seasoned art collector in Mexico City

Collector:
Gina Diez-Barroso de Franklin

Address:
Avenida Constituyentes 455
Col. América
Mexico City C.P. 11820
Mexico
www.coleccioncontemporanea.com

Opening Hours:
Mon–Sat: 10am–5pm

Colección Contemporánea is the remarkable addition to the growing private museum scene in Mexico City. The collector and entrepreneur Gina Diez-Barroso de Franklin opened her space to the public in late 2015, with a dual focus on art and design. Half of the museum houses Diez-Barroso's private collection, featuring artists including Lu Shengzhong, Robert Indiana, Liu Bolin, Marcus Lyon, and Iván Navarro; the other half hosts temporary exhibitions. The program features collaborations with, among others, Bard College, New York, as well as private galleries. Coming from a family of art collectors—Diego Rivera painted one of his *Calla Lilies* works for her mother—she has a long association with the Mexican art scene. In 2004, Diez-Barroso founded Centro, the first university in Mexico for art media and design, and the museum reflects this interdisciplinary approach.

COLLECTORS HOUSE

Cooperation between international collectors and a city museum

Collector:
Albert Groot

Address:
Raadhuisplein 19
6411 Heerlen
Netherlands
Tel +31 45 5711525
info@collectorshouse.eu
www.collectorshouse.eu

Opening Hours:
Thurs–Sun: 12–5pm

"Strength in unity," goes the saying. This is also the principle of the Collectors House, in Heerlen, a collaboration between the municipal museum Schunck, the Dutch collector Albert Groot, and several international collectors. Their shared goal is to show works of contemporary art that are otherwise rarely seen in public. The exhibitions at the Collectors House bring together works currently residing in different locations—in the Netherlands, Hong Kong, or Romania—and places them in a constructive dialogue with each other. Among the artists shown have been Marina Abramović, Mircea Cantor, Hans Op de Beeck, and Cao Fei. At a time when culture and museums are experiencing drastic cutbacks, initiatives that combine public and private certainly offer an alternative solution.

THE NARDA VAN 'T VEER COLLECTION

From nude photography to experimental imagery

Collector:
Narda van 't Veer

Address:
Monnickendam, Netherlands
narda@theravestijngallery.com

By appointment only.

Years ago, when Narda van 't Veer founded Unit, an agency for photography, illustration, animation, and film, she had a real passion for fashion photography. She was big fan of Frenchman Guy Bourdin, who had revolutionized fashion photography in the 1960s and 1970s. But over time, van 't Veer became more deeply invested in the medium's various other strands. At first she mainly collected nude photography, then she discovered her fondness for experimental and provocative work. Today, the Dutchwoman's private apartment showcases one of the most fascinating and extensive collections of photography, including newcomers such as Risk Hazekamp, as well as established artists like Helmut Newton, or the duo Inez van Lamsweerde & Vinoodh Matadin. For van 't Veer, who also runs a photo gallery, it's important that the works express something about the present and that they speak to her emotionally.

COLLECTOR & ARTIST

With the turbulent market for emerging art having calmed slightly, greater attention has once again been placed on those collectors who fervently support and push forward the careers of the artists they've chosen to acquire. Museum shows and biennials wouldn't happen without the many works that have been supported, sight unseen, owing to the lasting relationships and trust that exist between collector and artist. Varied models of patronage abound, of course. For instance, that of London supermarket heir Alex Sainsbury, whose family owns an already-enviable collection and whose father and uncles donated a wing to The National Gallery. Interested in delving deeper into contemporary art, he opened Raven Row in 2009. Located near Whitechapel Gallery, Sainsbury's exhibition space and residency program quickly became an important point of reference for Londoners on the lookout for new and notable contemporary artists. Collectors like Simon Franks and Robert Suss of the Franks-Suss Collection and Dominique and Sylvain Levy of the Dominique & Sylvain Levy Collection (DSLCollection), have for some time supported a new generation of artists primarily from China, with the latter employing the Internet as a platform for presenting work to a broader audience. Some collectors, like Francesca von Habsburg, take a multi-pronged approach and fund scores of artist projects for biennials and other exhibitions worldwide. While others take it upon themselves to establish a biennale and bring in international curators: the Dhaka Art Summit (DAS), for instance, founded by the Samdani Art Foundation in 2012, has allowed the collector couple of Nadia and Rajeeb Samdani to bolster the art and architecture scene in South Asia. The sculpture park, which opens in northern Bangladesh at the end of 2018, is being steadily expanded through commissioned work and artist residencies. Regardless of the methods they use, patrons like these are indispensable to keeping the art world in motion.

CONCORDIA COLLECTION

Local and international artists in a historic house

Collector:
Julian Oggel

Address:
Westersingel 103
3015 LD Rotterdam
Netherlands
Tel +31 653 771561
julian.oggel@xs4all.nl

By e-mail appointment only.

On one of the most beautiful streets of Rotterdam, between the lively Witte de Withstraat and the Museum Boijmans Van Beuningen, sits the home of Julian Oggel, a lawyer and the CEO of an investment firm. The house itself is worth a visit: built in 1904, it is one of the few buildings to have survived the destruction of World War II. Oggel's collection, which he has been amassing since 2002, is eclectic and yet retains a strong connection to the city. This has much to do with the presence of local artists like Ron van der Ende and Marin de Jong, and of international artists who have produced work while here, such as Keith Haring and Ivan Chermayeff. Oggel has a preference for Pop Art but also owns works of Hyperrealism and Conceptual Art. In the neighboring townhouse he rents luxury apartments—furnishing these with works from his collection upon request.

ALEXANDER RAMSELAAR COLLECTION

A townhouse of young talents from Rotterdam, the Netherlands, and around the world

Collector:
Alexander Ramselaar

Address:
Mathenesserplein 97
3023 LA Rotterdam
Netherlands
office@backinggrounds.com
www.alexander-ramselaar.com

Visitation permitted only occasionally. Please inquire by e-mail.

Rotterdam collector Alexander Ramselaar discovered his first artwork in a gallery on the way to work. He was immediately transfixed. After a longer period of collecting modern design, the real estate specialist, who now advises arts and cultural institutions, began to shift his focus toward contemporary art. In his unique 1920s penthouse, the hospitable collector presents art in the dining room and bedroom, in the stairwell, and even in the bathroom. Ramselaar, an avid traveler, first collected work from the Rotterdam art scene and now does so internationally: Diango Hernández, Rossella Biscotti, Giorgio Andreotta Calò, Pieter Hugo, Guy Tillim, James Beckett, or Michael Bauer are just some of the artists in his collection. Moreover, after becoming frustrated by the massive cuts in the Dutch cultural budget, Ramselaar and a few other collectors established the Foundation C. O. C. A. to support young artists.

MUSEUM BEELDEN AAN ZEE

Modern and contemporary sculpture nestled in the Netherlands' pristine dunes

Collectors:
Theo & Lida Scholten

Address:
Harteveltstraat 1
2586 EL The Hague/
Scheveningen
Netherlands
info@beeldenaanzee.nl
www.beeldenaanzee.nl

Opening Hours:
Tues–Sun: 11am–5pm

The Museum Beelden aan Zee is camouflaged so perfectly, you almost walk right past it. Located in the middle of sand dunes in the upscale seaside resort of Scheveningen, the entrance to the most important collection of sculptures in the Netherlands hides behind an exposed concrete façade. Though highly frequented tourist attractions—the spa hotel, the pier, or the casino—are right around the corner, it is extremely quiet inside the building, which opened in 1994. Under the leitmotif "man—the human image," Theo and Lida Scholten began in 1966 to bring together more than 1 000 sculptures from all major art centers around the world. The spectrum ranges from Armando to Marc Quinn, all the way to Berlinde De Bruyckere. Every year three to four thematic and monographic exhibitions are curated from the collection.

DE PONT MUSEUM

Masterpieces of contemporary art in the spacious halls of a former wool mill

Collector:
Jan de Pont

Address:
Wilhelminapark 1
5041 EA Tilburg
Netherlands
Tel +31 13 5438300
info@depont.nl
www.depont.nl

Opening Hours:
Tues–Sun: 11am–5pm

Katharina Grosse, Roni Horn, David Clearbout, Fiona Banner, Anri Sala, Philip-Lorca diCorcia, Fiona Tan, Sigmar Polke, Rosemarie Trockel, Luc Tuymans, and Mark Wallinger—the Tilburg-based collection of the De Pont Museum, in the southern Netherlands, is remarkable. Since opening its doors in 1992 around 700 works by international contemporary artists have come together to be presented in a 6 000-square-meter space. Benthem Crouwel Architects, from Amsterdam, renovated a wool mill from the 1930s so sensitively that one can still feel the industrial character of the building. The construction was made possible by Jan de Pont (1915–1987), a Tilburg businessman, who provided a large part of his estate for the promotion of contemporary art. In summer 2016, a new wing for film, video art, and photography was opened. At the same time the entrance underwent a gentle facelift.

MUSEUM VAN BOMMEL VAN DAM

An enthusiastic Dutch couple and their personalized collection

Collectors:
Maarten & Reina
van Bommel van Dam

Address:
Deken van Oppensingel 6
5911 AD Venlo
Netherlands
Tel +31 77 3513457
info@vanbommelvandam.nl
www.vanbommelvandam.nl

Opening Hours:
Tues–Sun: 11am–5pm

Maarten van Bommel acquired his first artwork at the age of sixteen. Later, as a stock trader, he continued growing his collection. He and his wife, Reina van Dam, both now deceased, began collecting together in 1944, but somewhat unsystematically: abstract Dutch paintings of the Informel and CoBrA, but also African masks and Japanese woodcuts. After searching extensively for an ideal location to house their 1 000 works, a solution was found in 1969 in the city of Venlo: a museum for their art and, next door, a residential bungalow. A connecting door allowed them to move freely between the two. Over the years, other collectors have added to the holdings, and under the current directorship it has become more contemporary and international.

KRC COLLECTION

Dutch and international artists with a critical-political approach

Collector:
Rattan Chadha

Address:
Voorschoten, Netherlands
info@krccapital.com
www.krccollection.com

Visitation permitted only occasionally. Please inquire by e-mail.

Curiosity aroused Rattan Chadha's enthusiasm for contemporary art. In the mid-1980s, he came across one of Andy Warhol's *Campbell's Soup* paintings and was shocked at the price: 50 000 US dollars for an image of soup cans? Chadha wanted to understand the valuation, so for six months he studied Warhol. He became convinced of Warhol's artistic strategy, and bought the work. Born in India in 1949, the entrepreneur had founded—and then sold—the fashion label Mexx. His collection, one of the largest in the Netherlands, is located in an expansive, modern space behind the historic façade of an old silver factory near Leiden. It includes works by Candice Breitz, Thomas Hirschhorn, Erik van Lieshout, and Marc Bijl—all artists who have taken a critical stance towards contemporary politics and society.

MUSEUM VOORLINDEN

A light-flooded museum in perfect harmony with nature

Collector:
Joop N. A. van Caldenborgh

Address:
Buurtweg 90
2244 AG Wassenaar
Netherlands
Tel +31 70 5121660
info@voorlinden.nl
www.voorlinden.nl

The museum is open daily from 11am–5pm.

Guided tours of the sculpture garden each Thursday from May to October. Please check the website to book your visit.

The industrialist Joop van Caldenborgh, who acquired his first work of art as a teenager, is considered one of the most important art collectors in the Netherlands. Since 1995, countless visitors have toured his impressive sculpture garden on the estate of Clingenbosch, which includes major works by Anish Kapoor and Sylvie Fleury. The Museum Voorlinden, a 4 000-square-meter exhibition space, opened in late 2016 and now serves as the main attraction. Located on the neighboring forty-hectare estate of Voorlinden in Wassenaar, near The Hague, the museum is home to an extensive collection of paintings, photography, installations, and video art, and also hosts temporary exhibitions. Among the permanently installed works are a monumental steel sculpture by Richard Serra, a *Skyspace* by James Turrell, and Leandro Erlich's *Swimming Pool.* The museum's floor-to-ceiling windows foster a harmonious coexistence between exhibition space and landscape.

KASTEEL WIJLRE ESTATE

Art from the 1960s to the present in a modern pavilion

Collectors:
Jo & Marlies Eyck

Address:
Kasteel Wijlreweg 1
6321 PP Wijlre
Netherlands
Tel +31 43 4502616
info@kasteelwijlre.nl
www.kasteelwijlre.nl

Please check the website for the most current information on opening hours.

Over the past several decades, collectors Marlies and Jo Eyck have turned their castle Wijlre, which they bought in Limburg in 1981, into a Gesamtkunstwerk. Here you'll encounter contemporary art in harmony with architecture, cultural heritage, and nature. Owners of a paint wholesale company, they began collecting abstract painting in the late 1960s. Over time they added other kinds of art. Today, their collection includes artists ranging from Donald Judd to René Daniëls, to Marlene Dumas. Sculptural works, mainly site-specific, can be found in the palace gardens, such as a fallen tree by Giuseppe Penone. Also located here is Hedge House, an exhibition pavilion and orchid greenhouse opened in 2001, designed by Wiel Arets Architects (WAA) out of concrete, glass, and steel. Since 2017, the Kasteel Wijlre Estate Foundation oversees the grounds as well as the arts and cultural program.

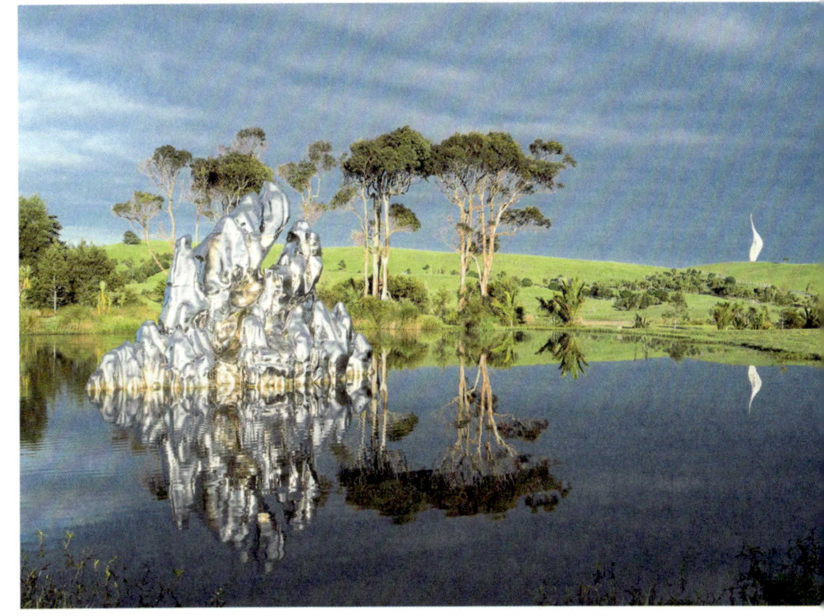

GIBBS FARM

A sculpture park in XXL format with monumental art in the grandness of nature

Collector:
Alan Gibbs

Address:
Kaipara Harbour
North Auckland Peninsula
New Zealand
info@gibbsfarm.org.nz
www.gibbsfarm.org.nz

By appointment only.
Please inquire via website.

It's as if giants had dropped their toys on green grass hills. At the Gibbs Farm sculpture park, opened in 1991, on the coast of New Zealand, art and nature correspond in a way that emphasizes the monumentality of both. Since the 1960s, entrepreneur Alan Gibbs has collected works by Richard Serra, Sol LeWitt, Andy Goldsworthy, George Rickey, and Daniel Buren—all artists known for grand outdoor gestures. But even art aficionados are amazed by the dimensions of these site-specific sculptures, some of which extend—in the case of Goldsworthy's Arches—into the water. It's not surprising that the park has become a visitor magnet. If you're looking to be one of them, however, book a tour as early as possible: Gibbs Farm is open to the public only one day a month.

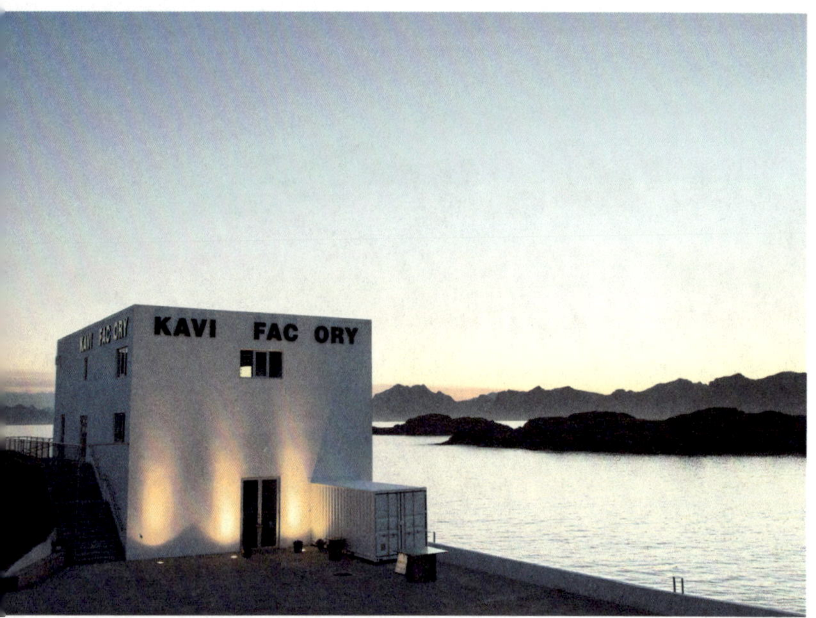

KAVIARFACTORY

Contemporary art projects on a picturesque island off the northern Norwegian coast

Collectors:
Venke & Rolf A. Hoff

Address:
Henningsværveien 13
8312 Henningsvær
Norway
Tel +47 907 34743
contact@kaviarfactory.no
www.kaviarfactory.com

Opening Hours:
Mon–Sun: 10am–6pm
And by appointment.

This exhibition space is as close to the Arctic Circle as it could be. In the summer of 2013, the Norwegian art collectors Venke and Rolf A. Hoff opened their art space in a former caviar factory on the Lofoten Islands. The KaviarFactory is located in the picturesque fishing village of Henningsvær, the gateway to the northern archipelago. The building was renovated by the Norwegian architecture firm Element; the lettering on the façade is the work of artist Michael Sailsdorfer. "Many international artists have visited us here," says Rolf A. Hoff. "They all love this place and want to come back." Equally popular is their lighthouse, which can be rented for special occasions. The collectors own works by Norwegian and international artists such as Bjarne Melgaard, Marguerite Humeau, Paulo Nimer Pjota, Katherine Bernhardt, or Jack Goldstein, and they invite artists from all over the world to realize exhibitions in the 500-square-meter former factory.

OSLO

As far as contemporary architecture goes, Oslo is currently becoming one of the world's hottest cities. It's not just the ice berg-esque opera house on the harbor that sets new standards. The new trendy district of Tjuvholmen, created directly on the fjord, is also a hotspot for creative people. Here you'll find a plethora of current architectural trends as well as top-notch galleries like Gerhardsen Gerner, Galleri Brandstrup, or Peder Lund, who works directly with artists like Ed Ruscha or Richard Serra on a project basis. Noteworthy are also installations encountered here and there, such as one by Oslo-based Fredrik Raddum: a gigantic foot seemingly crashing through a parking-garage ceiling. An important part of the neighborhood is the Astrup Fearnley Museet, a Renzo Piano building featuring a sail-shaped glass roof. Not only one of city's most idiosyncratic structures, it also boasts an exquisite private collection of contemporary art. Right next door is Tjuvholmen Sculpture Park, with a bathing beach and works by Louise Bourgeois, Anish Kapoor, and Franz West. Creative forces are also concentrated in the Kunstnernes Hus (English for artists' house), a striking functionalist building directly on the palace park, where you'll find Norway's largest artist-run gallery. It features exhibitions, a cinema, a bookstore, a restaurant, a variety of open studios, and a lecture room. Within a few minutes walk you'll reach the National Museum—the Nasjonalmuseet—with its excellent collection of modern Scandinavian and international art. Of course there are also works by Edvard Munch here. In any case, the city's most famous artist is hard to miss in Oslo. His paintings hang in the luxurious Hotel Continental's bar, where the passionate wine drinker paid his tabs in drawings, or in chocolate manufacturer Freia's canteen in the northeast of the city. Of course, you shouldn't miss the Munchmuseet, which moves into a spectacular new building in 2019. In 2020, the National Museum will also find a new home. If you come to the city now, you'll experience first-hand how it's reinventing itself.

HENIE ONSTAD KUNSTSENTER (HOK)

Modern art and exhibitions with contemporary artists in spectacular architecture

Collectors:
Sonja Henie & Niels Onstad

Address:
Sonja Henie vei 31
1311 Høvikodden
Norway
Tel +47 67 804880
post@hok.no
www.hok.no

Opening Hours:
Tues–Sun: 11am–5pm

Sonja Henie (1912–1969) is considered one of the most successful figure skaters in history. Together with her husband, Niels Onstad (1909–1978), a ship owner and art patron, she amassed a collection of modern art. In 1968 they opened the Henie Onstad Kunstsenter (HOK), high over the Oslo Fjord, south of the capital city. Norwegians Jon Eikvar and Svein Erik Engebretsen won the architectural competition, and erected a spectacular neo-expressionist structure that meshes nicely with the surrounding landscape. The building was extended in 1994, and again in 2003, and is now complemented by a sculpture park featuring works by Per Kirkeby and Tony Cragg, among others. Spread across 3500 square meters, the HOK offers highlights of its collection, from Henri Matisse through Hans Hartung to Fernand Léger, as well as temporary exhibitions with contemporaries such as Ilya Kabakov, Omer Fast, or Olav Christopher Jenssen.

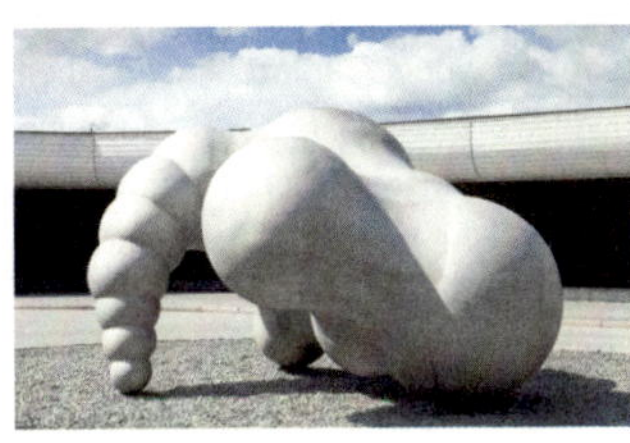

KISTEFOS-MUSEET

Prime public art park in the Norwegian woodlands north of Oslo

Collector:
Christen Sveaas

Address:
Samsmoveien 41
3520 Jevnaker
Norway
Tel +47 61 310383
post@kistefos.museum.no
www.kistefos.museum.no

The park is open at all times.

The small community of Jevnaker in the Norwegian province of Oppland is certainly not on the shortlist of art world hotspots. But for lovers of large-scale sculpture and the great outdoors, Kistefos Park is well worth a visit. The largest publicly accessible sculpture park in all of Scandinavia, Kistefos currently features almost forty artworks, by the likes of Marc Quinn, Elmgreen & Dragset, Tony Cragg, Ólafur Elíasson, and Jeppe Hein. The park is part of the Kistefos-Museet, which investor and industrialist Sveaas founded in 1996 to commemorate the pulp mill built by his grandfather on the Randselva River in 1889. The Industrial Museum now occupies that building, with sculptures spread across the vast, pristine grounds. Open to the public twenty-four hours a day, 365 days a year, the works, from Ilya Kabakov's *The Ball,* which looks out over the river, to Anish Kapoor's *S-Curve,* make Kistefos well worth the hour's trip north from Oslo.

ASTRUP FEARNLEY MUSEET

Major works of contemporary art in a Renzo Piano building

Collector:
Hans Rasmus Astrup

Address:
Strandpromenaden 2
0252 Oslo
Norway
Tel +47 22 936060
info@fearnleys.no
www.afmuseet.no

Opening Hours:
Tues–Wed, Fri: 12–5pm
Thurs: 12–7pm
Sat–Sun: 11am–5pm

Norwegians seldom complain about limited finances. Oil and gas resources supply an influx of capital, and Oslo has become one of the most expensive cities in the world. Perhaps this is why private museums are somewhat more grandiose in Norway than elsewhere, a fact perfectly illustrated by the brand new building of the Astrup Fearnley Museum, which was founded in 1993. Ship owner and collector Hans Rasmus Astrup commissioned none other than Italian architect Renzo Piano, still one of the most in-demand architects in the world. A 4 000-square-meter exhibition space, built in 2012, reflects maritime flair in glass, steel, and wood in an exposed location on a fjord, housing series of works by well-known, blue-chip artists such as Francis Bacon, Anselm Kiefer, Jeff Koons, Takashi Murakami, and Cindy Sherman. The collectors are also interested in young Norwegian art and, more recently, in newcomers from Asia and Latin America.

EKEBERGPARKEN— COLLECTION CHRISTIAN RINGNES

A three-kilometer-long sculpture trail with a harbor view

Collector:
Christian Ringnes

Address:
Kongsveien 23
0193 Oslo
Norway
Tel +47 21 421919
info@ekebergparken.com
www.ekebergparken.com

The park is open at all times.

In the hills framing the Norwegian capital of Oslo an enchanting sculpture park is hidden among the trees. The Ekebergparken—pictured in the background in Edvard Munch's famous painting *The Scream*—is an eighteenth-century public park featuring remains from the Stone, Bronze, and Viking Ages. Since September 2013, visitors have been able to encounter more than thirty sculptures, by artists from Aristide Maillol to Tony Cragg and Lynn Chadwick. The transformation of this previously neglected park is the brainchild of the collector Christian Ringnes, whose foundation loaned Oslo the artworks after the city declined a donation. The art here enters a fascinating dialogue with nature: an aluminum sculpture by Louise Bourgeois floats between trees, and bronze muses, lost in thought, by Guy Buseyne and Salvador Dalí, are located between a pavilion by Dan Graham and installations by James Turrell and Jenny Holzer.

WARSAW

Warsaw has two versions of an institution named Foksal. Galeria Foksal was initiated by artists and critics in 1966. Located in an annex to Zamoyski Palace, a protected historic landmark, the non-commercial art center features a program still organized by artists today. Established Polish positions are presented as well as international artists such as Andrea Fraser or Anselm Kiefer. The Foksal Gallery Foundation (FGF) developed out of this in 1997. Since 2001, however, both ventures have gone separate ways. The FGF has contributed significantly to the global boom of Polish contemporary art, with artists like Monika Sosnowska or Piotr Uklański, and the 1960s-era building it calls home, redesigned by Swiss architects Diener & Diener in 2015, is also well worth a visit. But Warsaw, a metropolis enlivened by increasing amounts of color in recent years, still has plenty more to offer art enthusiasts. For example, the Museum of Modern Art in Warsaw's three different venues: Austrian Adolf Krischanitz's Pavilion on the Weichsel—the Museum on the Vistula—opened in 2017, a sculpture park, and museum headquarters on Pańska street, to be replaced by a new building by New York architects Thomas Phifer and Partners by 2020. Other highlights are the Zachęta—National Gallery of Art, founded in 1860, which today often presents socially critical exhibitions of international artists, and the Centre for Contemporary Art Ujazdowski Castle (CCA), a space committed to interdisciplinary, experimental exhibition formats and internationality. Even the delightful castle gardens invite you to stay awhile. Also worth a visit is Raster Gallery, founded in the city center by two art critics in 2001. It represents important Polish artists such as Wilhelm Sasnal and Marcin Maciejowski, and the artist collective Slavs & Tatars, made up of primarily anonymous members. Anyone visiting Warsaw in the summer should attend the Chopin concert series in Łazienki Park. The lively social affairs are held on Sundays near the monument to the great composer and master pianist.

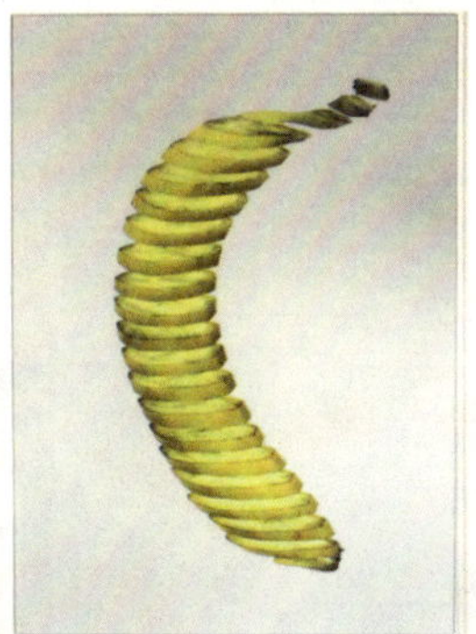

MICHAŁ BOROWIK COLLECTION

Young Polish art melding aesthetics and content

Collector:
Michał Borowik

Address:
Warsaw, Poland
contact@borowikcollection.com
www.borowikcollection.com

By e-mail appointment only.

"I collect artworks by young Polish artists in a variety of media. It gives me great pleasure to live with objects that reflect our times." This is how Michał Borowik describes his approach. When he chooses a piece to include in his discerning collection, he does so with an eye toward artworks that inject aesthetics with meaning. "I really dislike empty shells," he says, insisting at the same time that the artist's medium fit that message. This attitude has earned Borowik a place on the list of the world's fifty most interesting collections assembled by people under fifty years old, a list drawn up by American magazine *Modern Painters* in 2011. Among other artists, Michał Gayer, Magdalena Starska, and Michał Smandek are some of the young Polish artists one finds in Borowik's stunning assembly of works.

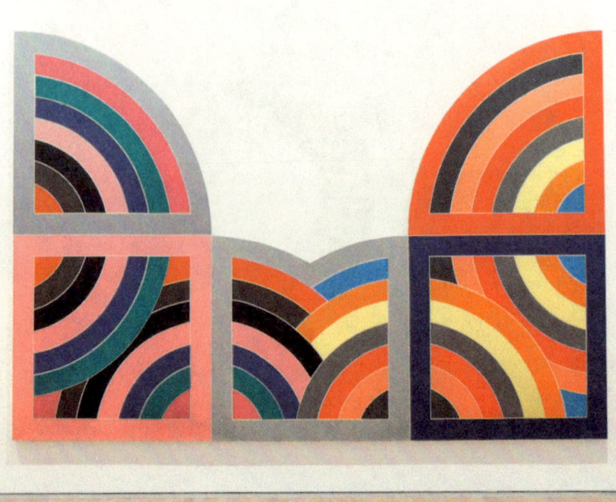

MUSEU COLEÇÃO BERARDO

One of Portugal's largest private collections in a public arts center

Collector:
José Berardo

Address:
Praça do Império
1449-003 Lisbon
Portugal
Tel +351 213 612878
museuberardo@museuberardo.pt
www.museuberardo.com

Opening Hours:
Mon–Sun: 10am–7pm
And by appointment.

Think big! Businessman, collector, and philanthropist José Berardo has achieved a lot in life. Born in Funchal on the island of Madeira and coming from humble stock, he emigrated to South Africa at age eighteen to try his luck there. What followed was the ascent from vegetable wholesaler to the owner of gold and diamond mines. Berardo returned to Portugal in 1986 and now oversees a multinational consortium of companies. With a focus on museum-quality and comprehensiveness, his art collection mirrors his entrepreneurial self-confidence. From Cubism to the Düsseldorfer School of Photography, nearly every art movement since 1900 is represented. Special attention is paid to Portuguese artists like Helena Almeida or Pedro Cabrita Reis. Since 2017, in addition to hosting temporary exhibitions, the more than 1 000 works of the collection are on permanent view at the Centro Cultural de Belém (CCB), a public arts center located on the Tagus River.

LEAL RIOS FOUNDATION—CONTEMPORARY ART

Portuguese and international art in a former auto repair shop

Collectors:
Manuel & Miguel Leal Rios

Address:
R. Centro Cultural, 17B
1700-106 Lisbon
Portugal
Tel +351 210 998623
contact@lealriosfoundation.com
www.lealriosfoundation.com

Opening Hours:
Thurs–Sat: 2:30–6:30pm
And by appointment.

Portuguese brothers Manuel and Miguel Leal Rios think of art as "a visionary, global language." The two have devoted themselves to building an art collection together since 2002, with designer Miguel Leal Rios serving as the curator for the collection, which has been open to the public since 2012. Located south of the Lisbon airport, the roughly 1 000-square-meter former auto repair shop has ample space to present works of all genres in temporary, themed exhibitions. Known for his clear, formal language, architect Alexandre Marques Pereira converted the premises into a multifunctional white cube, creating an optimal space for presenting painting, sculpture, photography, video, time-based media, and installation. In addition to native artists like Helena Almeida—a pioneer of Portuguese photographic and concept-based art who was born in 1934—the brothers' collection includes recognized names such as Erwin Wurm, Matt Mullican, Lawrence Weiner, or Tristan Perich.

QUETZAL ART CENTRE

Contemporary art on a winery in the picturesque Alentejo region

Collectors:
Inge & Cees de Bruin

Address:
Apartado 19
7960-909 Vidigueira
Portugal
Tel +351 284 441618
reservas@quintadoquetzal.com
www.quintadoquetzal.com

Opening Hours:
Wed–Thurs, Sun: 10am–8pm
Fri–Sat: 10–12am

For the de Bruins collecting art has always been a family affair. While Inge and Cees de Bruin built up one of the most important private collections in the Netherlands, their daughter Aveline made sure that the collection was joined by a little sister in Portugal's Alentejo region. At Quinta do Quetzal, a modern winery, the art enthusiasts have created—alongside wine production and a restaurant—an expansive exhibition space where works from the highly diverse collection are exhibited on a regular basis. Since 2016, visitors to the Quetzal Art Centre have been able to marvel at works by well-known artists such as John Baldessari, Ed Ruscha, Thomas Schütte, Rui Chafes, Mariana Silva, and Philippe Parreno. And since the family has always been closely associated not only with art, but also with the historic Alentejo wine-growing region, they invite local guest curators to present works by artists from Portugal among grapevines and wheat fields.

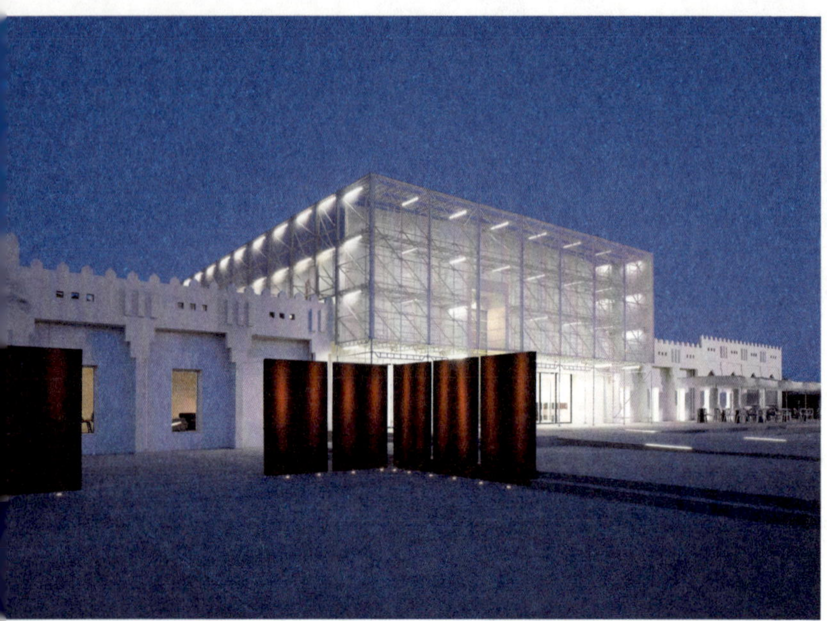

MATHAF—ARAB MUSEUM OF MODERN ART

A royal collection spanning 200 years of Arab art

Collector:
Sheikh Hassan bin Mohamed bin Ali Al Thani

Address:
Education City Student Center
Al-Luqta Street
Doha
Qatar
Tel +974 4402 8855
mathaf_info@qma.org.qa
www.mathaf.org.qa

Opening Hours:
Tues–Thurs: 11am–6pm
Fri: 3–8pm
Sat–Sun: 11am–6pm

The Art Newspaper once reported that Qatar is the world's biggest art buyer and has initiated some of the most important purchases of modern and contemporary art over the last few decades. Indeed Qatar's royal family has played an active role in acquisitions, with the aim of building a top-class collection for Qatar's growing network of museums. One of them is Mathaf, which is dedicated solely to Arab art. It opened in December 2010 thanks to the commitment of the Emir's son, Sheikh Hassan bin Mohamed bin Ali Al Thani, and thanks to the support of museum officials. The Sheikh began collecting in the 1980s and has amassed some 6 000 works, including pieces by artists throughout the Middle East, North Africa, and the Arab Diaspora, from 1840 to today.

MARE—MUZEUL DE ARTĂ RECENTĂ

A Bucharesti museum featuring the first comprehensive survey of Romanian postwar art

Collector:
Roger Akoury

Address:
15 Primăverii Boulevard
011972 Bucharest
Romania
office@mare.ro
www.mare.ro

Opening hours:
Wed–Mon: 10am–6pm

MARe, the Museum of Recent Art, is the outcome of a discussion between collector Roger Akoury and art critic and curator Erwin Kessler. The concept was to trace the trajectory of Romanian art from the 1960s through today. The collection now includes 450 works by approximately seventy prominent, mainly Romanian artists. It also features Romanian modernism and avant-garde works by artists such as Victor Brauner and Daniel Spoerri, and contemporary positions such as Miklos Onucsan, Dan Perjovschi, and Victor Man, among others. The museum fills an art-historical blind spot by providing a comprehensive overview of recent painting, sculpture, installation, and photography in Romania. In designing the museum, which opened in fall 2018, the Beirut-based architectural firm YTAA—Youssef Tohme Architects and Associates converted a 1930s-era villa into a spectacular black concrete building.

THE MIRCEA PINTE COLLECTION

An important collection of Romanian art of the past fifty years

Collector:
Mircea Pinte

Address:
Cluj, Romania
mircea.pinte@gmail.com

By e-mail appointment only.

Mircea Pinte began collecting in 2004, when the artists who later became known internationally under the label Cluj School were just starting out in their careers. By chance he met the painter Adrian Ghenie, whose work immediately cast a spell over him. Along with Ghenie and curator Mihai Pop, Pinte initiated the Plan B foundation in 2005 as a non-commercial exhibition space and research center for Romanian art from the 1960s to the present. Here he also got to know artists like Mircea Cantor, Victor Man, Ciprian Mureşan, Şerban Savu, or Marius Bercea, and continuously expanded his collection with their works. Over time, major works from the past fifty years of Romanian art were also added—such as by Paul Neagu, Ion Grigorescu, Geta Brătescu, or Horia Bernea—but also younger positions like George Crîngaşu or Mi Kafchin. The collection can be viewed at Pinte's private residence and occasionally in national and international exhibitions.

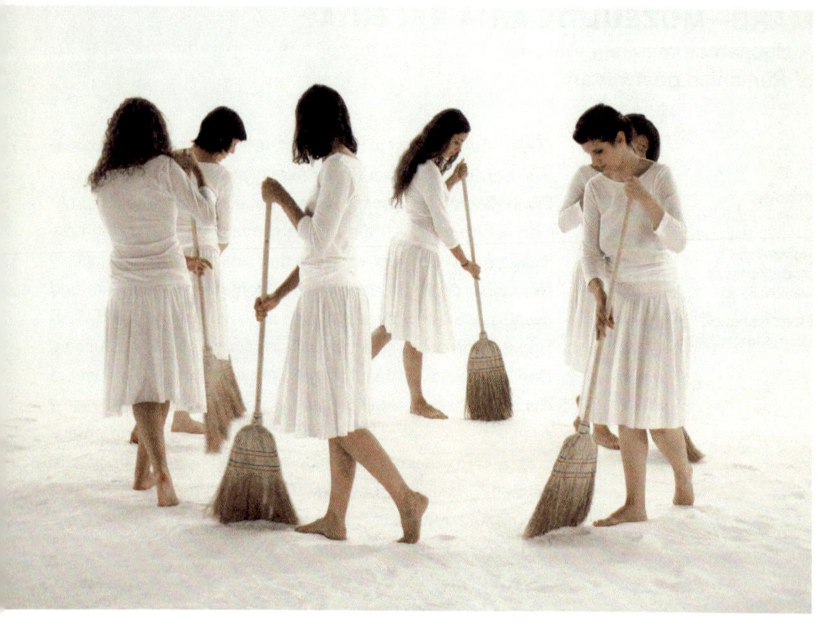

THE OVIDIU ȘANDOR COLLECTION

A Romanian collector fostering a contemporary art community in his hometown

Collector:
Ovidiu Șandor

Address:
Timișoara, Romania
contact@artencounters.ro

Visitation permitted only occasionally. Please inquire by e-mail.

It all began with an interest in antique maps. Now some twenty years later, Ovidiu Şandor's collection includes more than 300 works of Romanian contemporary art. Şandor started his collection by purchasing modern art from his home country, but soon a passion for younger artists took hold—in step with growing acclaim for artists of the so-called Cluj School. Key figures of that movement, such as Adrian Ghenie, Victor Man, Mircea Cantor, and Ciprian Mureşan all feature prominently in Şandor's collection. Additionally, he has made a particular effort to collect works by older figures from Romania who have been rediscovered in recent years, from Geta Brătescu and Ana Lupaş to artists of the Sigma Group—Ştefan Bertalan and Doru Tulcan among them—which was founded in Şandor's hometown Timişoara. The collector also launched the Art Encounters Foundation, which organized its first biennial in October 2015.

MOSCOW

Despite the omnipresent threat of censorship, Moscow has developed a vibrant and lively contemporary art scene, thanks primarily to Russian business tycoons and private collectors. The city's premier art center is the Garage Museum of Contemporary Art, founded in 2008 by collector Daria Zhukova. Named after the exhibition location where it all began—a former bus depot built in 1926—the institution moved into its permanent domicile in Gorki Park in 2015: a former 1960s-era restaurant extensively renovated and expanded by Rem Koolhaas. Another institution actively supporting art is the V-A-C Foundation, established in 2009 by businessman Leonid Mikhelson who is focused on integrating Russian contemporary art into national and international discourse. New exhibition spaces designed by star architect Renzo Piano are scheduled to open in spring 2019 in a former power station on the Moskva. And the collectors and patrons Vladimir Smirnov and Konstantine Sorokin have made studios available to young artists in a former factory building south of Gorki Park since 2011. Among the most important state-owned institutions are the Moscow Museum of Modern Art (MMOMA) and the National Centre for Contemporary Arts (NCCA), an exhibition and research institute focusing on the twenty-first century. Since 2008, the MMOMA and the NCCA have organized the Moscow International Biennale for Young Art, which is dedicated to a younger generation of artists. Russia's largest biennial, the Moscow Biennale of Contemporary Art, starts in September, around the same time as the art fair Cosmoscow. Another meeting point for the art scene is the Winzavod Centre for Contemporary Art, a former nineteenth-century wine-making facility, where artists' studios are situated alongside the 11.12 Gallery, the Regina Gallery, and the Pechersky Gallery. Other locations worth visiting for contemporary art around the city include the Triumph Gallery as well as Artwin Gallery, established in 2012.

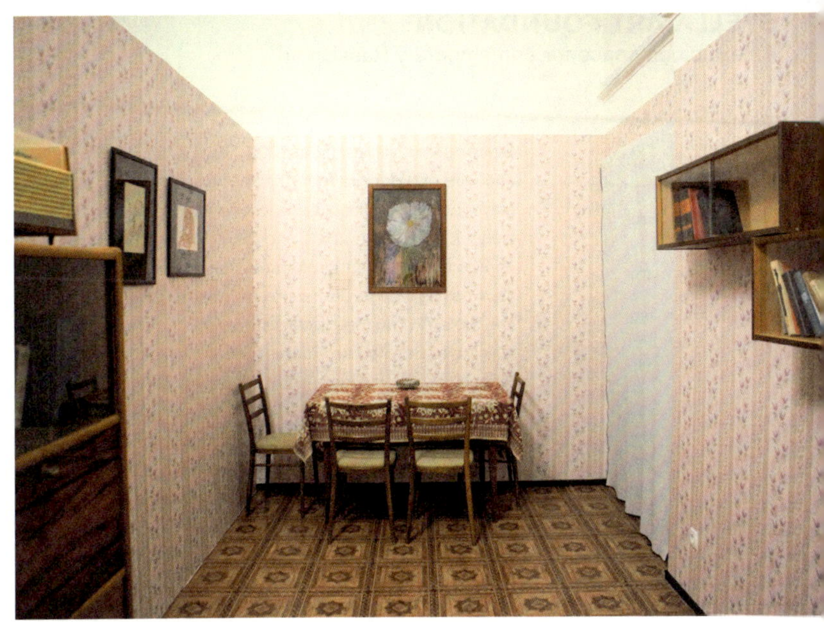

THE EKATERINA CULTURAL FOUNDATION

Russian and international contemporary art in a pioneering private museum

Collectors:
Ekaterina & Vladimir Seminikhin

Address:
Kuznetsky Most, 21/5
107996 Moscow
Russia
Tel +7 495 6215522
info@ekaterina-foundation.ru
www.ekaterina-fondation.ru

Opening Hours:
Tues–Sun: 11am–8pm

Ekaterina and Vladimir Semenikhin were among the first Russian collectors to open their collection to the public. In the catalogue to their first exhibition, in 2007, the couple wrote: "Those mysterious private collections that were treated with suspicion by both the state and society during Soviet times are now gradually stepping out of the shadows." The Semenikhins have been collecting international contemporary works since 2003, but they were such early supporters of the post-Soviet avant-garde that the *Financial Times* deemed them "pioneers among Russian private collectors" and "the unofficial patron saints of Russia's contemporary arts scene." The Ekaterina Cultural Foundation consists of 800 works of Russian art, from Ivan Shishkin to Komar & Melamid to Dubossarsky & Vinogradov.

STELLA ART FOUNDATION

An exhibition space for contemporary Russian art

Collector:
Stella Kesaeva

Address:
Skaryatinsky Pereulok, 7
121069 Moscow
Russia
Tel +7 495 6913407
info@safmuseum.org
www.safmuseum.org

Opening Hours:
Tues–Sun: 12–7pm

Since opening her gallery in 2003, Stella Kesaeva, art collector and wife of billionaire Igor Kesaev, has become an influential player on the Russian art scene. She was appointed commissioner for the 2011, 2013, and 2015 Russian Pavilions at the Venice Biennale, and in Moscow she runs a private space showcasing works from her personal collection and elsewhere. The Stella Art Foundation consists of approximately 800 pieces, mainly by contemporary Russian artists like Ilya Kabakov, Andrei Monastyrski, Yuri Albert, and Oleg Kulik. But it also features famed international talents like Yves Klein, Andy Warhol, Bill Viola, Alex Katz, Richard Prince, or Robert Mapplethorpe. Although Kesaevas's plans to build an art museum in a former bus depot in Moscow were ultimately halted by bureaucratic hurdles, an alternative solution is already in planning. The new museum is scheduled to open its doors in the coming years.

NOVY MUZEI

Soviet nonconformist art as an alternative to Socialist Realism

Collector:
Aslan Chekhoyev

Address:
6-ya Liniya, 29
199004 St. Petersburg
Russia
Tel +7 812 3235090
info@novymuseum.ru
www.novymuseum.ru

Opening Hours:
Wed–Fri: 11am–7pm
Sat–Sun: 12–8pm

If you think the only art movement in Russia before the end of the Soviet era was Socialist Realism, you should visit the Novy Muzei in Saint Petersburg. It holds Aslan Chekhoyev's collection of the unofficial movements of Russian modern art from the postwar era to the end of the twentieth century. After Josef Stalin died in 1953, there was an underground wave of liberalization in the arts in Russia, and artists began experimenting, even if they could not exhibit. One famous episode of state repression of unsanctioned art was in 1974, when police broke up a show with a bulldozer and water cannons. Chekhoyev's collection is an important effort to direct public attention to works by artists like Lydia Masterkova, Lev Kropivnitsky, and Vladimir Nemukhin. Figures in their contemporary collection are artists like Oleg Kulik and the AES + F group, among others.

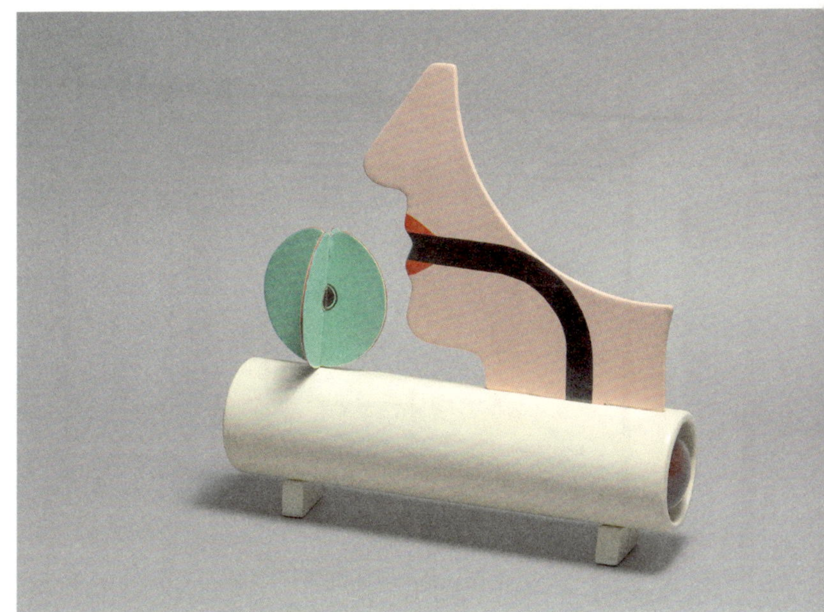

KOLEKCIJA TRAJKOVIĆ

A survey of postwar Serbian art in a private Belgrade apartment

Collectors:
Slavica & Daniel Trajković

Address:
Palmotićeva 33
11000 Belgrade
Serbia
office@kolekcijatrajkovic.com
www.kolekcijatrajkovic.com

By e-mail appointment only.

Slavica and Daniel Trajković's collection focuses exclusively on Serbian art, spanning the postwar period through the present day. Showcased in their home, a light, spacious nineteenth-century apartment in central Belgrade, the collection includes more than 1 000 works by over 150 artists. It ranges from paintings to works on paper to video, providing an impressive overview of Serbian art from the Communist period under Tito through today. Of special interest is their collection of Serbian radical art and its documentation through posters, catalogues, and letters. The Trajkovićs regularly lend works to local and international museums, and also established an eponymous foundation in 2010, dedicated to the preservation and promotion of their collection and to fostering discourse around artistic practices. The collectors have their sights firmly set on creating a wider, international audience for Serbian art.

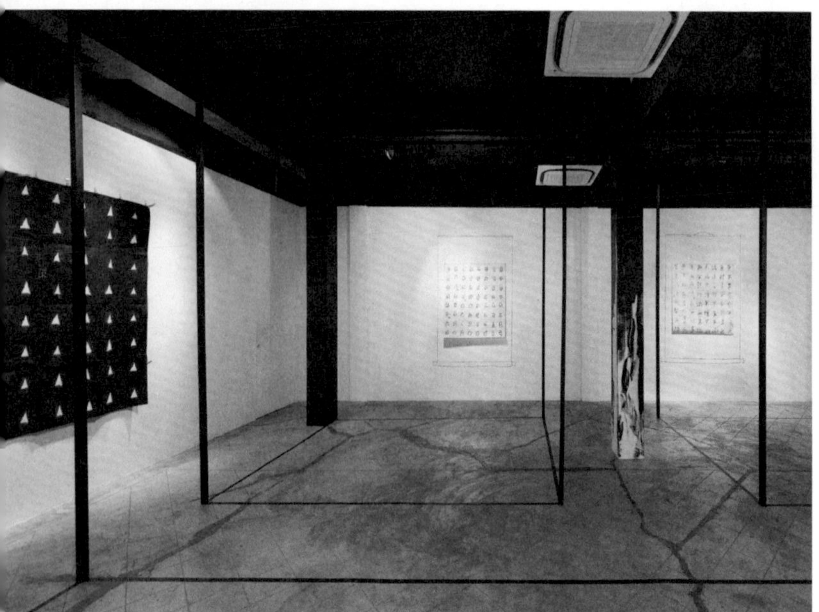

THE PRIVATE MUSEUM

A collector's room—also for other collectors

Collector:
Daniel Teo

Address:
51 Waterloo Street, #02–06
Singapore 187969
Singapore
Tel +65 6738 2872
mail@theprivatemuseum.org
www.theprivatemuseum.org

Opening Hours:
Mon–Fri: 10am–7pm
Sat–Sun: 11am–5pm
And by appointment.

The architect and real estate developer Daniel Teo began to collect art in the 1990s. His collecting intensified after 1994, when he teamed up with the Swede Björn Wetterling to open the Wetterling Teo Gallery in Singapore, one of the first international art galleries in Southeast Asia. Teo is particularly interested in Pop Art; the first work he acquired was by James Rosenquist. He also collects ink paintings and works by local artists. Alongside images by Roy Lichtenstein, Jim Dine, and Tom Wesselmann are those by Lim Tze Peng, Chua Ek Kay, and Kumari Nahappan. In 2008 he opened The Private Museum, where he exhibits his own collection—and that of fellow collectors. "I have met many collectors," Teo says, "and I would like to encourage more collectors to step forward to showcase their collections. It is an important way to establish relationships between artists, collectors, and the public."

SINGAPORE

Singapore is famous for its cleanliness and, of course, as a financial center. Office towers and huge shopping temples form the city's image. For a long time, contemporary art was not a concern in this tropical city-state—until former Art Basel director Lorenzo Rudolf established Art Stage Singapore in 2011. Since then, the art market is experiencing an enormous boom. New galleries and museums are springing up at a record pace and attracting not only a well-established audience but also hipsters. In the western harbor area, a dozen international and local art dealers have moved into Gillman Barracks, a former British military quarters, whose white colonial buildings are loosely scattered around a tropical green hillside, giving the impression of an historic enclave in the ultra-modern megacity. Here, Partners & Mucciaccia from Rome shows artists like Jean-Michel Basquiat or Robert Rauschenberg. Pearl Lam from Hong Kong showcases Chinese and international sculptors like Chun Kwang Young and Yinka Shonibare in their program. Also located on the former military site since 2013 is the Nanyang Technological University Centre for Contemporary Art Singapore (NTU CCA Singapore), which offers a sophisticated program under the direction of German curator Ute Meta Bauer. The fledgling art scene's prestige building, the National Gallery Singapore, which opened in 2015, is a fifteen-minute taxi-ride from the city center. It impresses with a notable contrast: the largest collection of modern art in Southeast Asia, spread over six thousand square meters, is housed in two historic buildings, the former City Hall and the Supreme Court. From the terrace you can take in a magnificent view of the skyline, including the spectacular Marina Bay Sands hotel, which was built in 2010 by Safdie Architects and looks like a huge surfboard lying across three towers. Housed in the steel lotus flower next door is the ArtScience Museum, which is known for revolving contemporary exhibitions. An end to the art and construction boom is not in sight. Singapore is still building its urban silhouette like no other city.

THE NEW CHURCH MUSEUM

Contemporary African art as a mirror of society

Collector:
New Church Foundation

Address:
102 New Church Street
Tamboerskloof, Cape Town
South Africa
info@thenewchurch.co

Please check the website for the most current information on opening hours.

The name "The New Church" does not refer to a sacred space but rather to the street on which the museum is located. What is church-like, however, is the museum's strong commitment to social issues: according to its founding idea, the institution is inspired by "art's ability to facilitate the examination of society's values and norms, and believes that this has tremendous social benefit." The New Church Museum comprises a collection of about 450 works of contemporary African art. Among them are works by renowned representatives such as Meschac Gaba, Willem Boshoff, and Pieter Hugo. Two to three times per year, guest curators work with the collection, occasionally bringing external loans into dialogue. The museum is located in a converted Victorian house, which has been renovated to include a minimalistic exhibition space at the rear.

ZEITZ MOCAA—ZEITZ MUSEUM OF CONTEMPORARY ART AFRICA

A venue for contemporary African art

Collector:
Jochen Zeitz

Address:
Silo District
V&A Waterfront
S Arm Road
Cape Town 0002
South Africa
Tel +27 87 3504777
info@zeitzmocaa.museum
www.zeitzmocaa.museum

Opening Hours:
Wed–Mon: 10am–6pm
Every first Friday of the month from 10am–9pm.

Since fall 2017, the first museum for contemporary African art has been located in a spectacular building in the port of Cape Town. It is hard to believe that no other venue with a similar focus existed anywhere else in the world. The Zeitz MOCAA was established through a partnership between the V&A Waterfront and former Puma CEO Jochen Zeitz, whose own collection serves as the museum's founding collection. Architect Thomas Heatherwick transformed a 1920s-era grain silo into an institution featuring six thousand square meters of exhibition space. In addition to temporary shows, works by important artists such as Marlene Dumas and William Kentridge are on view at Zeitz MOCAA, whose mission is to collect, preserve, research, and exhibit cutting-edge art from Africa and its diaspora. Featuring a light-filled atrium, the nine-story building also boasts a hotel, a restaurant, and a rooftop sculpture garden that offers breathtaking views of the city and ocean.

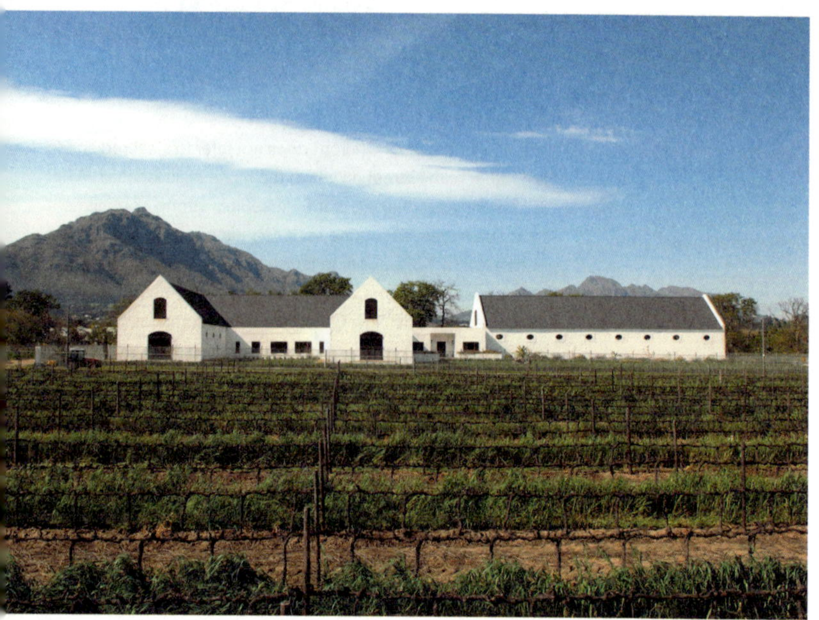

RUPERT MUSEUM

South African art highlights since 1940 in a region known for its wine

Collectors:
Huberte & Anton Rupert

Address:
Stellentia Avenue
Stellenbosch 7600
South Africa
Tel +27 21 8883344
rupertmuseum@remgro.com
www.rupertmuseum.org

Opening Hours:
Mon–Sat: 10am–4pm

A fire at their private home prompted collectors Huberte and Anton Rupert to build a museum for their extensive art collection. They found the right partner in Hannes Meiring, an artist and architect from Cape Town. Meiring's design updated the simple, seventeenth-century farmhouse to reflect contemporary tastes. In 2005 the Rupert Museum opened in South Africa's famous wine capital, Stellenbosch, and exhibits mainly South African art from 1940 to 2005 in a 2000-square-meter space. Artists shown include the New Objectivity landscape painter Jacobus Hendrik Pierneef, the sculptor Anton van Wouw and the painter Irma Stern, who was friends with the German Expressionists. Contemporary artists like William Kentridge have also found their way into this sizable collection.

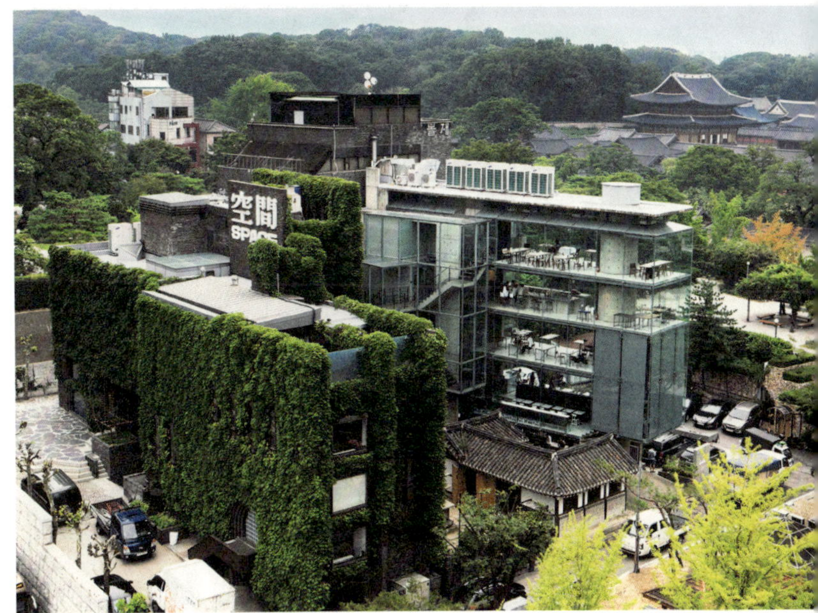

ARARIO MUSEUM IN SPACE

Wide-ranging collection of Korean and Western art by the country's leading collector and gallerist

Collector:
Kim Chang-il

Address:
83 Yulgok-ro, Jongno-gu
Seoul 110–280
South Korea
Tel +82 2 7365700
info@arariomuseum.org
www.arariomuseum.org

Opening Hours:
Mon–Sun: 10am–7pm

Collector and gallerist Kim Chang-il began collecting Korean art in the 1970s, but it was a visit to the Museum of Contemporary Art, Los Angeles (MOCA) in 1981 that sparked his interest in international contemporary art. In 2014, he resurrected a seminal 1970s office building in downtown Seoul to display his private art collection, which ranges from Korean contemporaries to the New Leipzig School to the Young British Artists. The building's labyrinthine corridors, narrow staircases, and low ceilings house works by Keith Haring, Mona Hatoum, and Subodh Gupta. Kim rotates the pieces regularly—his collection of 3 700 works is one of the largest and most significant in Southeast Asia. There are four additional branches of the Arario Museum, one on Jeju Island. The polymath restaurateur and department-store proprietor also manages to find time to sculpt, draw, and paint—adding his own pieces to his ever-growing collection.

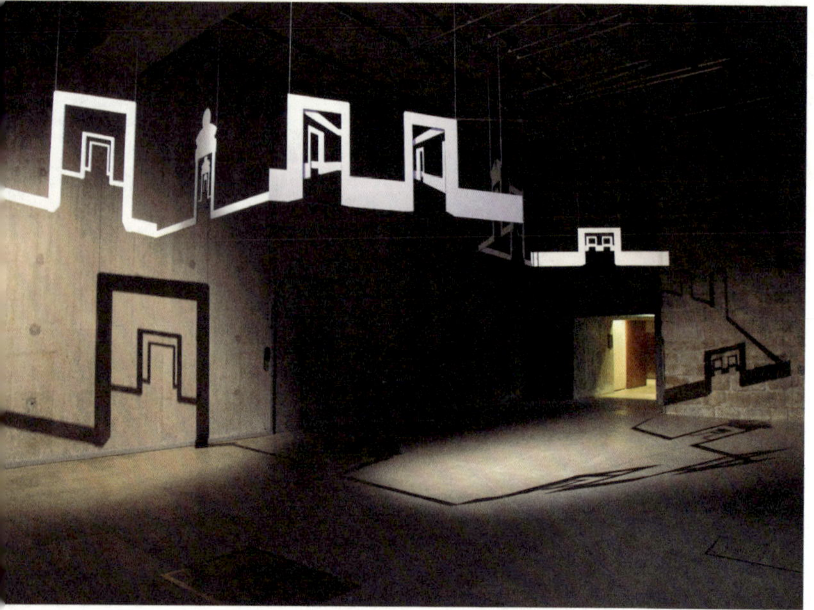

ADRASTUS COLLECTION—COLLEGIUM

A collection presenting the diversity of art in the age of globalization

Collectors:
Javier Lumbreras &
Lorena Pérez-Jácome

Address:
San Ignacio de Loyola 8
05200 Arévalo
Spain
info@adrastuscollection.org
www.adrastuscollection.org

Please check the website for the most current information on opening hours.

An enthusiasm for art runs in the family, now in its eighth generation: for the past twenty-seven years Javier Lumbreras has devoted himself to his passion for collecting. Together with his wife Lorena Pérez-Jácome, the Spanish investor founded the Adrastus Collection in 2000. Including over 600 works by artists from forty countries thus far, the collection features pieces by artists such as Walid Raad, Minerva Cuevas, Carol Bove, Adrián Villar Rojas, Yto Barrada, Iman Issa, Jonathas de Andrade, Tacita Dean, Tino Sehgal, and Paul Lee. Since 2016, a new home is being created for the collection: in Arévalo a former Jesuit boarding school and adjoining church is gradually being transformed into a cultural hub that makes special reference to the historical location. Scheduled to open by late 2019, the 15 000-square-meter space will provide enough room for a museum, an archive, as well as production and conservation workshops.

BARCELONA

Moving images in the windows of chic boutiques, in dimly lit bodegas, or stylish tapas bars—once a year, Barcelona transforms into a paradise for lovers of video art. During the ten-day springtime Loop Festival, artists' videos are shown in approximately one hundred spots around the city—sometimes in subtle locales, sometimes more prominently displayed. Toward the end of the festival, international art audiences regularly flock to the three-day Loop Fair, held in the converted "black-box" suites of a four-star hotel. This is perhaps the best opportunity to get to know the local institutions and galleries. While the Museu Picasso and the Fundació Joan Miró focus on the art of these two superstars, as well as presenting smaller rotating exhibitions, the Fundació Antoni Tàpies has consistently made a name for itself with a decidedly contemporary program showing artists ranging from Allan Kaprow to Harun Farocki, to Allora & Calzadilla, in addition to its collection. Carles Guerra, its well-connected director, was appointed in 2015 much to the enthusiasm of the local art scene. In the same year, Argentine-native Ferran Barenblit took over the helm of the

Museu d'Art Contemporani de Barcelona (MACBa). The blinding-white Richard Meier building was opened in 1995 in the trendy Raval district and showcases an excellent collection of Spanish and international art from the 1950s to today. Temporary exhibitions are devoted to the latest trends but also to earlier avant-garde movements. From here it's just a few steps to one of the most exciting commercial galleries: Àngels Barcelona focuses on conceptually charged and socially critical photography, film, and video art. An interesting new addition to the scene since 2015 is the local offshoot of the Madrid-based Fundación Mapfre. Located in the sumptuously designed Casa Garriga i Nogués, this foundation specializes in carefully crafted monographic exhibitions of major photographers such as Hiroshi Sugimoto or Shōmei Tōmatsu.

FUNDACIÓ SUÑOL

Two rooms, two ideas: Spanish classics meet new art

Collector:
Josep Suñol

Address:
Passeig de Gràcia 98
08008 Barcelona
Spain
www.fundaciosunol.org

Opening Hours:
Mon–Fri: 11am–2pm, 4–8pm
Sat: 4–8pm
And by appointment.

Real estate mogul Josep Suñol's 1 200-work collection, opened in 2007, counts as one of the largest in Catalonia. Represented are the three great Spaniards of the twentieth century—Pablo Picasso, Joan Miró, and Salvador Dalí—as well as artists of the subsequent generation, including Antonio Saura, Antoni Tàpies, and Eduardo Chillida. The collection also holds works from Italy and Switzerland, like those by Giacomo Balla, Lucio Fontana, and Alberto Giacometti, and by a younger generation of artists, mostly from Catalonia. Two yearly exhibitions allow the public to get acquainted with the collection. Nivell Zero, a second exhibition space with a separate entrance, leans toward the radically contemporary: events that take place there have a laboratory or workshop feel. Exhibitions and a smattering of film and video screenings deal with current themes.

FUNDACIÓ VILA CASAS

Three buildings, three points of focus: painting, sculpture, and photography

Collector:
Antoni Vila Casas

Addresses:
Museo Can Framis:
Carrer Roc Boronat 116–126
08018 Barcelona
Spain
Tel +34 93 3208736

Museo Can Mario:
Plaça Can Mario 7
17200 Palafrugell
Spain

Museo Palau Solterra:
Carrer de l'Església 10
17257 Torroella de Montgrí
Spain

www.fundaciovilacasas.com

Opening hours vary depending on exhibition and season. Please check the website for the most current information.

The Catalonian pharmaceutical businessman Antoni Vila Casas is fortunate to be able to show his foundation's extensive holdings of modern and contemporary art in three architecturally compelling museums around Catalonia. The Museo Can Framis, in Barcelona, is located in a former wool factory, replete with a new addition. Its 3 800 square meters are devoted to painting. Over 350 sculptures are housed at the Museo Can Mario, in a renovated cork factory in Palafrugell on the Costa Brava. And not far from there, at the Renaissance-era palace Palau Solterra, in Torroella de Montgrí, is where Vila Casas shows 300 works from his collection of photography. With names like Lluís Barba, Oriol Jolonch, or Francesca Llopis, Catalonian art dominates in a collection now comprising nearly 1 000 works.

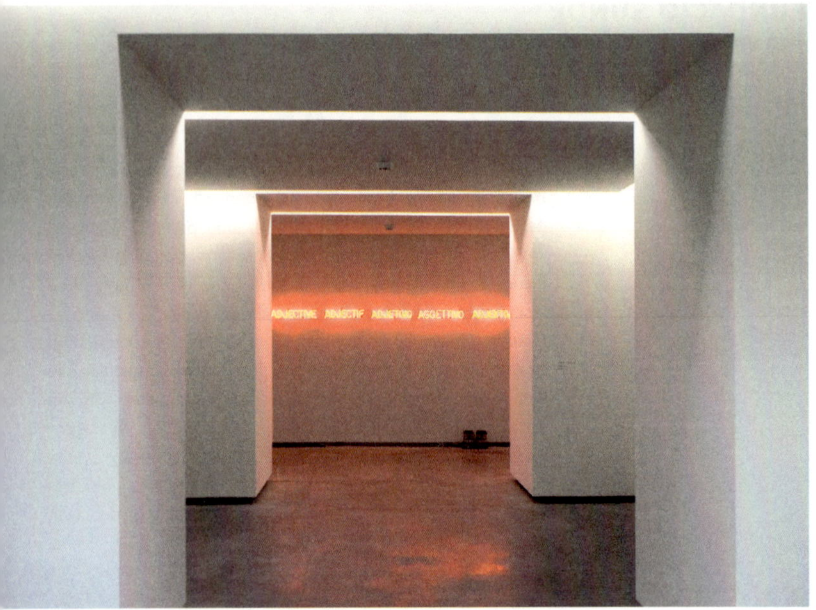

CENTRO DE ARTES VISUALES/ FUNDACIÓN HELGA DE ALVEAR

One of the world's most important collections of contemporary art

Collector:
Helga de Alvear

Address:
Calle Pizarro 8
10003 Cáceres
Spain
Tel +34 927 626414
general@fundacionhelgadealvear.es
www.fundacionhelgadealvear.es

Opening Hours:
June–September
Tues–Sat: 10am–2pm, 6–9pm
Sun: 10am–2:30pm
October–May
Tues–Sat: 10am–2pm, 5–8pm
Sun: 10am–2:30pm

German-native Helga de Alvear has lived in Madrid for over fifty years. She runs a successful gallery in the city with an international art program. But de Alvear not only sells art to collectors; she has often also been her own best client. This has allowed her to assemble a collection of roughly 3000 works by artists like Georg Baselitz, Martin Creed, Steve McQueen, Helena Almeida, Anri Sala, Elmgreen & Dragset, Thomas Demand, Jeff Wall, Juan Muñoz, or Louise Bourgeois—the remarkable list could go on. Since 2010, Alvear has been slowly presenting parts of her collection in the city of Cáceres in southwestern Spain. Her collection is housed in a 3000-square-meter patrician villa, redesigned by the highly sought-after Madrid architects Mansilla+Tuñón. A spectacular new 5000-square-meters expansion is currently under construction adding four more floors for exhibitions as well as an auditorium.

CDAN—CENTRO DE ARTE Y NATURALEZA/ FUNDACIÓN BEULAS

Spanish postwar painting and rotating exhibits relating to landscape

Collectors:
José Beulas & Maria Sarrate

Address:
Avenida Doctor Artero s/n
22004 Huesca
Spain
Tel +34 974 239893
cdan@cdan.es
www.cdan.es

Opening Hours:
April–October
Thurs–Fri: 6–9pm,
Sat: 11am–2pm, 6–9pm
Sun: 11am–2pm
November–March
Thurs–Fri: 5–8pm,
Sat: 11am–2pm, 5–8pm
Sun: 11am–2pm

Art and nature are the focus of activities at the CDAN—Centro de Arte y Naturaleza/Fundación Beulas, opened in 2006 near the northeastern Spanish city of Huesca. The core of CDAN is formed by a private collection owned by painter José Beulas, born in 1921. In the 1950s he began collecting the work of friends and companions: primarily regional landscape painters and sculptors, but also representatives of New Figuration and Informel, like stars Antonio Saura and Antoni Tàpies. In 2000, Beulas converted all of his assets and property into a public foundation. An organic, wavy building by star architect Rafael Moneo houses the art center. The surrounding landscape is spectacular, and with the help of the foundation, it has been blessed with land-art projects—eight so far—by artists including Richard Long, Per Kirkeby, and Ulrich Rückriem.

OTR ESPACIO DE ARTE

Perpetual surprises in a modern project space

Collectors:
José Antonio Trujillo & Elsa López

Address:
Calle de San Eugenio 10
28012 Madrid
Spain
info@espaciodearteotr.com
www.espaciodearteotr.com

By appointment only.

The aim of this downtown Madrid art space, opened in 2008, is not just to present a collection. Located near the Prado, the 300-square-meter OTR Espacio de Arte is dedicated to promoting young, not-yet-established art. Two to three thematic exhibits annually investigate artistic questions that cross into architecture. José Antonio Trujillo and Elsa López show work from their own collection, as well as that of guest artists. Spanish and Latin American positions dominate, among them Montserrat Soto and Ernesto Neto. Artists like John Baldessari, Imi Knoebel, Jenny Holzer, Katharina Grosse, Sol LeWitt, Ulrich Rückriem, Helena Almeida, Vik Muniz, Sean Scully, Jonathan Lasker, and Rémy Zaugg are also represented in the collection, displayed in exhibitions that nicely fuse concepts with sensual color.

FUNDACIÓN ROSÓN ARTE CONTEMPORÁNEO (RAC)

An award-winning concept art collection far from the Spanish art-metropolises

Collector:
Carlos Rosón Gasalla

Address:
Padre Sarmiento 41
36002 Pontevedra
Spain
Tel +34 986 842950
info@fundacionrac.org
www.fundacionrac.org

By appointment only.

The Galician city of Pontevedra lies in the outermost region of northwest Spain. Here, you have to be brave to open an ambitious exhibition hall. Luckily, the Madrid-educated architect Carlos Rosón Gasalla is a risk-taker. His collection of 280 artworks from more than 160 Spanish and international artists opened on the ground floor of his house in 2007. It's not the simple artistic positions that triggered his passion for collecting. Rather, Rosón Gasalla favors art with conceptual and ironic leanings: work by John Baldessari, Mateo López, Ana Mazzei, Baltazar Torres, and Philippe Parreno, for example. Accolades have come quickly for the carefully curated exhibitions, which take place twice a year: in 2009 he received the collector award of the Madrid art fair ArCo. Rosón Gasalla's foundation also sponsors an artist-in-residence program, which has hosted artists such as Tania Bruguera, Caio Reisewitz, and David Zink Yi.

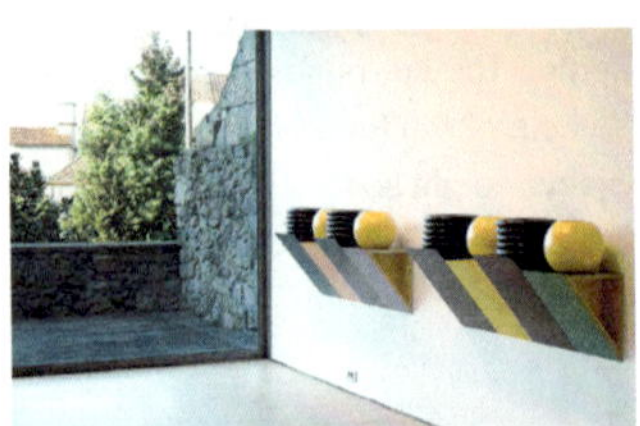

FUNDACIÓN CHIRIVELLA SORIANO

Spanish painting since 1957 in a beautifully restored gothic palace

Collectors:
Manuel Chirivella Bonet &
Alicia Soriano Lleó

Address:
Calle de Valeriola 13
46001 Valencia
Spain
Tel +34 196 3381215
info@chirivellasoriano.org
www.chirivellasoriano.org

Opening Hours:
Tues–Sat: 10am–2pm, 5–8pm
Sun: 10am–2pm

Notary Manuel Chirivella Bonet and his wife, Alicia Soriano Lleó, collected art for over twenty years before purchasing property containing a dilapidated gothic palace in the oldest section of Valencia in 2001. The permission to destroy the palace came a few days later. Apparently, a misunderstanding: the couple did not want to tear down the building; they wanted to restore it. They opened their collection—spread over 1 000 square meters—in 2005. The focus is on Spanish painting since 1957. That is the year both collectors were born, but the selection also serves an art historical purpose: in 1957 the followers of the Informel movement founded a breakaway artist group dedicated to new geometric abstraction and new kinds of figuration. Artists like Antonio Saura are well represented in the collection, which also shows more recent Spanish art.

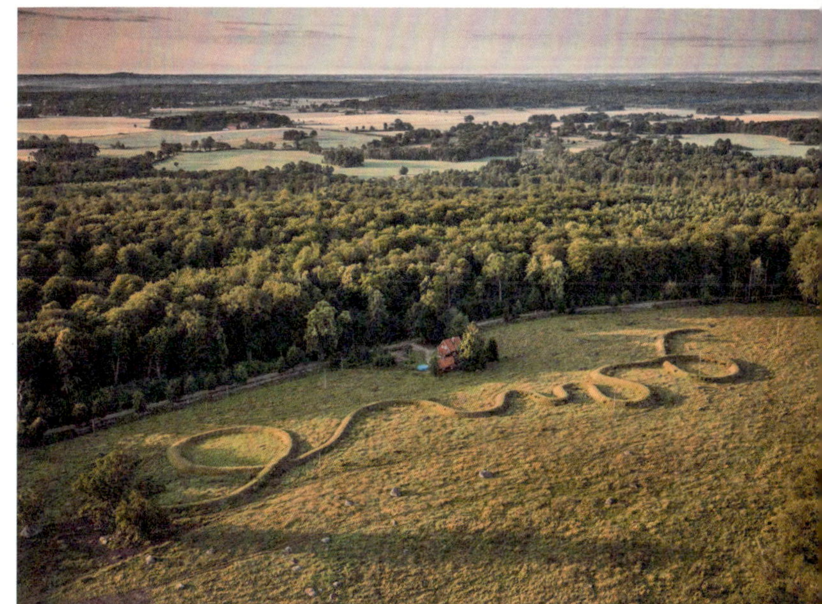

WANÅS FOUNDATION/WANÅS KONST

Site-specific contemporary art in southern Sweden

Collector:
Wanås Foundation

Address:
Knislinge, Sweden
Tel +46 44 66071
info@wanaskonst.se
www.wanaskonst.se

Opening hours vary depending on exhibition and season. Please check the website for the most current information.

The park is open daily from 8am–7pm.

Wanås castle in southern Sweden is a fortress from the fifteenth century and the private home of Charles and Marika Wachtmeister, located one-and-a-half-hours away from Copenhagen by car. In 1987, Marika Wachtmeister began to exhibit sculptures on the sprawling estate, featuring site-specific works by Igshaan Adams, Dan Graham, Ann Hamilton, Jeppe Hein, Jenny Holzer, Tadashi Kawamata, Maya Lin, and Yoko Ono. The Wanås Foundation is also known for its atmospheric sound works by artists Janet Cardiff and Robert Wilson. Today, more than seventy permanently installed works comprise the continuously expanding outdoor collection. A spacious stable, built in 1759, has been used to house temporary exhibitions and the Wanås Estate is also the site of an eco-friendly agricultural business. The Wanås Restaurant Hotel, opened in 2017, offers guests the chance to enjoy magical early morning walks in the park and locavore dinners in the old stable blocks.

KUNSTMUSEUM APPENZELL/ KUNSTHALLE ZIEGELHÜTTE

A perfect synthesis of the pristine with modern and avant-garde architecture

Collectors:
Myriam Gebert Macconi & Heinrich Gebert

Addresses:
Kunstmuseum Appenzell:
Unterrainstrasse 5
9050 Appenzell
Switzerland
Tel +41 71 7881800

Kunsthalle Ziegelhütte:
Ziegeleistrasse 14
9050 Appenzell
Switzerland
Tel +41 71 7881860

www.h-gebertka.ch

Please check the website for the most current information on opening hours.

A must-see for architecture fans: inspired by the vision of functional museum architecture—as the Swiss artist Rémy Zaugg dreamed of—the architect-duo Annette Gigon and Mike Guyer built the Kunstmuseum Appenzell (formerly: Museum Liner) in 1998, an architectural gem in the Appenzell region. Right next to the museum, the Heinrich Gebert Kulturstiftung opened a second venue in 2003, the Kunsthalle Ziegelhütte, which was restored by architect Robert Bamert and extended with an exhibition hall. Wood, iron, brick, and exposed concrete are unified in a successful synthesis of modernity and the local in this multifunctional industrial monument. Up to six special exhibitions a year showcase the broad range of the collection, from classic modernism to contemporary art, which includes more than 1 000 works by the artists Carl August and Carl Walter Liner, alongside 400 works by the likes of Hans Arp, Frank Stella, or Beat Zoderer.

FONDAZIONE ROLLA/ROLLA.INFO

A collection of modern and contemporary photography

Collectors:
Rosella & Philip Rolla

Address:
La Stráda
6837 Bruzella
Switzerland
Tel +41 77 4740549
rosella@rolla.info
www.rolla.info

By appointment only.

What began as a collection of modern and contemporary photography that was running out of space, took shape in a vacant former kindergarten in the small community in the Valle di Muggio, Ticino. This is where the Fondazione Rolla found its home in 2010. With the help of their foundation, Rosella and Philip Rolla provide researchers and photography enthusiasts access to important works by representatives like Robert Adams, Josef Sudek, and Eugène Atget, but also to works by contemporary photographers such as Thomas Struth, James Welling, and Vincenzo Castella. The Rollas' collection is, however, not only devoted to photography: Phil Rolla, an engineer who grew up in the US, is also mainly interested in American Minimal Art. His professional background may explain the couple's preference for German photography, in particular for the architectural and industrial photography of Albert Renger-Patzsch, Bernd & Hilla Becher, and Christof Klute.

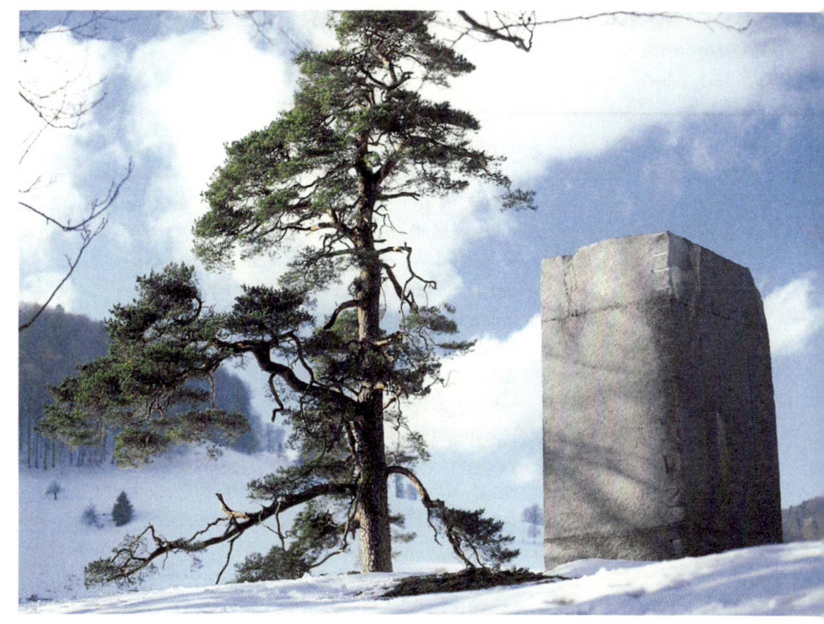

KLOSTER SCHOENTHAL

Nature-inspired sculptures in a pristine landscape

Collector:
John Schmid

Address:
Schönthalstrasse 158
4438 Langenbruck
Switzerland
Tel +41 61 7067676
mail@schoenthal.ch
www.schoenthal.ch

The park is open at all times.

There is a special place about thirty-five kilometers southeast of Basel in the gentle foothills of the Swiss canton of Jura. Basel-based entrepreneur and collector John Schmid has created a sculptural landscape with more than thirty works by Swiss and international artists around the former Schoenthal monastery. But urban art lovers had better exchange their nice shoes for rubber boots to walk the sculpture trail, which meanders through fifty hectares of fields, meadows, and forest. Twenty-four artists, from Richard Long to Ulrich Rückriem, to Nicola Hicks, David Nash, Tony Cragg, Ian Hamilton Finlay, or Roman Signer, have engaged the natural environs with great sensitivity and realized works that meld perfectly into the landscape. Schmid, who maintains friendly relations with all the artists, acquired the estate and its landmark building in 1985.

MUSEUM SAMMLUNG ROSENGART

The crème de la crème of classic modernism:
Picasso, Klee, and peers

Collectors:
Siegfried & Angela Rosengart

Address:
Pilatusstrasse 10
6003 Lucerne
Switzerland
Tel +41 41 2201660
info@rosengart.ch
www.rosengart.ch

Opening Hours:
April–October
Mon–Sun: 10am–6pm
November–March
Mon–Sun: 11am–5pm

The Lucerne-based Rosengart collection occupies a neoclassical building formerly owned by the Swiss National Bank. Carefully remodeled by the Basel firm Diener & Diener Architects, the building, finished in 2002, provides the perfect setting for this impressive collection of classic modernism. Art dealer Siegfried Rosengart (1894–1985) didn't just collect Pablo Picasso, Georges Braque, and Henri Matisse; he and his daughter Angela, who entered the family business at age sixteen, were actually close friends with all of them. And thus, "all the paintings were chosen with the heart," Angela Rosengart says. The ground floor is devoted to Picasso, and paintings by his contemporaries Fernand Léger and Wassily Kandinsky are featured on the first floor. Presented in the reinforced basement, where bolted safes once held the gold reserves of the Swiss National Bank, is an exquisite hanging of carefully illuminated Paul Klee works.

COLLEZIONE GIANCARLO E DANNA OLGIATI

Avant-garde art of the twentieth and twenty-first centuries
on Lake Lugano

Collectors:
Giancarlo & Danna Olgiati

Address:
Riva Caccia 1
6900 Lugano
Switzerland
Tel +41 58 8667214
mediazione@lugano.ch
www.collezioneolgiati.ch

Opening Hours:
Fri–Sun: 11am–6pm

Initially devoted to the German Expressionist avant-garde, attorney Giancarlo Olgiati shifted his attention to the contemporary art scene in the early 1960s while still a young collector. In so doing, he discovered the artists of the Nouveaux Réalisme, whose work he began to collect systematically in the second half of the 1970s. Since 1985, his wife, Danna Olgiati, a gallerist specialized in Italian Futurism, has assisted his building up of the collection, which also includes positions of Spatialism, Arte Povera, and the latest tendencies of neo-abstraction. In 2012 the Olgiatis gave the city a part of their collection on permanent loan, which is now stored and presented in temporary exhibitions in an underground area in Lugano's Central Park. The space's name, "-1", mirrors its location; since 2015, it is managed by the new cultural center LAC Lugano Arte e Cultura.

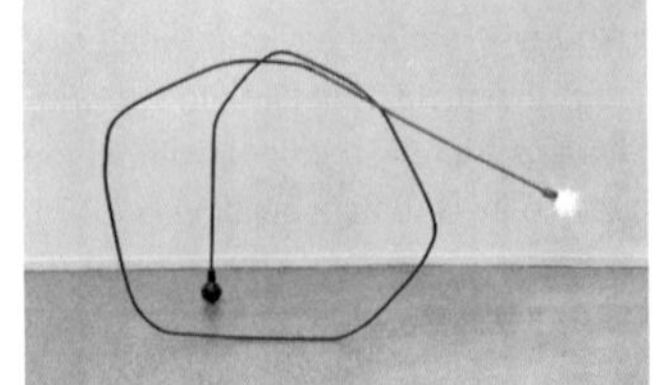

BASEL

Basel's flagship event is Art Basel, undisputedly the most important art fair in the world. Held each year in mid-June, the elite of international collectors meet here or at one of the half-dozen side fairs taking place simultaneously. Approximately 300 participating galleries at the main fair offer the most exquisite, most sought-after contemporary artworks of the twentieth and twenty-first century. Given this spectacle, visitors are apt to overlook the city's expansive range of top-notch art institutions: Kunstmuseum Basel, with its collection ranging from Lucas Cranach the Elder to Wolfgang Tillmans, has, since 2016, a new building for temporary exhibitions, designed by Basel architects Christ & Gantenbein and financed primarily by private capital. Specializing in young avant-garde positions, Kunsthalle Basel attracts visitors with its consistently fascinating program. Opened in 2014, the Haus der elektronischen Künste (HEK) has become an important institution focused on the links between art, technology, and the influences of digitization on our lives. Also forging new paths is the neighboring Schaulager, a hybrid combination of museum, art depot, and research facility, located in a polygonal-shaped building by the Basel architect super-duo Herzog & de Meuron, where art stars like Bruce Nauman or Francis Alÿs are fêted with monographic exhibitions. Just outside the Basel city gates in Riehen, the Fondation Beyeler scores big not only with its Renzo Piano museum building, which fits perfectly into the surrounding landscape, but also with exhibitions of classical modernism, postwar art, and established contemporaries like Marlene Dumas, Georg Baselitz, or Gerhard Richter. Interesting exhibitions of international and Swiss contemporary artists can also be found at Stampa gallery. The Kunsthaus Baselland, in Muttenz, renowned for its discourse-friendly program, and the Vitra Design Museum, in Weil am Rhein, housed in a deconstructivist Frank O. Gehry building, are additional worthwhile destinations when visiting Basel.

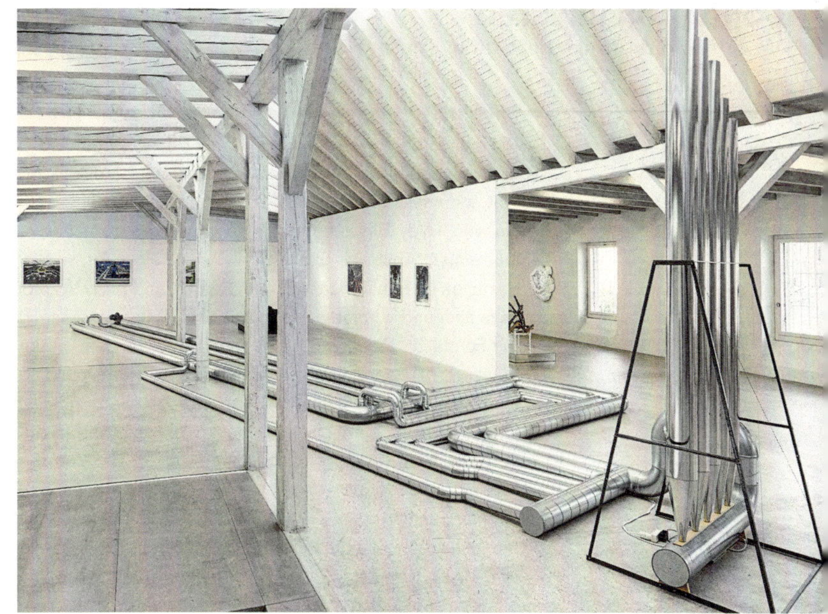

KUNST(ZEUG)HAUS

An extensive private collection of Swiss contemporary art of the last fifty years

Collectors:
Peter & Elisabeth Bosshard

Address:
Schönbodenstrasse 1
8640 Rapperswil-Jona
Switzerland
Tel +41 55 2202080
info@kunstzeughaus.ch
www.kunstzeughaus.ch

Opening Hours:
Wed–Fri: 2–6pm
Sat–Sun: 11am–6pm

The now-late, Zurich-based lawyer Peter Bosshard and his wife, Elisabeth, started collecting art in the 1970s. At that time they had just returned to Switzerland after living in New York City for two years. Then came a decades-long engagement with the Swiss contemporary art scene. The collector couple has always supported artists and art projects, and have since amassed roughly 5 000 works of art. In May 2008, the Bosshards opened an art center in a former armory building in the city of Rapperswil-Jona. Zurich architects Isa Stürm and Urs Wolf meticulously transformed the long and bulky structure into a voluminous 1 500-square-meter space, providing enough room for an annually changing exhibit of the collection and eight to twelve dedicated solo shows each year. Alongside established Swiss art stars like Silvia Bächli, Fischli/Weiss, or Roman Signer, the focus is also on younger positions such as Mario Sala or Yves Netzhammer.

FONDATION BEYELER

World-famous art in a building by Renzo Piano

Collectors:
Ernst & Hildy Beyeler

Address:
Baselstrasse 101
4125 Riehen
Switzerland
Tel +41 61 6459700
info@fondationbeyeler.ch
www.fondationbeyeler.ch

Opening Hours:
Wed: 10am–8pm
Thurs–Tues: 10am–6pm

His standards were always high. Ernst Beyeler, who died in 2010, turned his gallery in Basel into one of the most important addresses of the international art market. Together with his wife, Hildy Beyeler, he built an impressive collection of modernist, Abstract Expressionist, and Pop Art works. Paintings by Pablo Picasso, Mark Rothko, and Andy Warhol have all found a home here. In 1997, the collectors opened the Fondation Beyeler in their hometown of Riehen, on the outskirts of Basel. The elongated Renzo Piano building blends perfectly into the landscape. Every year the foundation stages three large exhibitions of modern or contemporary art. In 2008, Sam Keller, a former director of Art Basel and a hyper-connected art-world figure, became the foundation's director, lending a sense of continuity and inventiveness to the collection. If you think the Museum of Modern Art (MOMA) in New York City is too far to travel, a visit here might be just as rewarding.

SAMMLUNG RUEDI BECHTLER—KUNST IM CASTELL

Contemporary art of the highest quality in a hotel

Collector:
Ruedi Bechtler

Address:
Via Castell 300
7524 Zuoz
Switzerland
Tel +41 81 8515253
info@hotelcastell.ch
www.hotelcastell.ch

Open visitation during hotel hours. Guided tours every Thursday at 5pm.

There are simply too many so-called art hotels showcasing works by unknown regional artists usually purchased in a frenzy right before the hotel's grand opening. Hotel Castell, in Zuoz, in the Engadin region, however, goes about things differently. Both inside and outside the building, the visitor encounters works by Pipilotti Rist, Tadashi Kawamata, Simon Starling, or Andrea Büttner—most of them created specifically for the location. Hotel owner Ruedi Bechtler is an artist in his own right, and sensible enough not to feed his guests standard artistic fare. In 1955, his father, Walter A. Bechtler, started one of the largest Swiss art foundations, whose mission is to make contemporary art accessible. As its current president, Ruedi Bechtler is deeply devoted to this goal. One of the hotel's highlights, James Turrell's *Skyspace,* offers the opportunity for a contemplative experience both night and day.

ELGIZ MUSEUM OF CONTEMPORARY ART

Prominent Turkish and international contemporary art

Collectors:
Sevda & Can Elgiz

Address:
Maslak Meydan Sokak
Beybi Giz Plaza
Maslak-Sarıyer
34398 Istanbul
Turkey
Tel +90 212 2902525
info@elgizmuseumistanbul.org
www.elgizmuseum.org

Opening Hours:
Wed–Fri: 10am–5pm
Sat: 10am–4pm
Tues: by appointment only

Long before contemporary Turkish art came into the spotlight, Sevda and Can Elgiz knew its inherent worth. The couple has been eagerly collecting since the early 1980s, even knocking down walls of their own home to fit the artworks inside, as they told the American magazine *Art + Auction*. Initially they focused on Turkish artists; at the end of the 1990s they began to acquire works by international artists. The private Elgiz Museum—opened in 2001 as one of the first institutions for contemporary art in Turkey—now holds works by influential Turkish artists like Ömer Uluç and Güngör Taner, as well as those by international names like Chiharu Shiota and Erwin Wurm. In 2012, the museum was supplemented by 2 000 square meters of open-air, rooftop exhibition space.

PAPKO ART COLLECTION

Works of Turkish Modernism at the legendary Ralli Apartment

Collector:
Öner Kocabeyoğlu

Address:
Maçka Caddesi Ralli Apartmanı
No:37/4
Teşvikiye-Şişli
34367 Istanbul
Turkey
Tel +90 212 2969380
zelihaunal@papko.com

By appointment only.

Textile magnate Öner Kocabeyoğlu is considered one of the most passionate collectors on the Bosporus. At the age of thirty he fell in love with a gouache by Selim Turan. Since that time his enthusiasm for art has never wavered. It took a decade to assemble the basis of his collection, which now boasts 1 500 works by over 100 artists such as Fikret Mualla Saygı, Mübin Orhon, and Abidin Dino, as well as international names such as Julian Schnabel, Jannis Kounellis, Sarah Morris, or Andreas Gursky. The Papko Art Collection is housed in the Ralli Apartment, where Turkish avant-garde artist Fahrelnissa Zeid—who is also featured in the collection—once lived and presented her first exhibition in 1945. It's no coincidence that some of the works in the collection have a French flair: Kocabeyoğlu is particularly interested in Turkish artists who lived in exile in France after 1940 and whose works are strongly inspired by the École de Paris.

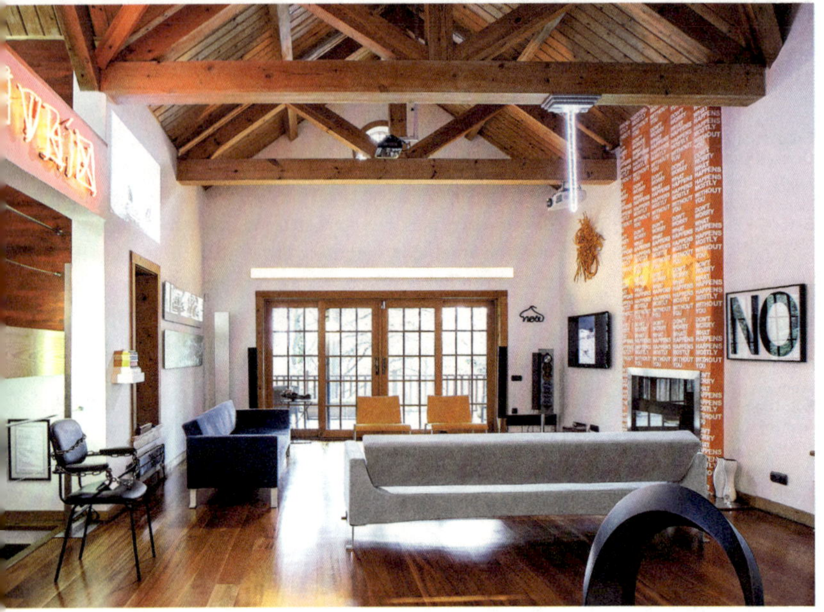

THE AGAH UĞUR COLLECTION

One of the largest video art collections in Turkey

Collector:
Agah Uğur

Address:
Gökmahal Sitesi
Istanbul Caddesi, Nazlı Sok.
No:28, A Blok/Apt. 18
Göktürk
34077 Istanbul
Turkey
Tel +90 533 7240084
info@whynot-art.com

By appointment only.

In the early 1990s, Agah Uğur was still collecting modernist Turkish painting. As the CEO of the giant Turkish industrial group Borusan explains, at that time he was primarily concerned with beauty. In 2008, however, he began to radically reorient his collection's concept. Since then, he has focused on provocative art that grapples with social and political themes, such as the abuse of power or issues related to ethnic and religious identity. Many of the artists in the collection are from Turkey, like Füsun Onur, Cevdet Erek, or Aslı Çavuşoğlu, but international names are also represented, such as Bouchra Khalili or James Richards. In order to make the exquisite video collection available to a broader public, Uğur opened Why Not—a 170-square-meter exhibition space with five rooms for screening videos and an area for installations, not far from his own residence. Half of the exhibits are rotated every six months.

ISTANBUL

Despite political tensions, Istanbul remains an important international art metropolis, not least because of the Istanbul Biennial. Held every two years from mid-September to mid-November since 1987, it is one of the world's most important art biennials, alongside Venice, São Paulo, and Sydney. In addition, the Contemporary Istanbul art fair, which is especially prized by local collectors, is held every year in September. But the art scene in Istanbul also benefits from private sector support, with corporations and banks generously subsidizing the city's institutions. One example is a platform for contemporary art in Taksim, Akbank Sanat, founded in 1993, which is sponsored by a financial institution. Or Istanbul Modern, a private museum of modern and contemporary art established in 2004 by an industry group. Both institutions are located in the sprawling Beyoğlu district, which unites several neighborhoods including the art hubs of Taksim, Karaköy, Dolapdere, and Çukurcuma and forms at the same time the western focal point of the city. Here you'll find a number of galleries, such as Pilot, Galerist, Öktem & Aykut, and Zilberman Gallery. Since 2016, several galleries well worth visiting have relocated within Beyoğlu and have injected new energy into their surroundings: DirimArt, Gaia Gallery, and Pilevneli Gallery moved to Dolapdere in the north, C.A.M. Galeri and PG Art Gallery southwest to Çukurcuma. The nonprofit center SALT, undoubtedly one of the city's most significant art initiatives, is located in a former bank in Karaköy—once the Galata district. A fifteen-minute walk away and well worth a visit is the exhibition space Arter, founded in 2010 by the Vehbi Koç Foundation (VKF) of the well-known entrepreneurial Koç family. End of 2018, the VKF is also opening a museum, which will present its own collection as well as external exhibitions and a multidisciplinary accompanying program.

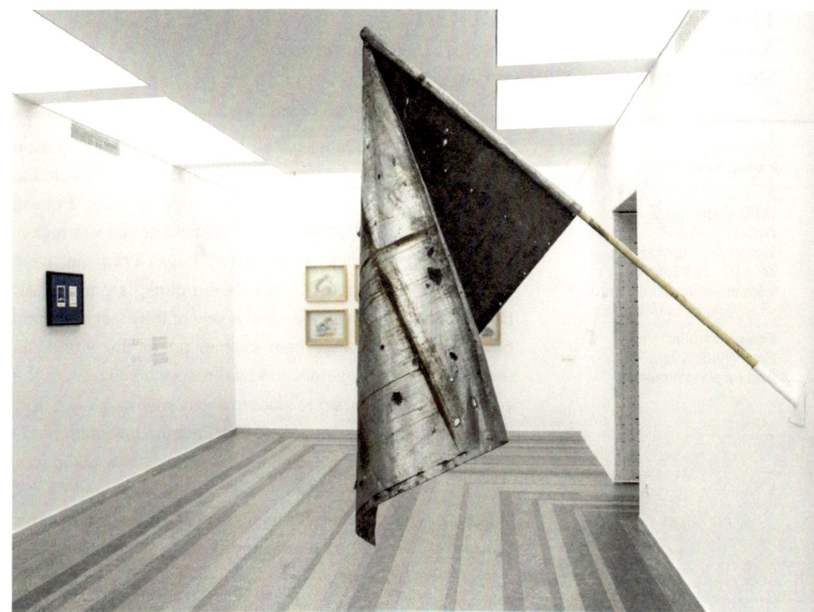

PINCHUK ART CENTRE

Blue-chip contemporary in the first private museum in the former USSR

Collector:
Victor Pinchuk

Address:
1/3-2, "A" Block
Velyka Vasylkivska/Baseyna vul.
01004 Kiev
Ukraine
Tel +00 44 5000858
info@pinchukartcentre.org
www.pinchukartcentre.org

Opening Hours:
Tues–Sun: 12–9pm

Within the span of a few years, Ukrainian billionaire Victor Pinchuk has asserted himself as one of the most powerful collectors on the international scene. He bought *Hanging Heart (Magenta/Gold),* by Jeff Koons, for a reported 23.6 million US dollars, and *99 Cent II Diptychon,* by Andreas Gursky, for a reported 3.3 million US dollars, setting a record price for both artists. Pinchuk has purchased other million-dollar artworks by the likes of blue-chip stars Peter Doig and Takashi Murakami. He reveals it all at his very popular Pinchuk Art Centre, founded in 2006, a colossal six-story building that was the first private museum opened in the former USSR; nearly a million visitors have already passed through its doors. "There is only one queue in the country," Pinchuk told *The New Yorker* in 2009: "ours."

THE FARJAM COLLECTION

A voyage from ancient Islamic art to contemporary Middle Eastern and Western art

Collector:
Farhad Farjam

Address:
DIFC Gate Village 4
Dubai
United Arab Emirates
Tel +971 4 3230303
info@farjamfoundation.org
www.farjamfoundation.org

Opening Hours:
Sun–Thurs: 10am–8pm
And by appointment.

Farhad Farjam, a Dubai-based Iranian industrialist, started his collection when he was still a student in New York in the 1970s. He bought the first piece of his collection of Persian miniatures for 2 000 US dollars, the cost of a semester's tuition. This resulted in, well, a lost semester. "It was a dramatic story for me that I never forget," he recalled during a panel at Art Dubai in 2010. Today Farjam owns one of the most important collections of privately held Islamic art in the world, an undertaking he considers a social responsibility. Over the years Farjam has turned to modern and contemporary art from the Middle East and the West. The Farjam Collection today includes artists like Mohammad Ehsai and Nja Mahdaoui, as well as Western icons Andy Warhol and Jean-Michel Basquiat. The collection forms the core of the eponymous foundation, which has committed itself to the promotion of intercultural dialogue.

JEAN-PAUL NAJAR FOUNDATION (JPNF)

European-American Post-Minimalist Art in a Bauhaus-inspired building

Collector:
Jean-Paul Najar

Address:
45 Alserkal Avenue
Street 17, Al Quoz
PO Box 928040
Dubai
United Arab Emirates
info@jpnajarfoundation.com
www.jpnajarfoundation.com

Opening Hours:
Sat–Thurs: 11am–6pm

Situated on Alserkal Avenue in the heart of Dubai's art quarter, the Jean-Paul Najar Foundation opened its doors to the public in 2016. Najar—an economist, photographer, and sculptor who spent most of his life in Paris—began collecting art in the mid-1960s, engaging in dialogues with many artists of that time. A pivotal figure for abstract art, he curated various exhibitions and published in-depth texts on the artists he had befriended. His exceptional collection includes works by Jene Highstein, Gordon Matta-Clark, Suzanne Harris, Marcia Hafif, and Linda Francis, among others. To create a private museum for her father's collected works, Deborah Najar Jossa brought the legendary architect, Mario Jossa, out of retirement to design a building with a Bauhaus-inspired interior. The foundation aims to ensure and expand on Najar's legacy through a mix of new acquisitions, educational programs, and temporary exhibitions.

DUBAI

Cities rarely feel as contradictory as Dubai: an artificial giant created virtually overnight, embedded within a seemingly surreal desert landscape. Nevertheless, a highly interesting art scene has taken root and grown at a blistering pace. One hotspot is Gate Village, where, next to large financial corporations, you'll find galleries like Cuadro Fine Art Gallery, Ayyam Gallery, and Tabari ArtSpace. Christie's is also here, which launched the first auction for international modern and contemporary art in the Middle East in 2006, making Dubai the region's most important center for the international secondary art market. Another pulsating focal point for the creative art scene is Alserkal Avenue in the Al Quoz district, where Rem Koolhaas's Concrete complex, opened in 2017, offers a variety of cultural events like exhibitions, performances, and conferences. Alongside installations in public spaces, cafes, and studios, you'll also find galleries like The Third Line, the Green Art Gallery, Grey Noise, the Gallery Isabelle van den Eynde, and New York's Leila Heller Gallery, as well as the Salsali Private Museum, featured in this publication. March is the best time to discover

Dubai's art scene, when Art Dubai is held at the Madinat Jumeirah—a fair that has played a key role in the development of the scene since 2007. At the same time as Art Dubai are other events like the Sikka Art Fair in the historical district of Al Fahidi, focusing on young art from around the Emirates. The Jameel Arts Center, one of the city's first nonprofit venues for contemporary art, opens at the end of 2018, giving visitors another reason to explore the diverse region. While Dubai represents more of the art market, neighboring Emirates impress with large-scale exhibitions and new institutions: the Sharhaj Biennial is held every two years in Sharhaj; the Louvre Abu Dhabi was completed in Abu Dhabi in 2017; and the National Museum of Qatar, also designed by star architect Jean Nouvel, opens its doors in Doha in late 2018.

SALSALI PRIVATE MUSEUM

A platform for collectors in Dubai's hub of creativity

Collector:
Ramin Salsali

Address:
Complex/Unit 14, Alserkal Avenue
Street 8, Al Quoz 1
Dubai
United Arab Emirates
Tel +971 4 3809600
spm@salsalipm.com
www.salsalipm.com

Opening Hours:
Sat: 1–5pm
Sun–Thurs: 11am–6pm
And by appointment.

Located in the industrial area Al Quoz 1—one of Dubai's designated hubs for arts and creativity—the Salsali Private Museum, which opened in 2011, is not just an exhibition space for Ramin Salsali's collection of contemporary art. It is also a platform for collectors who want to meet and exchange ideas, or to exhibit their own collections. "An art collection is an art in itself," Salsali says. "It should reveal to its audience a story more significant than any individual viewpoint." An Iranian consultant for the petrochemical industry, Salsali started collecting when he was a twenty-one-year-old student in Germany. Today he owns over 300 works by Middle Eastern artists such as Reza Derakshani, Mona Hatoum, and Shirin Neshat, which sit alongside international stars like Arman, Niki de Saint Phalle, Jonathan Meese, André Butzer, Fischli/Weiss, Meret Oppenheim, and Daniel Richter.

BARJEEL ART FOUNDATION

Modern and contemporary art from four corners of the Arab world

Collector:
Sultan Sooud Al-Qassemi

Address:
Maraya Art Centre
Al Qasba
Sharjah
United Arab Emirates
Tel +971 6 5566555
info@barjeelartfoundation.com
www.barjeelartfoundation.com

Opening hours vary depending on exhibition. Please check the website for the most current information.

The term "Arab world" comprises a vast territory spanning from the Middle East to North Africa, subsuming the Levant, Maghreb, Egypt, the Gulf Arab, and Iraq—places strongly characterized by their own history and culture. This internal diversity of the Arab world's countries lies at the basis of Sultan Sooud Al-Qassemi's art collection, which includes over 500 works by both modern and contemporary Arab artists, such as Shakir Hassan Al Said, Khaled Hafez, and Lara Baladi. Sultan Al-Qassemi spent over a decade amassing his collection, which was opened to the public in 2010, on the second floor of the Maraya Art Centre, in Al Qasba, the entertainment hub of Sharjah. "What's the point of art," he asked in the local daily newspaper *The National,* "if it is not shared?"

CLARINDA CARNEGIE ART MUSEUM (CCAM)

A double feature of contemporary art in the heart of America

Collectors:
Robert & Karen Duncan

Addresses:
300 N 16th Street
Clarinda, IA 51632
United States of America
Tel +1 712 8501175
www.clarindacarnegieartmuseum.com

Lincoln:
1828 N Street
Lincoln, NE 68508
United States of America

Opening Hours:
Clarinda:
Wed, Sun: 1–4pm
Lincoln:
By appointment only.

Over eighteen months, in 2013 and 2014, Robert and Karen Duncan opened not one but two exhibition spaces in the American heartland. The couple has spent the past thirty years building a collection of over 2000 works, by a varied cast of artists such as Bruce Nauman, Bernar Venet, and George Segal. Female artists are particularly well represented with major works by Louise Bourgeois, Georgia O'Keeffe, and Kiki Smith. While the Duncans periodically welcome visitors at their home by-appointment, they decided to open up their holdings even further. Wanting to give back to their hometown of Clarinda they purchased the city's former Carnegie Library, completely restored and refurbished it, and then turned it into an art museum for works from their collection. It follows The Assemblage, an exhibition space opened in 2013 in Lincoln, Nebraska, together with fellow collectors Marc and Kathryn LeBaron, providing access on a by-appointment basis.

TRANSFORMER STATION

International photographic art and a unique collaboration

Collectors:
Laura Ruth & Fred Bidwell

Address:
1460 West 29th Street
Cleveland, OH 44113
United States of America
Tel +1 216 9385429
info@transformerstation.org
www.transformerstation.org

Opening Hours:
Wed, Fri–Sat: 12–5pm
Thurs: 12–8pm
Sat–Sun: 10am–5pm

Laura Ruth and Fred Bidwell exhibit their collection in an erstwhile transformer station six months out of the year. Then they leave the exhibition rooms to the watchful eyes of the Cleveland Museum of Art, which uses the atmosphere of the old industrial building for exhibitions suited to the cool ambiance. This unique collaboration was decided before the Transformer Station's February 2013 opening, because both the Bidwells and the museum pursue the same goal of bringing smartly curated contemporary art exhibits to Cleveland. The collector couple's emphasis is on photography, having purchased works by Jessica Backhaus, Hiroshi Sugimoto, Philip-Lorca diCorcia, and Martin Parr. They also offer a perfect link to the curatorial mission of the museum by presenting historical positions like Walker Evans and Lee Friedlander.

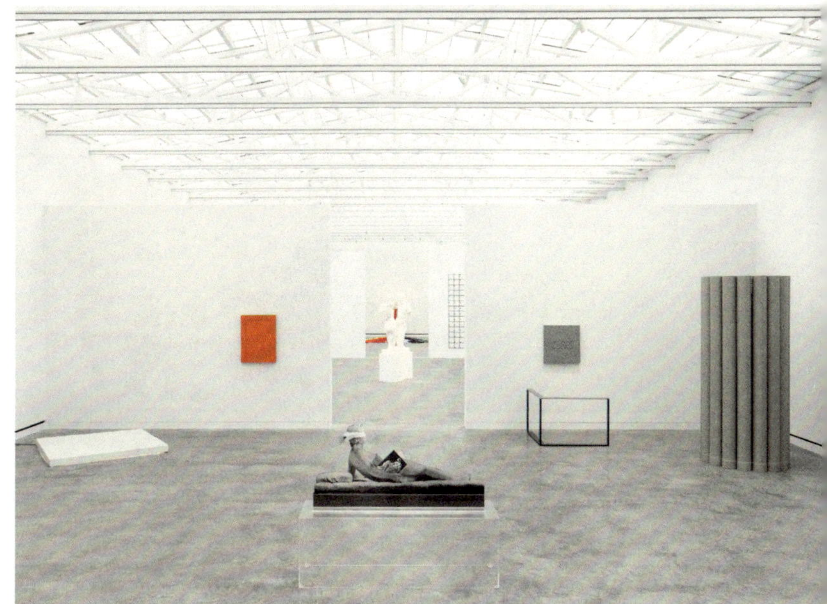

MAGAZZINO ITALIAN ART

Contemporary Italian Art on the Hudson River

Collectors:
Nancy Olnick & Giorgio Spanu

Address:
2700 Route 9
Cold Spring, NY 10516
United States of America
Tel. +1 845 6667202
info@magazzino.art
www.magazzino.art

Opening Hours:
Thurs–Mon: 11am–5pm
By appointment only.

It takes just over an hour's train ride from Grand Central Station, New York up the Hudson River to reach Cold Spring, and it is there that Nancy Olnick and Giorgio Spanu transformed the warehouse—*magazzino* in Italian—of a former computer manufacturing plant in 2017 into an elegant space for exhibiting contemporary Italian art from the 1960s to the present. Assembled over decades by the American-Italian couple, the collection focuses on Arte Povera, with plans to add a research library. The philosophy of an art form that typically combines natural and industrial materials is perfectly suited to the austere minimalism of the concrete buildings, which blend harmoniously into the landscape. Thematically curated shows are presented on over 1 600 square meters of exhibition space and feature works by artists such as Giulio Paolini, Michelangelo Pistoletto, Jannis Kounellis, Mario Merz, Giuseppe Penone, and Luciano Fabro.

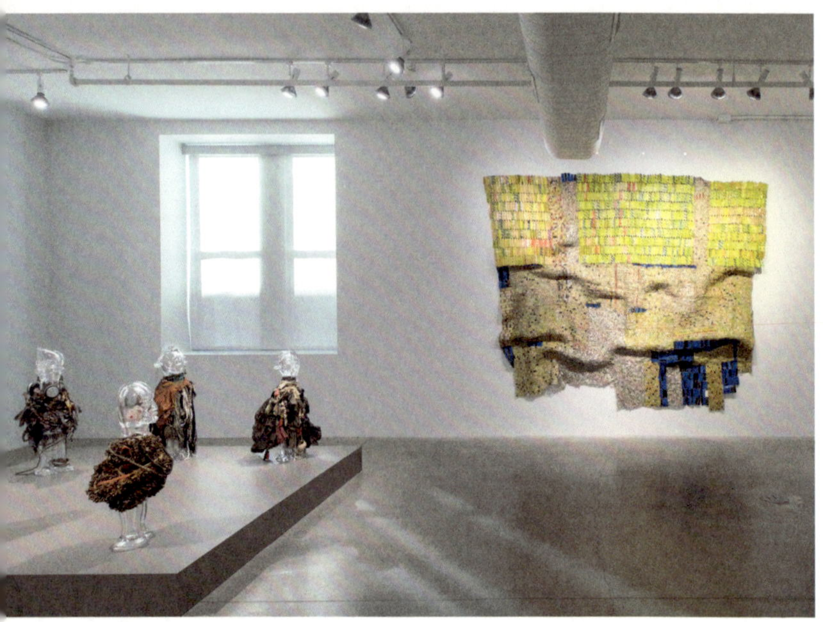

PIZZUTI COLLECTION

Meritorious Midwestern assemblage of the now

Collectors:
Ron & Ann Pizzuti

Address:
632 Park Street
Columbus, OH 43215
United States of America
Tel +1 614 2804004
info@pizzuticollection.org
www.pizzuticollection.org

Opening Hours:
Wed, Fri–Sat: 10am–5pm
Thurs: 10am–8pm
Sun: 12–5pm

The Pizzuti Collection is one of the newest entrants onto the American private museum circuit—one of the most dynamic, too. Real-estate mogul Ron Pizzuti assembled the estimated 2 000-work collection over the past four decades, starting with Karel Appel's *Circus People,* in 1974. The print hung in the collection's inaugural exhibition, in September 2013. Spread over a three-story building, which formerly served as the headquarters of an insurance company, the Pizzuti Collection rotates at least once per year. It features a wide range of artists from the collection, from established names like Carroll Dunham and David Hammons to emerging exponents like Florian Meisenberg. Pizzuti is particularly keen on works by Cuban artists, a passion that began after a trip to the country in 2009. He also recently launched a sculpture garden on the premises with works by Tom Friedman, Thomas Houseago, and Jason Middlebrook, among others.

THE GOSS-MICHAEL FOUNDATION

A must-see for all fans of Young British Artists

Collectors:
Kenny Goss & George Michael

Address:
1305 Wycliff Avenue
Suite 120
Dallas, TX 75207
United States of America
Tel +1 214 6960555
info@g-mf.org
www.g-mf.org

Opening hours:
Tues–Fri: 10am–4pm

The strong contingent of Young British Artists in Dallas, Texas, is the result of a longstanding alliance between art dealer Kenny Goss and the now-late pop star George Michael. Both shared a great sympathy for Damien Hirst's marinated cadavers and their themes of death and ephemerality, and for Tracey Emin's often eroticized installations. Sarah Lucas's feminist statements are also represented in the collection. Getting a feel for the criteria that the Goss-Michael Foundation employed in assembling its collection has been possible since 2007. Today, approximately 500 works by over a hundred artists are represented, including Gilbert & George, Op Art-queen Bridget Riley, or provocateurs Jake & Dinos Chapman. Many works are from the 1990s, which, according to the collector duo, were the formative years for an entire artistic generation.

NASHER SCULPTURE CENTER

A private collection of masterpieces every museum dreams of

Collectors:
Patsy & Raymond Nasher

Address:
2001 Flora Street
Dallas, TX 75201
United States of America
Tel +1 214 2425100
www.nashersculpturecenter.org

Opening Hours:
Tues–Sun: 11am–5pm

Patsy and Raymond Nasher began obeying one command in the 1950s, and they have stayed true to it ever since: only collect sculpture. More specifically, by modernist artists like Henry Moore, August Rodin, Pablo Picasso, and Raymond Duchamp-Villon. These works are accompanied by masterpieces by Alexander Calder, Richard Serra, and Claes Oldenburg. Every single object in this collection is museum-worthy; taken as a whole, they show the development of an entire epoch. Since 2003 the Nasher Sculpture Center has presented its holdings in exciting contrasts and supplemented by matching new acquisitions. Built by architect and Pritzker-Prize winner Renzo Piano, the pavilion-like structure, situated at the end of a park in Dallas's arts district, allows for a perspective that establishes a relationship between the robust outdoor sculptures and the fragile objects located inside.

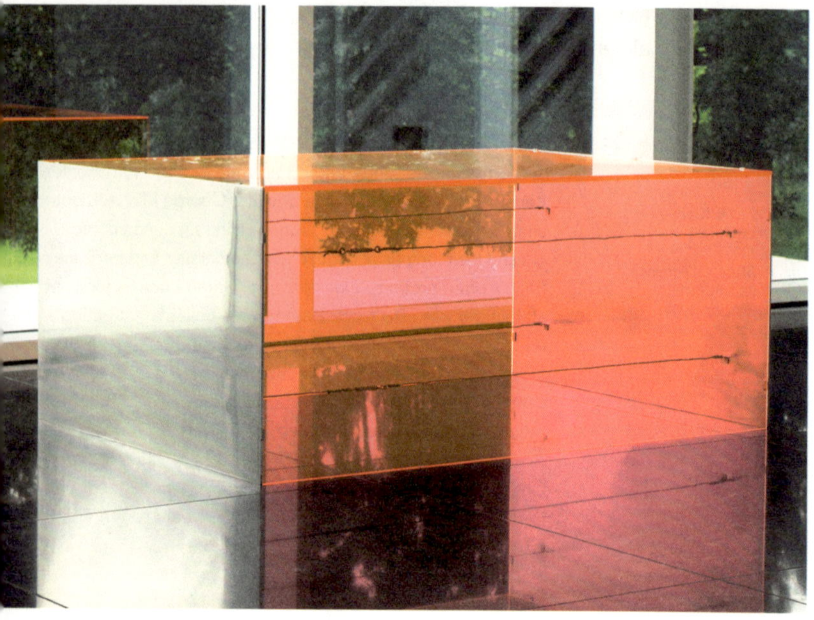

THE WAREHOUSE

Two major United States collections in dialogue

Collectors:
Cindy & Howard Rachofsky
Amy & Vernon Faulconer

Address:
14105 Inwood Road
Dallas, TX 75244
United States of America
Tel +1 214 4422875
www.thewarehousedallas.org

By appointment only.

Cindy and Howard Rachofsky open their Rachofsky House, designed by Richard Meier, for events devoted to their charitable interests. But art lovers can find parts of the collection with works by Gerhard Richter, Lucio Fontana, Sigmar Polke, Piero Manzoni, Mario Merz, Kazuo Shiraga, and Atsuko Tanaka at a second address. Since 2013 Cindy and Howard Rachofsky have shared a large industrial building called The Warehouse—divided into sixteen galleries—with fellow collector Amy Faulconer, who, together with her now-deceased husband, also assembled an impressive collection with works by artists such as Anselm Kiefer, Anish Kapoor, Bridget Riley, Cecily Brown, Jaume Plensa, Kara Walker, and James Turrell. The result is an exciting dialogue of exhibits and, because collaborating collectors are a rarity elsewhere, a truly innovative experiment.

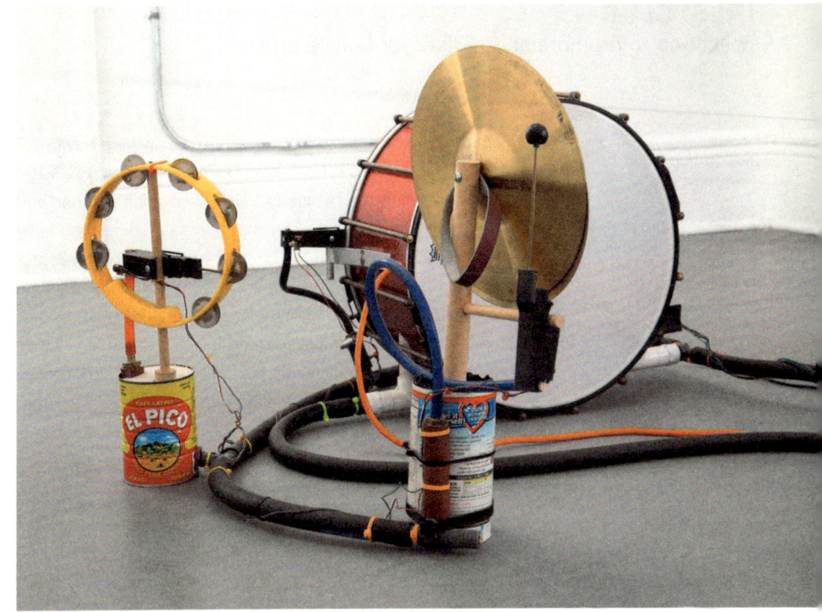

THE DIKEOU COLLECTION

Siblings collect artists they find to be inspiring

Collectors:
Devon & Pany Dikeou

Addresses:
1615 California Street, Suite 515
Denver, CO 80202
United States of America
Tel +1 303 6233001

Dikeou Pop-Up:
Colfax
312 East Colfax Avenue
Denver, CO 80203
United States of America

info@dikeoucollection.org
www.dikeoucollection.org

Opening Hours:
Wed–Fri: 11am–5pm
And by appointment.

Artist Devon Dikeou and her brother Pany are less interested in establishing themselves than in making known the colleagues they deem important. Among them are established names like Momoyo Torimitsu, Vik Muniz, and Wade Guyton. Above all, the collection suggests a preference for subtle humor, which can be found in the works by Dan Asher, Jonathan Horowitz, Johannes VanDerBeek, or Margaret Lee. The Dikeou's exhibition space, in Denver, matches their taste in art: an odd bricolage of styles in the form of an historical office building from 1902 that has retained its retro charm. For the most recent acquisitions the collection has expanded to include work by painter Joshua Abelow and installations by Devon Dikeou. Another specialty lies a few blocks away—Dikeou Pop-Up: Colfax, a second address featuring the work by Rainer Ganahl, Lizzi Bougatsos, Anicka Yi, among others—as well as an enormous archive of vinyl records.

GIRLS' CLUB

A collection to promote and rediscover female artists

Collectors:
Francie Bishop Good &
David Horvitz

Address:
723 Northeast 2nd Avenue
Fort Lauderdale, FL 33304
United States of America
Tel +1 954 8289151
admin@girlsclubcollection.org
www.girlsclubcollection.org

Please check the website for the most current information on opening hours.

With dazzling names like Beatriz Milhazes, Elizabeth Peyton, or the American concept art-icon Barbara Kruger, you'll get noticed fast in the art business. But Francie Bishop Good and David Horvitz could name dozens of female artists who have been unjustly overlooked, which is why the American collector pair created a private foundation called the Girls' Club in 2006. Housed in a former warehouse in the Fort Lauderdale area, which has been transformed into a bona-fide creative hub in recent years, the couple always comes up with inventive new ways of presenting its collection, now comprising more than 900 works by female artists. The two collectors have directed their attention, for example, toward the elaborate works of Sandy Winters, born in 1949, or the stunning photography of Tracey Baran, who documented the inhabitants of a small New York town before her untimely death at age thirty-three, in 2008.

OLIVER RANCH FOUNDATION

A sculpture park where art responds to nature

Collectors:
Nancy & Steve Oliver

Address:
22205 River Road
Geyserville, CA 95441
United States of America
Tel +1 510 4129090-210
www.oliverranchfoundation.org

Opening Hours:
Fri–Sun: Only guided tours with prior registration. Group tours upon request.

Driving through the countryside north of San Francisco to visit the region's vineyards is no longer a hidden secret. But Nancy and Steve Oliver's sculpture park still is. In the mid-1980s the two decided to complement the picturesque landscape with art. The first sculpture was *Shepherd's Muse,* by Judith Shea, an allusion to sheep farming, the collectors' shared hobby. Sculptures by Miroslaw Balka, Fred Sandback, Richard Serra, Bill Fontana, and Bruce Nauman soon followed. The Oliver Ranch Foundation is based on the idea that art must directly respond to nature. Each work is created in dialogue with the artist. The realization of a work often takes several years, as was the case with Ann Hamilton's accessible *Tower,* the centerpiece of the Olivers' collection. Visitors can take a seat on one of two curiously constructed staircases, while performances and plays are presented on the other.

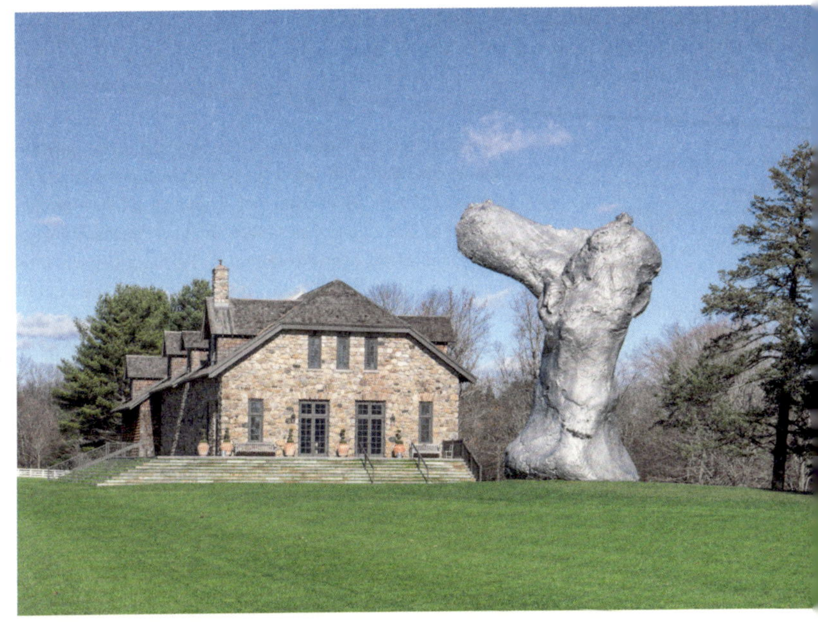

THE BRANT FOUNDATION ART STUDY CENTER

Important American art from the 1960s to the present

Collector:
Peter M. Brant

Address:
941 North Street
Greenwich, CT 06831
United States of America
Tel +1 203 8690611
info@brantfoundation.org
www.brantfoundation.org

Opening Hours:
Mon–Fri: 10am–4pm
By appointment only.

He sits at the source and is one of the first to know who the artists of tomorrow will be: Peter M. Brant—the owner of Brant Publications, chairman and CEO of a large paper manufacturing concern, and a coproducer of movies about important artists of the twentieth century, such as Jean-Michel Basquiat and Jackson Pollock. Over the decades, Brant has amassed one of the world's largest and most distinguished collections of American contemporary artists, including Andy Warhol, Julian Schnabel, and Keith Haring. His focus on American art stems from his interest in the American sense of life, which he finds in every work anew. The spectrum runs from the positive attitude of Jeff Koons to the provocative criticism of performer-sculptor Paul McCarthy. Appropriately, since 2009, a large part of the collection has been exhibited in something quite traditionally American: a former barn.

THE MENIL COLLECTION

An amazing collection with the format of a metropolitan museum

Collectors:
Dominique & John de Menil

Address:
1533 Sul Ross Street
Houston, TX 77006
United States of America
Tel +1 713 5259400
info@menil.org
www.menil.org

Opening Hours:
Wed–Sun: 11am–7pm

The legacy of Dominique und John de Menil is not only the imposing museum with numerous individual galleries for works by Mark Rothko, Cy Twombly, or Byzantine art. The couple began their collection in the 1940s and have amassed invaluable works of art over the decades: Fernand Léger, Henri Matisse, or Pablo Picasso mark the entry point of this incredible collection, and Jean-Michel Basquiat, Eric Fischl, Cindy Sherman, and Robert Gober belong to the list of later additions. Between the two groups hang the heroes of American postwar painting: Barnett Newman, Willem de Kooning, or Jasper Johns. Dominique de Menil, who passed away in 1997, had survived her husband for more than twenty years. She founded their museum in 1987. Mid-2017 marks the opening of the Menil Drawing Institute (MDI), the first independent institution in the country dedicated exclusively to the presentation and research of contemporary drawing.

THE SETH STOLBUN COLLECTION

Today's patronage of contemporary art

Collector:
Seth Stolbun

Address:
Houston, TX
United States of America
seth@stolbun.org
www.stolbun.org

By e-mail appointment only.

Seth Stolbun comes from a family of art enthusiasts. As a child he loved the prints of Joan Miró that hung on the wall at home. His first work—by Damien Hirst—he bought in 2010, followed by various works on paper. But he no longer concentrates solely on graphic works. Stolbun's collection, which is spread around several residences in Houston, New York, and Aspen, includes works by artists such as Anish Kapoor, Grayson Perry, and Rafaël Rozendaal, among others. "The collection is focused on a larger question of what it means to be a patron of the arts in the twenty-first century," explains Stolbun, who has a Master of Fine Arts himself. The collector, who finances various exhibitions in the US and also supports artist residencies, primarily seeks out artists who question standard models of art production. An example is the New York artist partnership Ultraviolet Production House, which supplies collectors with do-it-yourself art kits.

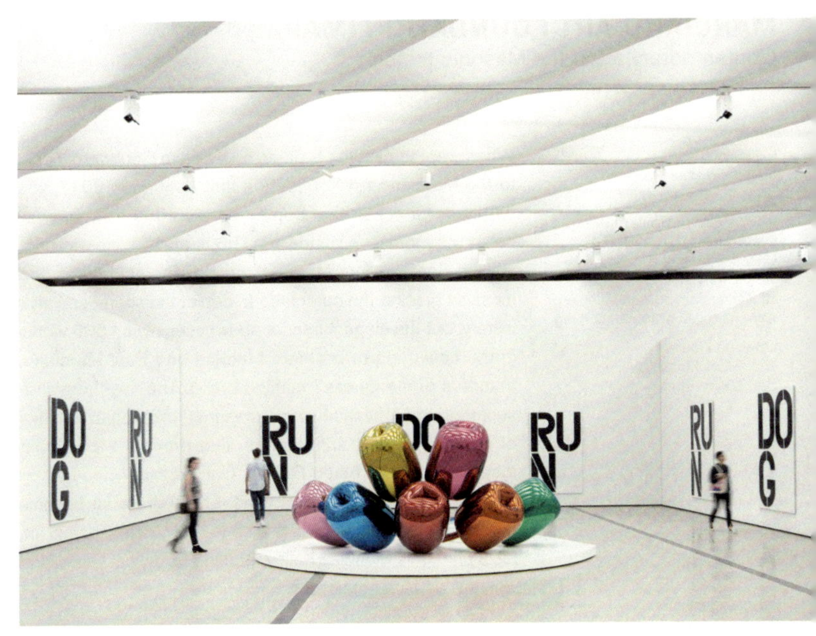

THE BROAD

A compendium of contemporary art in downtown L.A.

Collectors:
Eli & Edythe Broad

Address:
221 S. Grand Avenue
Los Angeles, CA 90012
United States of America
curator@thebroad.org
www.thebroad.org

Opening Hours:
Tues–Wed: 11am–5pm
Thurs–Fri: 11am–8pm
Sat: 10am–8pm
Sun: 10am–6pm

Eli and Edythe Broad's philanthropic efforts in the arts are so extensive it can be hard to keep them straight. Their gifts have earned them names on two museums—the Broad Contemporary Art Museum at the Los Angeles County Museum of Art (LACMA) and the Eli and Edythe Broad Art Museum at Michigan State University (Broad MSU). But the collectors opened a more private affair in 2015, called, simply, The Broad. It's the first of the three institutions to focus solely on the couple's private collection and that of The Broad Art Foundation, which they founded in 1984. Together, the over 2 000 works by more than 200 artists, among them Jeff Koons, Kara Walker, and William Kentridge, represent a veritable compendium of the very best contemporary art. Located in downtown L.A., in a building designed by Diller Scofidio + Renfro, The Broad sports two floors of exhibition space and a vast vault that houses the couple's immense catalogue of works.

MARCIANO ART FOUNDATION (MAF)

Contemporary art at the Masonic temple

Collectors:
Maurice & Paul Marciano

Address:
4357 Wilshire Boulevard
Los Angeles, CA 90010
United States of America
Tel +1 424 204 7555
info@marcianoartfoundation.org
www.marcianoartfoundation.org

Opening Hours:
Thurs–Fri: 11am–5pm
Sat: 10am–6pm

When walking past the building on Wilshire Boulevard, home to the Marciano Art Foundation that opened in 2017, you hardly get a sense that contemporary art is tucked away behind its impressive façade: the 1960s-era building was originally a Scottish Rite Masonic temple. The sculptures and mosaics gracing the outer façade depict the secret society's history, but the elegant interior showcases over 1 500 works in the collection of brothers Maurice and Paul Marciano, founders of the Guess? fashion brand. The five-thousand-square-meter exhibition space presents revolving exhibitions of international art-scene stars, and there is a particular focus on works by Albert Oehlen, Christopher Wool, Takashi Murakami, and Paul McCarthy. Since Los Angeles has become one of the most important global centers for contemporary art, local phenoms like Mike Kelley, Sterling Ruby, Jim Shaw, and Jonas Wood are not to be omitted here.

FREDERICK R. WEISMAN ART FOUNDATION

The Who's Who of Modernism, from Surrealism to Pop

Collectors:
Frederick R. & Billie Milam Weisman

Address:
265 North Carolwood Drive
Los Angeles, CA 90077
United States of America
Tel +1 310 2775321
tours@weismanfoundation.org
www.weismanfoundation.org

Opening Hours:
Mon–Fri: 10:30am and 2pm
Only guided tours with prior registration.

It's as if Billie Milam and Frederick R. Weisman were still living in their mansion. Paintings by Abstract Expressionists like Willem de Kooning or Mark Rothko hang together with Pop Art works over the fireplace and sectional sofas. Yet the collector couple had purchased the 1920s house only as an exhibition space. Weisman, the son of Russian immigrants, and a passionate art buyer, established a foundation in 1982 to preserve his esteemed collection after his death. Now, guided tours through the villa and adjacent gallery showcase the work that was most important to him: European Modernism from Paul Cézanne and Pablo Picasso, Surrealists like Max Ernst, and postwar art by Alberto Giacometti, Alexander Calder, or Robert Rauschenberg. Way too much art for a mansion, and all of it museum-worthy, which why the forward-looking collector founded several American museums before his death, in 1994.

LOS ANGELES

Los Angeles's chief cultural contribution might be found up on the silver screen, but the city's art scene is booming too. Artists are moving to the city in droves, from the art meccas of New York and the somewhat more artist-friendly Berlin. L.A.'s advantages are obvious: its rents are still relatively reasonable and its populace is affluent, and there's an ever-growing cadre of contemporary art enthusiasts. The city's institutions are also flourishing. The Broad, which opened its doors to the public in 2015, houses the collection of real-estate magnate Eli Broad and his wife Edythe. Just a few paces away from the arts and culture hub of Grand Avenue is one of three venues belonging to the Museum of Contemporary Art, Los Angeles (MOCA). The museum's largest space, the Geffen Contemporary, is just minutes away as well. Also located nearby is the Institute of Contemporary Art, Los Angeles (ICA LA), which opened in late 2017. From here, head half an hour west by car (traffic allowing) and you'll hit the Los Angeles County Museum of Art (LACMA), the largest of the city's art institutions. On the way there, it's worth stopping by the Underground Museum, where artists like Josef Albers or Imi Knoebel are presented in a part of the city where you'll otherwise only find car repair shops or self-storage spaces. But L.A. has much more than just museums to offer. Fairs like Art Los Angeles Contemporary (ALAC) or the LA Art Show draw numerous collectors to the city each year. And some of the world's most influential galleries have also opened outposts here: Sprüth Magers can be found across from LACMA since 2016, and Hauser & Wirth resides in a former flour mill in downtown L.A. What's more, there are exciting exhibition spaces like Night Gallery, Ghebaly Gallery, or Freedman Fitzpatrick. In East Hollywood, Lauri Firstenberg and Anthony James at There-There, show new works straight out of the artists' studios. As the saying goes, if you want to see what's next in North American art, go west, young man!

DEPART FOUNDATION

Young American art in Miami Beach, Malibu, and Rome

Collectors:
Pierpaolo Barzan & Valeria Sorci

Addresses:
1825 Collins Avenue
Miami Beach, FL 33139
United States of America

Malibu:
3822 Cross Creek Road, Suite 3844
Malibu, CA 90265
United States of America

info@departfoundation.org
www.departfoundation.org

By e-mail appointment only.

Since 2005, Pierpaolo Barzan has collected primarily young American art. "At first I was driven by the desire to build a collection that reflects my generation," Barzan explains. "So I was interested in artists like Sterling Ruby, Joe Bradley, and Nate Lowman. After that, it was only natural to continue with the next generation." Today, the collector and his wife Valeria Sorci own about 600 works by artists like Cory Arcangel, Grear Patterson, Lucien Smith, or Kour Pour. Parts of the collection have been on view in a permanent project space inside the Hotel Nautilus in Miami Beach since 2015. In addition, the couple organizes presentations in collaboration with institutions in Rome and establishes temporary project spaces, including a two-year exhibition concept in Malibu, started in 2017. By collaborating with young emerging artists in particular, it seeks to promote cross-cultural exchange between artists from Europe and America.

CIFO—CISNEROS FONTANALS ART FOUNDATION

A Latin American art evades pigeonholing in this expansive collection

Collector:
Ella Fontanals-Cisneros

Address:
1018 North Miami Avenue
Miami, FL 33136
United States of America
Tel +1 305 4553380
info@cifo.org
www.cifo.org

Opening Hours:
Thurs–Fri: 12–6pm
Sat–Sun: 10am–4pm

Anyone who equates Latin American art with colorful, mythical painting will be pleasantly challenged by Ella Fontals Cisnero's collection. Forty years of continuous collecting offers stellar insight into the abstract, geometric language of Jesús Rafael Soto or Lygia Clark. The centerpiece is a work by Julio Le Parc, whose hulking sculpture at Documenta 3, the *Continuel-Mobile*, was comprised of flexible metal discs that scattered light about the room. It was stored in boxes for decades, but now it fits perfectly in a former department store that was transformed into an exhibition hall by the prize-winning architect Rene Gonzalez in 2005. Photography, video, and installation art form the 1 400-work collection, each given equal treatment. There's also an increasing amount of contemporary art—by Francis Alÿs or Ernesto Neto, for example—unrestrained by either geography or theme.

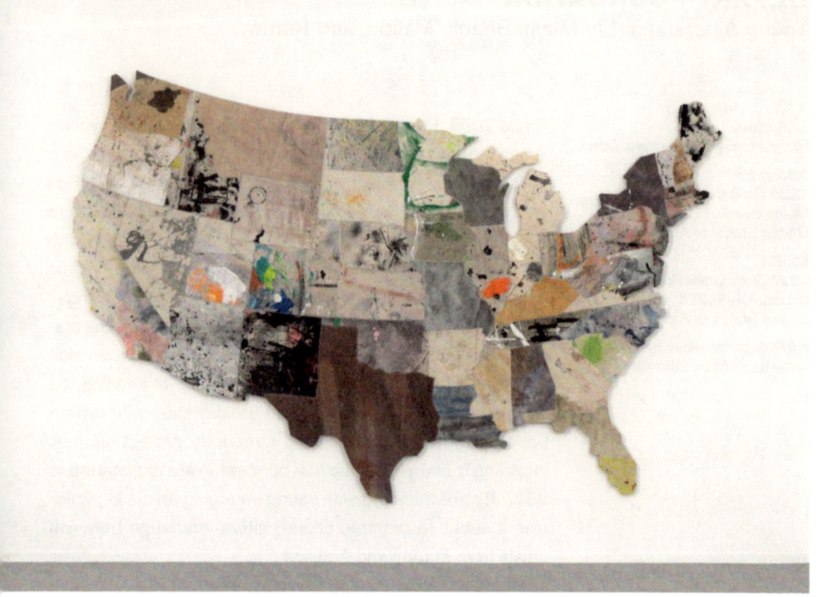

DE LA CRUZ COLLECTION—CONTEMPORARY ART SPACE

Emerging artists mix with established positions

Collectors:
Rosa & Carlos de la Cruz

Address:
23 Northeast 41st Street
Miami, FL 33137
United States of America
Tel +1 305 5766112
info@delacruzcollection.org
www.delacruzcollection.org

Opening Hours:
Tues–Sat: 10am–4pm

Wherever Rosa and Carlos de la Cruz show up art dealers get nervous. They count among the so-called group of super-collectors, whose enthusiasm and joy for acquiring art seem to have no limits. There's always room in the collection for one more work—preferably a large-scale one—by Thomas Houseago, Sterling Ruby, or Glenn Ligon. The couple is intensely interested in new movements, acquiring them for their private museum, which opened in Miami's Design District in 2009. This is how the work of up-and-coming artists like Nate Lowman or Dan Colen made it into the collection. With purchases of Cosima von Bonin, Isa Genzken, Félix González-Torres, Wade Guyton, Martin Creed, or Christopher Wool, the de la Cruzes demonstrate that their interests also extend to complex theoretical works. Each year the exhibition is rotated for Art Basel Miami Beach. Additionally, the museum offers an extensive program of lectures and workshops by artists, all free of charge.

MIAMI

For many in the art world, Miami represents an annual December pilgrimage to Art Basel Miami Beach and its numerous satellite fairs. In its nearly sixteen-year existence, the fair has transformed into one of the true magnets of the global art scene. The captivating strength of this event, however, means that so many of the city's highlights can easily be overlooked. One of these is unquestionably the Pérez Art Museum Miami (PAMM), which opened its doors to the public in 2013. Thanks to a major gift from real estate mogul Jorge M. Pérez, the museum is housed in an architectural masterpiece designed by Swiss architects Herzog & de Meuron. Since 2015, Franklin Sirmans, a curator known for his long-time advocacy of greater diversity in the art world, continues PAMM's efforts to strengthen the importance of Latin American art. The PAMM is part of the Miami Art Museums Alliance (MAMA), initiated to increase the profile of the institutions in the fifty-one weeks of the year when Art Basel isn't in town. Other highlights outside of the fair season include the Bass Museum of Art, a museum for contemporary art that reopened in Miami Beach in 2016, as well as the Institute of Contemporary Art, Miami (ICA Miami). For Art Basel Miami Beach 2017, the latter inaugurated its new building in Miami's Design District—featuring more than twice the amount of exhibition space as its former building—with heavyweight artist names like Roy Lichtenstein, Pablo Picasso, and Anna Oppermann. Alongside these institutions, the city leads the US in its number of publicly accessible, private collections, all of which are well worth a look. But, the ever-more-popular field of street art is where Miami truly shines—especially in Wynwood. Compared to other cities that have clamped down on street art in recent years, late real-estate magnate Tony Goldman essentially legalized it in the neighborhood when he began redeveloping its warehouses in 2009, attracting landmark works by Shepard Fairey, Os Gemeos, Ryan McGinnes, and AVAF, among others.

THE MARGULIES COLLECTION AT THE WAREHOUSE

Big-name photographers and sculptors

Collector:
Martin Z. Margulies

Address:
591 Northwest 27th Street
Miami, FL 33127
United States of America
Tel +1 305 5761051
mcollection@bellsouth.net
www.marguliesware house.com

Opening Hours:
October–April
Tues–Sat: 11am–4pm

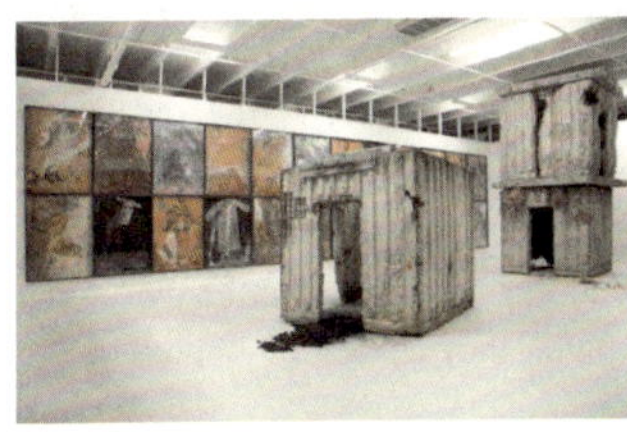

Old and new photography, from Helen Levitt to Cindy Sherman, videos and installations by Sara Barker, Bill Viola, or minimalistic light artist Iván Navarro count among the interests of the real-estate tycoon Martin Z. Margulies—a special niche not for everyone. His collection, which has been overseen by curator Katherine Hinds since the 1980s, is situated in a former warehouse. There you also find must-haves for any international collection: Richard Serra, Donald Judd, Dan Flavin, Jannis Kounellis, Michelangelo Pistoletto. Margulies combines these with Surrealist sculptures by Joan Miró, objects by Franz West, or a large-scale installation work by Anselm Kiefer—artists separated chronologically by just a few decades but also by entire artistic epochs. Such fissures, however, excite the collector and uniquely mark his rotating exhibits.

CRAIG ROBINS COLLECTION

A collection where art meets design

Collector:
Craig Robins

Address:
3841 Northeast 2nd Avenue,
Suite 400
Miami, FL 33137
United States of America
Tel +1 305 5318700
tiffany@dacra.com

Opening Hours:
Mon–Fri: 9am–5pm
By appointment only.

If anyone knows how art and design should be displayed together, it's Craig Robins. The real-estate agent founded Design Miami in 2005 as a companion to Art Basel Miami Beach and thereby managed to make a discredited Art Déco district chic and expensive once again. His collection, housed in his office building, brings together both fine art and fine design with consistency: paintings by Thomas Scheibitz, Kai Althoff, or Marlene Dumas meet classical furniture by Jean Prouvé, Charlotte Perriand, or Ron Arad, a contemporary design icon. Robins arranges the works with an eye toward form and content. It's not surprising that Cosima von Bonin or Mike Kelley are on the list of his favorite artists: both have extended their range to create sculptures that integrate furniture, plush, and even ambient music.

RUBELL FAMILY COLLECTION/ CONTEMPORARY ARTS FOUNDATION

The most resonant names in Western art united in one collection

Collectors:
Mera & Donald Rubell

Address:
Miami, FL
United States of America
Tel +1 305 5736090
info@rfc.museum
www.rfc.museum

Please check the website for the most current information on opening hours.

They are America's super-collectors, with museum-sized exhibition spaces, and are also exhibition project sponsors. Their philosophy is clear and consistent: for four decades Mera and Donald Rubell have only purchased art that resonates with both of them. They have seen eye-to-eye over 1 500 times thus far, and have acquired work by artists including Bruce Nauman, Jeff Koons, Lawrence Weiner, Gerhard Richter, Richard Prince, and Keith Haring. Another highlight is German photography, from August Sander to the Düsseldorf Becher School, including Thomas Ruff and Andreas Gursky. Since 1993, part of their collection has been shown in a remodeled warehouse and adjacent sculpture garden. In 2019, however, the collection is moving: this time a warehouse is being renovated in the neighboring, up-and-coming district of Allapattah. The Rubells are aware that their market power can influence artists' careers—but ultimately they collect out of passion.

THE HESS ART COLLECTION, NAPA

Museum highlights from Europe and America in the gentle hills of Napa Valley

Collector:
Donald M. Hess

Address:
4411 Redwood Road
Napa, CA 94558
United States of America
Tel +1 707 2551144
info@hesscollection.com
www.hesscollection.com/art

Opening Hours:
Mon–Sun: 10am–5:30pm

Additional exhibition locations:
Salta, Argentina, p. 17

He sold the family brewery. He started and successfully built up a Swiss mineral water brand and later sold it to Coca-Cola. From that day on, Donald M. Hess, the son of Swiss-American parents, was able to devote his time to his two true passions: wine and art. Hess now owns vineyards and art collections in two locations: the Argentine Andes and the US. He purchased his primary residence in California's Napa Valley in 1978. At Mount Veeder, wine tasting is not the only attraction. The two-hour drive from San Francisco is worth making for other reasons as well: integrated into the rustic 1903 building is roughly one-quarter of Hess's 1 000-work art collection, spread over two expansive levels. Works by Francis Bacon, Franz Gertsch, Anselm Kiefer, Gerhard Richter, or Per Kirkeby are true jewels: nowhere else in California can you see a greater concentration of such high-quality pieces.

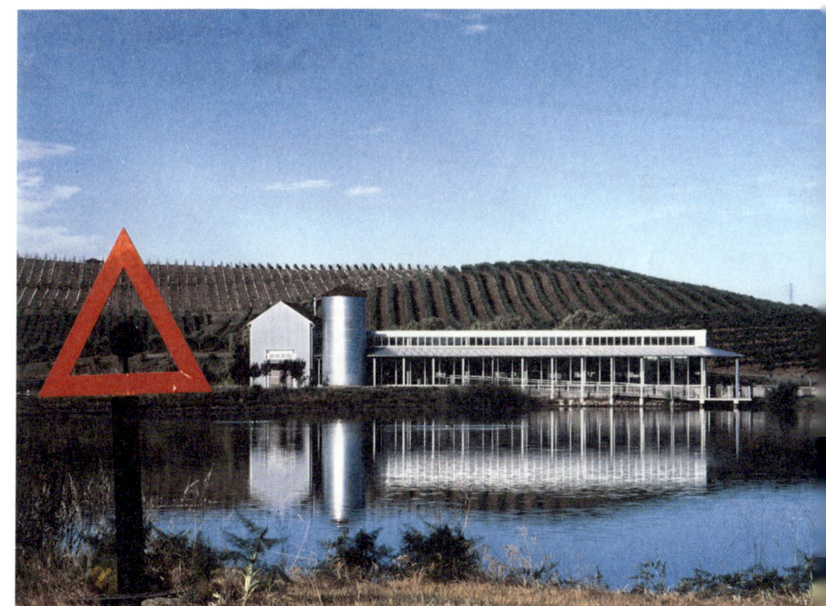

DI ROSA CENTER FOR CONTEMPORARY ART

Nature and art in almost equal standing

Collectors:
Rene & Veronica di Rosa

Address:
5200 Sonoma Highway
Napa, CA 94559
United States of America
Tel +1 707 2265991
tours@dirosaart.org
www.dirosaart.org

Opening Hours:
Wed–Sun: 10am–4pm
Only guided tours with prior online registration.

Nestled between vineyards and expansive open space, the collection of the now-late Rene di Rosa and his wife Veronica has been open to the public since 1997. Everything here seems to be focused on the local: the large outdoor sculptures as well as the works presented in four elongated buildings were all made by regional artists. The painterly landscape is just as important to the collectors as the animals who make it their home. What shouldn't be overlooked: artists like Mark di Suvero, Bruce Nauman, and Larry Sultan, or the painter Raymond Saunders all spent a number of years in California, and are therefore included in the portfolio of the collection alongside artists who are not as known internationally, such as Mildred Howard or Joan Brown. Today the collection—including newly added commissioned works—can be viewed in a variety of guided tours throughout the year.

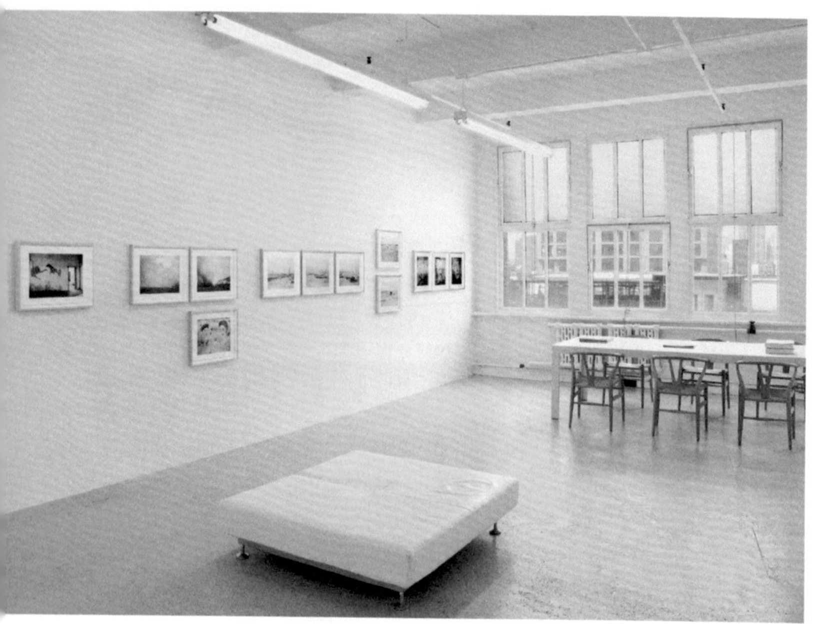

THE WALTHER COLLECTION— PROJECT SPACE NEW YORK

African and Asian photo art in dialogue with Western classics

Collector:
Artur Walther

Address:
526 West 26th Street, Suite 718
New York, NY 10001
United States of America
Tel +1 212 3520683
contact@walthercollection.com
www.walthercollection.com

Opening Hours:
Tues–Sat: 12–6pm
And by appointment.

Additional exhibition locations:
Neu-Ulm, Germany, p. 112

Having a second space in New York City makes sense, particularly for globally connected collectors like Artur Walther, founder of the Neu-Ulm-based Walther Collection, a top-notch German venue opened in 2010 that specializes in contemporary and classic photography. For Walther, who has long lived on the Hudson, establishing an address in New York City was entirely logical. Here, he sits on the committee of both the Whitney Museum of American Art and the International Center of Photography (ICP), and the city is also where he makes numerous international contacts, which benefit his German location as well. Since 2011, the Walther Collection has been located in a 160-square-meter space inside a historical landmark, the West Chelsea Art Building—ten floors of galleries and artists' studios. The collection's cosmopolitan perspective includes African and Asian works, and its rotating three-month schedule offers both new discoveries and modern masters.

NEW YORK

The New York art scene is thriving like never before. With this growth comes a shifting and expanding geographic landscape for the city's dealers, artists, and museums. A majority of New York's most important galleries showing established and blue-chip artists still remain in Chelsea—including Hauser & Wirth, which is moving into its own building designed by Selldorf Architects in 2019. Meanwhile, the more classical environs of the Upper East Side also attract an increasing number of major dealers who occupy spaces in historical townhouses. Cologne and Berlin veteran Daniel Buchholz, for instance, opened his first New York space in 2015, placing it a stone's throw away from the Metropolitan Museum of Art, and longtime Chelsea inhabitant Barbara Gladstone quietly launched an additional space uptown the same year. While a select number of spaces uptown such as Venus Over Manhattan and Half Gallery offer up a roster of emerging artists, the most-exciting young talents are to be found on the Lower East Side. Here the artists run the galleries themselves, like Essex Flowers, Bodega, and Regina Rex, or are represented by dynamic young art dealers like

Bridget Donahue and 56 Henry. Brooklyn remains home to the greatest number of artists—and increasingly prominent galleries such as Clearing and The Journal Gallery. Brooklyn's most southern points have continued to expand their offerings of contemporary art as well. Pioneer Works, a nonprofit exhibition space and residency, continues to put on impressive programming in Red Hook. But it's not just the galleries that are on the move. The Whitney Museum of American Art inaugurated its new Meatpacking District location in 2015. Meanwhile, the Breuer Building—the Whitney's home for nearly fifty years—reopened in March 2016 as The Met Breuer under the temporary guardianship of the Metropolitan Museum of Art, breathing new life into the museum's contemporary art department. The only real challenge to seeing unparalleled art in New York? Keeping up with where to go next.

WEST COLLECTION

Key names in international art meet new voices

Collectors:
Paige & Al West

Address:
1 Freedom Valley Drive
Oaks, PA 19456
United States of America
Tel +1 610 8837368
lee@westcollection.org
www.westcollection.org

By appointment only.

Financial services professional Al West is a man of action. He doesn't wait for gallerists or curators to recommend emerging voices to him; he lures them in himself. In 2011, for example, he and his daughter, Paige West, asked artists to apply for the West Collection Art Prize. Everyone who downloaded the app, looked at the art, then gave an evaluation and became part of the extended jury. This kind of participation is continued in the public spaces of West's business, SEI Investments. Approximately 1 200 works are installed in SEI's main building and can be viewed by appointment. The collection has grown since 1996, now encompassing nearly 3 000 works, including those by Donald Judd, Richard Artschwager, Martin Boyce, and Candice Breitz. Many of the works are loaned to museums or curated traveling exhibitions.

BUCKHORN SCULPTURE PARK

Magic sculpture garden in Upstate New York

Collectors:
Sherry & Joel Mallin

Address:
60 Pound Ridge Road
Pound Ridge, NY 10576
United States of America
sherryhmaf@gmail.com

By appointment only.

Nestled on six hectares in the scenic town of Pound Ridge, New York, is the Buckhorn Sculpture Park and the private home of collector couple Sherry and Joel Mallin. It features gardens, woodlands, a lake, an orchard, and over seventy outdoor sculptures each discreetly and creatively placed to be viewed as individual works of art in extraordinary settings. Some of the artists featured include Richard Serra, Sol LeWitt, Joel Shapiro, Andy Goldsworthy, Ursula von Rydingsvard, Anish Kapoor, and Dan Graham. The collection also includes pieces by young sculptors whose work is showcased for the first time. In 2001, a 930-square-meter facility known as the Art Barn was completed in order to highlight an ever-changing collection of installations, paintings, photographs, videos, and sculptures. Works by masters such as Chuck Close, Yayoi Kusama, and Sean Scully are installed alongside works by mid-career artists and young, emerging talent.

HALL ART FOUNDATION

Impressive presentations of art in an eighteenth-century building

Collectors:
Christine & Andrew Hall

Address:
551 VT Route 106
Reading, VT 05062
United States of America
Tel +1 802 9521056
info@hallartfoundation.org
www.hallartfoundation.org

Opening Hours:
May–November
Wed, Sat–Sun by appointment only.
Every first Friday of the month from 5–8pm.

Additional exhibition locations:
Holle, Germany, p. 105

Christine and Andrew Hall are not just long-standing collectors of Georg Baselitz. In 2006, the American commodities trader and his wife also bought the artist's former castle near Hildesheim, Germany to house works from their collection, and, since 2017, also exhibit works there. Lexington Farm, an eighteenth-century former dairy farm located in Vermont, has been part the art foundation since 2012 and is where the Halls exhibit parts of their vast collection. But unlike many of their colleagues, whose collections read like a Who's Who of the international art scene, the Halls have decided to concentrate on a few positions, preferring to collect these extensively. This allows them to present their collected works of Neo-Expressionists A. R. Penck and Georg Baselitz in imposing solo exhibitions. These are flanked by other monographic exhibitions including, among others, Neil Jenney's figurative paintings and the photographs of Edward Burtynsky.

LINDA PACE FOUNDATION

The legacy of a patroness who promoted young art

Collector:
Linda Pace

Address:
111 Camp Street
San Antonio, TX 78204
United States of America
Tel +1 210 2266663
info@pacefound.org
www.lindapacefoundation.org

Opening Hours:
Wed–Sat: 12–5pm
And by appointment.

Linda Pace was an artist. But she was even more than that. Starting in 1993, she organized a scholarship and exhibition program for artists in San Antonio, Texas. The artists often went on to have fantastic careers. Before she died in 2007, the passionate patroness had acquired roughly 500 works by artists including Isaac Julien, Susan Philipsz, Lynda Benglis, Arturo Herrera, Mona Hatoum, Jesse Amado, and Gabriel Orozco. Pace installed part of her sculpture collection in a park dedicated to her young deceased son. The publicly accessible terrain is located next to Space, one of the foundation's buildings where works from the collection are presented in temporary exhibitions. The foundation continues to acquire artworks in order to continue Pace's legacy. Now with over 800 pieces, the collection will move into a spacious new home in 2019: Ruby City, a bright red structure designed by David Adjaye, is being built on site.

PIER 24 PHOTOGRAPHY

Photography shines at this outsized venue in the heart of San Francisco

Collectors:
Andrew & Mary Pilara

Address:
Pier 24 The Embarcadero
San Francisco, CA 94105
United States of America
Tel +1 415 5127424
info@pier24.org
www.pier24.org

Opening Hours:
Mon–Fri: 9am–5:15pm
By appointment only.

Collectors have long had a tenuous relationship to photography. It's a fickle medium: one difficult to preserve and with a relatively recently established market. But that hasn't dissuaded collector Andrew Pilara, who is fairly new to the pursuit: his Pilara Foundation, located on Pier 24, purchased its first photograph just over a decade ago. So entranced was Pilara with Diane Arbus's 2003 San Francisco Museum of Modern Art (SFMOMA) retrospective that he immediately embarked on assembling a collection, which now boasts over 4 000 photographs. The collection's works are practically an A-to-Z of the medium's greats: from classics like Ansel Adams and Irving Penn to contemporary stars like Doug Aitken, Philip-Lorca diCorcia, and Jeff Wall. The works are stored and displayed on a rotating basis in what is perhaps America's largest photo-centric exhibition hall: a 2 600-square-meter space under the Bay Bridge.

THOMA FOUNDATION

Two intimate art spaces that encourage dialogue between work and viewer

Collectors:
Carl & Marilynn Thoma

Addresses:
Art House Santa Fe:
231 Delgado Street
Santa Fe, NM 87501
United States of America

Orange Door:
Chicago, Illinois
United States of America

info@thomafoundation.org
www.thomafoundation.org

Opening Hours:
Santa Fe:
Thurs–Sat: 10am–5pm
Chicago:
By appointment only.

Since 1975 Carl and Marilynn Thoma have amassed a diverse array of over 1 000 works, often in highly specialized areas that require a deep level of personal commitment. Ranging from digital and electronic art, to Japanese bamboo sculptures, postwar art including Color Field and Hard-edge, and one of the world's largest concentrations of Spanish Colonial paintings, the Thomas' continually growing collection is impressive. Opened to the public in 2014, the Thoma Foundation presides over two different sites: Orange Door in Chicago and the Art House in Santa Fe. The Art House, located in the historic Canyon Road arts district, is a traditional adobe house that has been converted into an art space. The focus here is on contemporary works from the collection, including digital art, light installations, and Color Field works. Orange Door, open by appointment only, is housed in an old warehouse space and showcases work from the entire collection.

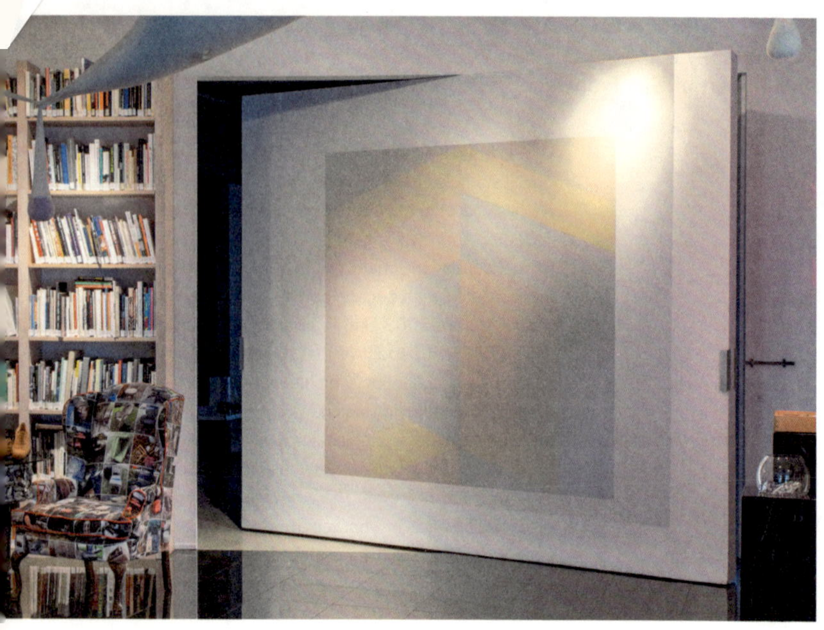

WHITESPACE

International art stars in a former warehouse

Collector:
Elayne Mordes

Address:
2805 N. Australian Avenue
West Palm Beach, FL 33407
United States of America
Tel +1 561 8424131
whitespace@mordes.com
www.whitespacecollection.com

Opening Hours:
November–April
Sat–Sun: 1–4pm
And by appointment.

The collector couple Elayne and Marvin Mordes has assembled works by established artist-teams like Teresa Hubbard & Alexander Birchler, or Elmgreen & Dragset. Their collection also includes international names like Jonathan Meese, Thomas Houseago, Mat Collishaw, Christian Boltanski, and Anish Kapoor. The couple's treasures, comprised primarily of sculptures and installations, are housed in an unassuming warehouse in Palm Beach that was previously used for the manufacturing of one of the city's most in-demand products: dentures. Marvin Mordes was a longtime board member at the Hirshhorn Museum in Washington D.C. Since his death, his wife continues to fulfill the couple's mission: sharing knowledge and art with others, and opening Whitespace's rooms upon request for groups, private events, and, on Saturdays and Sundays, for all interested art lovers.

A project like this can never be complete. Almost every month, collectors worldwide open new showrooms or make their private collections available to the public in a variety of ways. If you know of any private collection of contemporary art that is publicly accessible and not listed here, we would be delighted to hear about it. We would be equally pleased to hear of any plans you might have for opening your own collection to interested art lovers. Doing so will help us keep the *BMW Art Guide by Independent Collectors* up to date.

Please write to us at:
bmwartguide@independent-collectors.com

Silvia Anna Barrilà is a freelance journalist based in Milan and Berlin who specializes in the art market. Since 2008 she has written for the Italian financial newspaper *Il Sole 24 Ore (ArtEconomy24)* and for *Icon*, *Il Corriere del Ticino*, as well as for other international media, including *Damn*. She is also co-founder of the international art gallery blog, Contemporary Art Galleries. For this guide she wrote about collections in southern and eastern Europe: Greece, Hungary, Italy, Poland, Russia, Turkey, and Ukraine. She also covered several countries in Asia—Bangladesh, China, India, and Japan—as well as a few collections in Germany, the Netherlands, Qatar, South Africa, Spain, Switzerland, and the United Arab Emirates.

The journalist couple **Nicole Büsing & Heiko Klaas**, based in Hamburg and Berlin, have written freelance art journalism and criticism since 1997 for a variety of national and international art magazines and newspapers including *Monopol, Artmapp, Artist Kunstmagazin*, *Dare, Zeitkunst, Kunstmarkt Media, Photonews*, and *Next Level*. They also write catalogue essays for artists and institutions. For this guide they focused on collections from Europe and South America—Argentina, Austria, Belgium, Brazil, Denmark, Finland, France, Germany, Iceland, Israel, Luxembourg, Mexico, the Netherlands, Norway, Portugal, Spain, and Switzerland—as well as individual collections in Japan, South Africa, and the United States of America.

Sandra Danicke lives in Frankfurt am Main and is a correspondent for the art magazine *Art*, where she reports on contemporary artists and all art historical time periods. In addition, she holds a PhD in art history and works as an editor for the *Frankfurter Rundschau* and as a freelance journalist for *Die Zeit* and the *Süddeutsche Zeitung*. She is also the author of numerous catalogue essays and publications on contemporary art. Her focus in this guide was on individual collections in Austria, Cyprus, the Czech Republic, Denmark, Germany, Italy, the Netherlands, Romania, Turkey, and the United States of America.

Alexander Forbes is a New York-based art writer and critic who works as executive editor for the global collector's platform Artsy, where he has been responsible for developing editorial content on art world trends and art market analysis since 2015. Prior to that he was based in Berlin, where he worked as the European art market editor for *Artnet News* and served as the bureau chief for German-speaking countries at Louise Blouin Media publishers. For this guide he focused on collections in the United States of America, as well as on several collections in Canada, Finland, France, Germany, Great Britain, Italy, Israel, Norway, and Romania.

Jeni Fulton is a writer and editor based in Basel, where she has worked as executive editor for the Art Basel art fair since 2018. Previously she was editor-in-chief for *Sleek Magazine* and contributed to *Frieze.com, Spike Art Quarterly, Randian*, and *Apollo*. She holds a degree in philosophy from the University of Cambridge, and received her PhD from the Department of Cultural History and Theory at the Humboldt Universität of Berlin in 2016. Her focus in this guide was on individual collections in China, Lebanon, Mexico, Romania, Serbia, South Korea, and the United Arab Emirates.

Independent art critic **Christiane Meixner**, based in Berlin, has served as editor of *Der Tagesspiegel*'s Art & Market section since 2008. She has worked as an editor for the magazine *Weltkunst* and also writes for a variety of magazines, daily newspapers, and *Zeit Online*. Her focus in this guide was on collections from Australia, Canada, and New Zealand—as well as several collections in Great Britain and the United States of America.

Anne Reimers lives in London. Since 2006 she has been a freelance arts journalist for the *Frankfurter Allgemeine Zeitung* reporting on auctions, art fairs, and exhibitions in the British capital and internationally. An art historian, Reimers has taught cultural theory since 2005 and is senior lecturer at the University for the Creative Arts (UCA) in Rochester, as well as associate lecturer at the Central Saint Martins College of Art and Design in London. Her focus in this guide was on collections in Great Britain, as well as several collections in Australia, Belgium, France, Germany, Norway, and the United States of America.

Berlin-based journalist **Frauke Schlieckau** works as deputy editorial director at Kobalt Productions where she oversees the European cultural magazine show Metropolis by Arte. She holds a PhD in literature studies, and as a writer and director spezializing in art reporting she produces documentaries, reportages, and artist portraits for Arte, 3Sat, ZDF, and Deutsche Welle. She also reported on the Venice Biennale and Documenta 14 in Athens for ZDF and Arte. Her focus in this guide was on individual collections in Brazil, Germany, Lebanon, Portugal, and Turkey.

* new in the Art Guide

K

L

M

* new in the Art Guide

* new in the Art Guide

p. 13 Fundación Amalia Lacroze de Fortabat; photo: Bernardo Galmarini/Alamy Stock Photo **p. 14** Amalia Pica, *Monumento a Intersecciones #7*, 2013; photo: Pablo Jantus, for the media ARSOmnibus **p. 18** MONA/Rémi Chauvin; courtesy: the artist and MONA Museum of Old and New Art, Hobart, Tasmania, Australia **p. 20** Patricia Piccinini, *Lustre*, 1999, and *Car Nuggets: They're good for you* (detail), 1998; photo: Dianna Snape; courtesy: Lyon Housemuseum **p. 23** Installation view, Peter Atkins, 2018; courtesy: Tolarno, Melbourne and GAGPROJECTS, Adelaide **p. 24** The artists and White Rabbit Collection **p. 25** Stanislav Kolíbal, *Fundort Dachboden*, 1992, permanent installation, Kunstraum Buchberg; photo: Franz Schachinger **p. 26** Sol LeWitt, *Eybesfeld*; photo: Paul Ott **p. 27** Tony Cragg, *Early Forms (Molly)*, 1999; © Museum Liaunig **p. 31** Installation view; courtesy: Samdani Art Foundation; photo: Noor Photoface **p. 32** *Private Choices*, 2017, Galila's P.O.C.; photo: Philippe De Gobert **p. 33** Valerie Snobeck, *Reservoirs with Stains*, 2015; Sergio Verastegui, *A Single Vertical Line*, 2014; Evan Roberts, *Field No. 12*, 2015; photo: Hugard & Vanoverschelde Photography **p. 34** Photo: Pascal Vanneau **p. 37** Haroon Mirza, *Digital Switchover*, 2012, © Haroon Mirza/hrm199 Ltd., Vanhaerents Art Collection, Brussels **p. 39** Art Center Hugo Voeten, Herentals, Belgium **p. 41** Instituto Inhotim—Centro de Arte Contemporânea e Jardim Botânico/Galeria Adriana Varejão; photo: Eduardo Eckenfels **p. 45** *Somebody, Everybody, Nobody* (installation view); photo: courtesy Scrap Metal, Toronto **p. 47** Martin Creed, *Work No. 329*, 2004, © Martin Creed; photo: SITE Photography; courtesy: Rennie Museum, Vancouver **p. 48** Guido van der Werve, *Nummer veertien, home*, 2013; M Woods Collection, Beijing; photo: Tian Yu **p. 52** Haegue Yang, *Journal of Mundane and Uncertain Days 4*, Sifang Art Museum, Nanjing **p. 56** T.A. Gkekas/ The Office Collection. Dimitris Merantzas, *Self-portrait*, 2003 and *Trust*, 2013; photo: Antonis Minas **p. 58** Peter Ibsen/Peter Ibsen Collection **p. 59** Henry Moore, *Reclining Figure on Pedestal*, 1960; courtesy: Henry Moore Foundation; photo: Rauno Träskelin **p. 60** Sara Hildén Art Museum **p. 61** Installation view *Ailleurs*, 2014; © La FabriC—Fondation pour l'art contemporain Claudine et Jean-Marc Salomon **p. 62** Vincent Ganivet, 1976, Suresnes (Hauts-de-Seins, France), *Entrevous*, 2010, deux arches constituées de parpaings assemblés béton, cale en bois et sangles de sécurisation, 556 x 1005 x 950 cm, n° inv.: FNAC 2013-0312 (1 et 2). Centre National des Arts Plastiques, France, gift of Yvon Lambert, Dépôt du Centre National des Arts Plastiques, France à la Collection Lambert, Avignon; © Adagp, Paris, 2018/CNAP; photo: François Deladerrière **p. 64** Venet Foundation, the steel corridor of the factory; © Serge Demailly; courtesy: Bernar Venet Archives, New York **p. 65** Louise Bourgeois, *Crouching Spider*, 2003; © Easton Foundation, New York; photo: Andrew Pattman **p. 67** François Morellet, *Red Beaming Pi 300*, 2002; courtesy: the artist and Galerie Jean Brolly; photo: Denis Prisset **p. 68** Gao Weigang, *No Way!*, 2013; courtesy: the artist and dslcollection **p. 74** Tatiana Trouvé, *Untitled*, 2014; photo: Maya Claussen **p. 78** Boros Collection, Berlin; Katja Novitskova, *Pattern of Activation*, 2014; photo: NOSHE **p. 79** Salon Dahlmann, Miettinen Collection; photo: Nick Ash **p. 80** The Feuerle Collection; photo: Holger Niehaus **p. 81** Moritz Hirsch, *Autofiction*, 2004–2012; photo: Moritz Hirsch **p. 82** Hoffmann Collection, Berlin **p. 84** *The Missing—or: One Thing Next to Another*, installation view, Kunstsaele Berlin, 2014; photo: Jan Brockhaus **p. 88** Rose Wylie, *Korean Children Singing*, 2013; Zachary Armstrong, *Large Self-Portrait*, 2014; photo: Kasia Gatkowska **p. 94** HGN Collection; photo: Stefan Lucks **p. 95** Richard Long, *Cornish Slate Circle*, 1983; Richard Long, *A Walk of Thirteen Days in the Swiss Alps*, 2000; Richard Long, *Stones Along the Way*, 1998; © Stiftung DKM; photo: Werner J. Hannappel **p. 97** Julia Stoschek Collection, Düsseldorf; photo: Ulrich Schwarz, Berlin **p. 101** Kunstraum Alexander Bürkle: Lori Hersberger, *Ghost Rider*, 2004/2013; background: Paul Schwer, *Neuschnee*, 2013; photo: Bernhard Strauss **p. 102** Photo: Bernhard Strauss **p. 103** Wolfgang Tillmans, *Man Pissing on Chair*, 1997; Ed Ruscha, *Parking Lots*, 1967–1972; Martha Rosler, *Bringing the War Home*, 1967–1999; photo: Egbert Haneke, Hamburg **p. 104** Wemhöner Collection, Herford **p. 106** Michael Wesely, *Schloss Kummerow*, 2016; photo: Thomas Wesely **p. 107** Famed, *Building Something Out of Something*, installation view Arbeitswohnung Stiftung Federkiel, 2009/2015; photo: Stefan Fischer **p. 112** Photo: Walter Vorjohann **p. 114** Photo: Tomas Riehle/Artur Images **p. 117** Sylvie Fleury, *First Spaceship on Venus (14)*, 1996, fiberglass, in eight parts, each 3.5 x 1 x 1 m, Schauwerk Sindelfingen, © Sylvie Fleury; photo: Frank Kleinbach **p. 118** François Morellet, ϖ-Rococo, n°18, 1=40°, 2001; Bosse Sudenburg, *IF-THEN*, 2009; Heiner Thiel, *Untitled (wvz 508)*, 2009; © Stiftung Konzeptuelle Kunst; photo: Ulli Sowa, Soest **p. 119** Reinhard Mucha, *Der Bau* [2002], 1980–1984; photo: Wolfgang Günzel, Offenbach **p. 120** DasMaximum, new exhibition hall with works by Walter De Maria; © Estate of Walter De Maria; photo: Velux **p. 126** Barry Flanagan, *Drummer Hare* **p. 127** Tara Donovan, *Untitled (Plastic Cups)*, 2006; courtesy: Jupiter Artland; photo: Ruth Clark **p. 128** Richard Long, *A Line in Norfolk*, 2016; photo: Pete Huggins **p. 129** Roe Ethridge, *Gisele on the Phone*, 2013; courtesy: Cranford Collection, London; photo: Mark Griffiths, www.mdrgriffiths.com **p. 134** Installation view

Sam Falls; courtesy: the artist and Zabludowicz Collection; photo: Stuart Whipps **p. 135** Urs Fischer, *Thank You Fuck You*, 2007 and *Death of a Moment*, 2007 and *Chair for a Ghost: Thomas*, 2003 and *Untitled (Door)*, 2006 und *Spinoza Rhapsody*, 2006; photo: Stefan Altenburger **p. 136** The George Economou Collection, Athens; photo: Erieta Attali **p. 138** Vorres Museum **p. 139** Vass Collection **p. 140** Installation view *No Site*, 2015; photo: Áslaug Íris Friðjónsdóttir **p. 142** *The Window of Jendela*, 2012, OHD Museum, Magelang, Indonesia **p. 146** Fondazione Antonio Dalle Nogare; photo: Jürgen Eheim **p. 149** Courtesy: Il Giardino dei Lauri **p. 151** Photo: Alessandro Moggi **p. 156** Collezione Maramotti, installation view, works by Mario Merz; photo: C. Dario Lasagni **p. 157** Gianni Piacentino 1965–2000, installation view, 2014, Fondazione Giuliani, Rome; photo: Giorgio Benni **p. 158** Marina Abramović, *Count on Us (Chorus)*, 2003, chromogenic-print; Giacinto Cerone, *Untitled, (Green Table—Two Pieces)*, 1999, ceramics; Campana brothers, *Crocodile*, 2012, object; Giacinto Cerone, *Untitled, (Violet Sculptures—Three Pieces)*, 2000, ceramics; Flavio Favelli, *Coppia grande oriente A (Installation—Lights)*, 2005; Alessandro Sarra, *Untitled #03m*, 2012, oil on canvas; Grazia Toderi, *Olympia (Barcellona Blue)*, 2001, cibachrome digital print, plexiglass; Gianni Caravaggio, *Cosmicomiche (Marbles—Two Pieces, B&W)*, 2006; Zhan Wang, *Untitled*, 2001, stainless steel rock, aluminum sculpture; photo: Giovanni De Angelis **p. 159** Marko Lluliä, *Death of the Monument*, 2009; courtesy: the artist and Nomas Foundation; photo: Luciano Mandato **p. 161** Goshka Macuga, *Plus Ultra*, 2009; courtesy: the artist and Kate MacGarry, London **p. 162** Paola Pivi, *Don't disturb me*, 2009; courtesy: Videoinsight® Collection **p. 165** Punta della Dogana; © Palazzo Grassi; photo: Andrea Jemolo **p. 169** Dominique Gonzalez-Foerster, *Moment Dream House*, 2003; © Dominique Gonzalez-Foerster; courtesy: Gallery Koyanagi, Tokyo and Tokyo Opera City Art Gallery; photo: Keizo Kioku **p. 170** Aïshti Foundation, installation view *Trick Brain*, 2017, curator: Massimiliano Gioni; photo: Guillaume Ziccarelli **p. 171** KA Art Space, Beirut, Lebanon; photo: Walid Rachid **p. 172** Avery K Singer, Ólafur Elíasson, Mladen Stilinović; courtesy: the artists and Kraupa-Tuskany Zeidler, Neugerriemschneider, and Espaivisor **p. 181** Gibbs Farm; photo: David Hartley-Mitchell **p. 182** Photo: John Stenersen **p. 185** Per Inge Bjørlo, *Larger Body*, 2003; photo: Øystein Thorvaldsen/Henie Onstad Kunstsenter **p. 189** Mateusz Sadowski, *Half a Banana*, 2014; courtesy: Michał Borowik Collection and Stereo, Warsaw **p. 190** Frank Stella, *Hagamatana II*, 1967; Museu Coleção Berardo; photo: David Rato **p. 192** Courtesy: Mathaf—Arab Museum of Modern Art **p. 194** Mircea Cantor, *Tracking Happiness*, 2009 **p. 197** Anatoly Zverev, *Lion*, 1979; Vladimir Yakovlev, *Flower*, 1974; Anatoly Zverev, *Elephant*, 1952; courtesy: The Ekaterina Cultural Foundation **p. 199** Dušan Otašević, *To Eat*, 1967; courtesy: Kolekcija Trajković, Belgrade **p. 200** Fung Ming Chip, *To Be & Not To Be*, 2012; photo: Jeremy San; The Private Museum Ltd., Singapore **p. 204** The Rupert Museum, Stellenbosch **p. 205** Arario Museum in Space, Seoul **p. 206** Walid Raad; courtesy: Paula Cooper Gallery, New York **p. 210** Joseph Kosuth, *Five Adjectives*, 1965; courtesy: Fundación Helga de Alvear, Cáceres; photo: Luis Asín **p. 212** Haim Steinbach, *Together Naturally (Doubled)*, 1986; Fundación Rosón Arte Contemporáneo **p. 213** Maya Lin, *Eleven Minute Line*, 2004; courtesy: the artist; photo: Per Pixel **p. 215** Ulrich Rückriem, *Tempel*, 1987; photo: Heiner Grieder **p. 216** Tatiana Trouvé, *I tempi doppi*, 2013; Collection Giancarlo & Danna Olgiati, Lugano **p. 219** Kunst(Zeug)Haus, Maya Bringolf, *Air Transfer*, 2015; photo: Bernhard Strauss **p. 222** The Agah Uğur Collection **p. 225** Pinchuk Art Centre, 2016; photo: Sergey Illin **p. 231** Giulio Paolini, *Saffo*, 1981; Giovanni Anselmo, *Untitled*, 1990; Alighiero Boetti, *Clino*, 1966; Alighiero Boetti, *Mazzo di tubi*, 1966; courtesy: Magazzino Italian Art, Cold Spring; photo: Marco Anelli, 2017 **p. 232** courtesy: Ralphoto Studio; photo: Alan Geho **p. 234** Donald Judd, *Untitled*, 1965, The Rachofsky Collection; photo: Kevin Todora **p. 235** Paul Ramírez Jonas, *Pause and Play*, 2000; courtesy: The Dikeou Collection **p. 237** Christopher Burke Studio; courtesy: The Brant Foundation, Greenwich **p. 239** Jeff Koons, *Tulips*, 1995–2004, © Jeff Koons; Christopher Wool, *Untitled*, 1990, © Christopher Wool; courtesy; the artist and Luhring Augustine, New York; The Broad Art Foundation; photo: Bruce Damonte **p. 244** Nate Lowman, *In Pieces And In Stiches*, 2017; courtesy: the artist and Massimo de Carlo, Milan, London, and Hong Kong **p. 247** Anselm Kiefer, *Sprache der Vögel*, 1989; The Margulies Collection at the Warehouse **p. 249** courtesy: di Rosa Center for Contemporary Art, Napa; photo: Erhard Pfeiffer **p. 250** Jo Ractliffe, (works from the series) *Terreno Ocupado*, 2007 and *As Terras do Fim do Mundo*, 2010; courtesy: The Walther Collection; photo: EPW Studio/Maris Hutchinson, 2011 **p. 256** Sol LeWitt, *Wall Drawing #1023 and Isometric Form*, 2002; photo: Reese Hendrik Blanke **Maps** designed by Freepik

BMW ART GUIDE by Independent Collectors

EDITORS
BMW Group, Munich
Independent Collectors, Berlin

CONCEPTION & IMPLEMENTATION
Independent Collectors, Berlin
Buero NOC, Berlin

PROJECT DIRECTORS
Hedwig Solis Weinstein, BMW Group
Cathérine Seibold
Karoline Pfeiffer, Independent Collectors
Juliane Eisele, Hatje Cantz
Sarah Nöllenheidt, Buero NOC

EXECUTIVE EDITOR
Sylvia Dominique Volz, Berlin

AUTHORS
Silvia Anna Barrilà, Berlin/Milan
Nicole Büsing, Hamburg/Berlin
Sandra Danicke, Frankfurt a. M.
Alexander Forbes, New York
Jeni Fulton, Berlin
Heiko Klaas, Hamburg/Berlin
Christiane Meixner, Berlin
Anne Reimers, London
Frauke Schlieckau, Berlin

ADDITIONAL TEXTS
Independent Collectors

ADDITIONAL CONTRIBUTORS
Amy Binding, Korinna Boring,
Sophie Eliot, Kira Pohl,
Christina Werner, Elena Winkler

TRANSLATION & PROOFREADING
R. Jay Magill & Tanja Maka, Berlin
Erik Smith, Berlin

GRAPHIC DESIGN
Anna Bauer, Miriam Busch,
Friederike Hamann, Buero NOC

TYPEFACES
Arial by Robin Nicholas &
Patricia Saunders,
The Monotype Corporation, Woburn,
Akzidenz Grotesk BQ
by Hermann Berthold,
H. Berthold AG, Berlin

PRODUCTION
Janine Lattich, Hatje Cantz

PRINTED BY
Offsetdruckerei Karl Grammlich GmbH,
Pliezhausen

PAPER
Invercote G, 180 g/m²
Fly 06, extraweiss, 90 g/m²

BINDING
Josef Spinner Großbuchbinderei,
Ottersweier

Published by
Hatje Cantz Verlag GmbH
Mommsenstrasse 27
10629 Berlin
Tel. +49 30 3464678-00
Fax +49 30 3464678-29
www.hatjecantz.com
A Ganske Publishing
Group Company

Hatje Cantz books are available
internationally at selected bookstores.
For more information about our
distribution partners, please visit
www.hatjecantz.com.

ISBN 978-3-7757-4474-4 (English)
ISBN 978-3-7757-4473-7 (German)

Printed in Germany

The BMW Art Guide by Independent
Collectors is also available as eBook:
ISBN 978-3-7757-4499-7 (English)
ISBN 978-3-7757-4497-3 (German)

Art is a gift. When we look at a work, are pulled into and interact with it, we say a wordless "thank you" to all the artists that fascinate, inspire, and sometimes even change us. With this book, BMW and Independent Collectors wish to thank everyone who lives with art and who has opened their spaces to like-minded spirits from around the world. Our heartfelt thanks go to all the collectors who appear in this edition of the *BMW Art Guide by Independent Collectors.* Your support and confidence in our project are what have made this book possible. Our deepest thanks go also to our committed team of authors and editors, and to the many contributors in the Independent Collectors and BMW network. You never turned away from the challenge. Thank you.

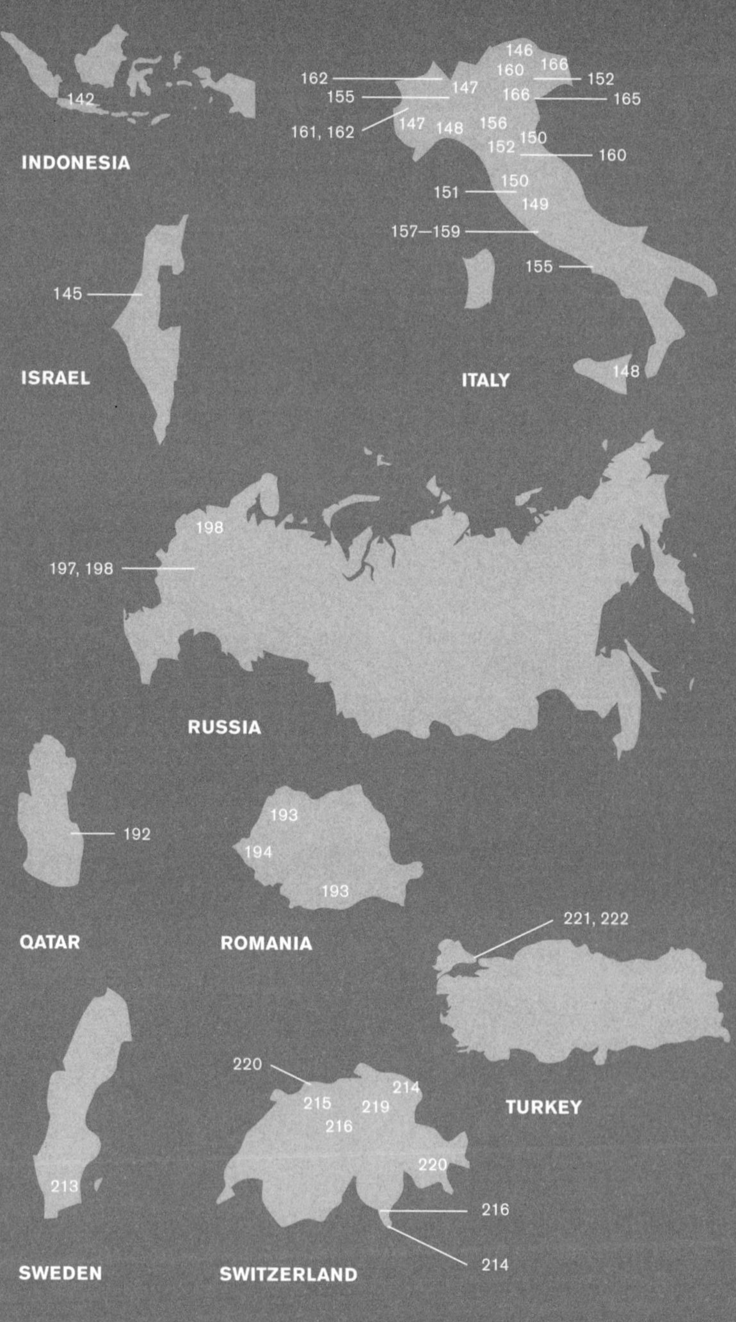

142
INDONESIA
162
155
161, 162
147
147
148
146
160
166
152
166
165
156
150
152
160
151
150
149
157—159
155
148
ITALY
145
ISRAEL
198
197, 198
RUSSIA
192
QATAR
193
194
193
ROMANIA
221, 222
TURKEY
220
215
214
219
216
220
216
214
213
SWEDEN
SWITZERLAND